HOLOCAUST SURVIVOR COOKBOOK

Published by:
Caras & Associates, Inc.
P.O. Box 9017
Port St. Lucie, FL 34985
United States of America
Printed in China

International Standard Book Number 978-1-61658-944-8

NINTH EDITION

To order additional copies please visit our website:
www.survivorcookbook.org
or call 443-604-2643

*This cookbook is dedicated to the memory of Abe Malnik from Dewey Beach, DE.
Abe told us his amazing story of survival but sadly he passed away on April 3, 2007,
the first day of Pesach, just prior to the publication of this cookbook.*

*In addition we dedicate this book to our beloved "Zeidy" Sam Zerykier of Teaneck, NJ.
Sam passed away on January 23, 2008. His courage, love, and good humor
were an inspiration to our entire family.*

*We are also dedicating the cookbook to the
six million Jews who did not survive the Holocaust.*
May their lives never be forgotten.

INTRODUCTION

In 2005, Sarah and Jonathan Caras, a young, newly married American couple, made aliyah and established their new home in Jerusalem. As part of their desire to give something back to the people of their new homeland they both volunteered time at the Carmei Ha'ir Soup Kitchen. Carmei Ha'ir serves over 500 meals every day to poor hungry Israelis.

Later that same year their two mothers, Joanne Caras and Gisela Zerykier, traveled together to visit their children. Among the many sites they visited in Israel was Carmei Ha'ir. Joanne was so impressed with the soup kitchen that she thought they were in a restaurant. Waiters take orders and serve meals to people at their tables. Everyone is treated with dignity and respect. Those who can afford to pay do so and those who can not afford to pay do not. Money is collected after meals in a tzedekah box near the door.

Joanne was so moved by what she saw that she decided to raise money to support the soup kitchen. Jonathan and Sarah came up with the idea to put together a cookbook of great Jewish recipes.

A short while later, Gisela's beloved mother from Belgium passed away. Gisela wrote a very moving tribute to her mother, who was a Holocaust Survivor. After reading Gisela's beautiful e-mail, Joanne immediately thought of a new concept for the cookbook- great Jewish recipes from the families of Holocaust Survivors, accompanied by the stories of those Survivors.

And so the **Holocaust Survivor Cookbook** was born.

Sarah, Jonathan, and Joanne solicited the support of Rachel, Mickey, and Harvey Caras and set out to collect 100 stories from all over the world. And they succeeded. This cookbook contains stories from across the United States, Canada, South America, Israel, Australia, New Zealand, Europe, South Africa, and even some that came from people who escaped to Asia.

Some of the stories are very detailed, as the Survivors took advantage of this forum to share with us their entire journey. Others were reluctant to give too many details. Some told us that they had never before told their story to anyone, even to their own children.

This cookbook is an opportunity for all of us to honor the courage, determination, intelligence, and fortune of those Survivors. In addition, it will allow us to help feed poor Israelis.

This has truly been a labor of love.

Gisela (left) and Joanne (right)

Yonatan, Zahava, and Sarah Caras

How to Use This Cookbook

Typical cookbooks are divided into sections- appetizers, salads, soups, main courses, side dishes, desserts, etc.

This cookbook is different. Since many of the Survivors submitted more than one recipe we chose to keep them together, even though they may run the entire gamut of categories. So you may find one page with a soup and a dessert recipe side by side.

The best way to find a recipe in this cookbook is to use the recipe index. There you will find the recipes by categories and the page numbers on which to find them. In some cases you will find more than one recipe for the same item.

We hope that you will open this cookbook often and use all of the recipes you find inside. And when you do use the cookbook here is the most important thing you can do.

Whenever you serve a recipe from this cookbook to your family please be sure to read them the story of the Survivor that goes with the recipe.

As your family enjoys their meal hopefully they will take the time to discuss the story they have heard. By doing this you will keep both the recipes and the stories alive for generations to come.

If you recognize a survivor or their family and would like to get in touch with them please send your contact information to us via our email survivorcookbook@aol.com and we will pass on your name to the survivor family.

These are family recipes, in many cases handed down through several generations. They are as we received them and they have not been "tested" as many cookbooks do. Many are lacking in detail that would help in the preparation of the food, others suggest several variations on the basic recipe, and others are very detailed. Try them, accept them as they are, modify them, or use them as a starting point to let your imagination go. Remember the history that they contain. A note has been added to each recipe to indicate whether it is meat, dairy or parve.

Acknowledgements

We greatly appreciate the support of the following people who helped to make this book possible:

Gisela Zerykier - Original art design and poem
Ronna Caras - Donated cover design by Vicki Cash
Deborah Adler - Howard County Jewish Federation
Reagan Kimball - RK Design & Printing
Melissa C. Halpern - Graphic Design/Layout
Phil, Rachel, and Debbie Katz - PK Graphics
Howard Mindek & Tali Mindek - Howard Photography
Beth Sellman (Head Proofreader) and Jennifer Sellman(Proofreader & Bat-Mitzvah project)
Dr. Abraham Zerykier - Proofreader
Chanie Baron - Proofreader
Lynda Gluck - Proofreader
Dr. Constance Rubler - Proofreader
Andy Bates- Recipe Editor
Rabbi Hillel Baron
Esther Finder - Gen Shoah
Hadassah Magazine
Hadassah groups around the world
Joy Lepola - Fox News
Billy Robbins- Fox News and Tracey Robbins
Jewish Times
Jewish Week
Jewish News Weekly
The Jewish Magazine
Washington, DC Holocaust Museum
Shoah Foundation
Jacques Fein
Dr. Harvey Levy
Sam Lauber
Debby Elstein - *Engagement Cookbook*
Tammy Rubin - Jewish Community Federation of Cleveland
Jewish Federations around the world
Jewish publications all over the world who printed our story

And special thanks to all of the brave Survivors and their families.
We honor all of you.

The Caras Family

Carmei Ha'ir

Reprinted from the Carmei Ha'ir website http://carmeihair.org.il

December 2003. The unemployment rate in Israel was reaching new heights, poverty and the social gap were becoming more and more acute, and the hundreds of charitable organizations in the country were finding it increasingly difficult to function properly. What could be

done to change the situation? What kind of agency, organization or institution could be established in order to enable people to emerge from the vicious cycle of poverty and get back on their own two feet? To answer these questions, three young energetic social activists racked their brains: Rabbi Yehuda Azrad, Yitzhak Levitan and Momi Ben Zeruel.

The answer they came up with can be summed up in one word: "Dignity." Poverty and the need to rely on others for assistance, first and foremost, deal a savage blow to the pride and dignity of needy individuals. They lose their self-confidence and their belief in their own abilities. Not only is their self-image impaired; they feel that their standing in the community has been sadly and significantly diminished. What is also crucial is that they no longer have any hope that their

situation will ever improve. Burdened with such feelings, their chances of ever emerging from the vicious cycle of poverty are very slim indeed. That is why our mission at Carmei Ha'ir is to restore to our clients their dignity, to enable them to recognize their self-worth and to encourage them to believe in themselves once more and in their capacity for once again being capable of financially supporting themselves and their family. In short, the bottom line at Carmei Ha'ir is to turn our clients from recipients of assistance to active contributors to society.

This insight was the guiding philosophy when we created Carmei Ha'ir, which has undertaken two ambitious goals: To restore the lost dignity of the tens of thousands of impoverished individuals in Israel and to establish a network that can provide comprehensive assistance to the needy; rescue them from a life of abject, humiliating poverty; renew their faith in themselves; restore their self-image; and enable them to soon reintegrate themselves into the job market.

Carmei Ha'ir's first project was the founding of a restaurant in the very heart of downtown Jerusalem – adjacent to the MahaneYehuda open marketplace. The restaurant's doors are open to all those who require our help. Although it is essentially a soup kitchen, it has the look of an elegant restaurant and the level of the meals it serves is comparable to the level of cuisine in the other eating establishments in the immediate area. The only difference between Carmei Ha'ir and counterpart businesses in its vicinity is the manner of payment. At Carmei Ha'ir, the customers themselves determine how much or how they will pay for their meal. There is a little box at the front entrance and many of our patrons, who simply do not have the funds to pay for what they

have been served, leave a note of thanks there that includes a brief description of their severe economic distress. Anyone can come into Carmei Ha'ir for a meal: The poor and the affluent, men and women, religious and secular individuals, the young and the elderly.

With this kind of approach, we preserve the dignity of our needy patrons who do not sense that they are lepers in Israeli society but instead feel that they are equals among equals.

Within a short while after its creation, our restaurant became a magnet and it has continued to attract immense interest. Many people enter our premises – some to have a good, satisfying meal and others to volunteer and help us prepare and serve meals. Carmei Ha'ir's patrons do not feel dejected; rather they sense that they are among friends who love and respect them. Every day, we can observe how the needy whom we serve straighten their backs with pride and how the glimmer of hope can be seen once more in their eyes. The restaurant's facilities are used not only at lunchtime from Sunday through Thursday each week. The restaurant is, in effect, a community center with a varied program, which includes, for example, communal festive meals on Jewish holidays, Bar- and Bat-Mitzvah celebrations and birthday parties for families with very limited means, parties for the members of Israel's armed forces, counseling sessions given in the evening to enable our patrons to return to the working world and to reintegrate into the community, and literary and artistic evenings.

 In addition to the many activities carried out on our premises, the building that houses the Carmei Ha'ir restaurant serves as a nerve center for daily volunteer programs. At Carmei Ha'ir, our volunteers prepare hundreds of sandwiches that are sent directly to elementary schools for those children who have come to the classroom with an empty lunch-bag. The sandwiches are distributed among them confidentially without the knowledge of their classmates in order to preserve the dignity and social standing of the children who receive our assistance. This program is conducted in cooperation with both the directors of the educational institutions attended by our young clients and the social services department of the Jerusalem municipality.

Every week, we package hundreds of food baskets that contain basic commodities and which are distributed along needy families, who are thus able to celebrate the Sabbath in a worthy manner. At the start of the school year, we hand out textbooks, pens, pencils, notebooks and rulers to children from socio-economically deprived families. With the approach of winter, we distribute space heaters and blankets to help fight the cold that penetrates the homes and hearts of many needy families in Jerusalem.

The goal of all these programs is to offer an overall solution to the economic distress of our clients and, at the same time, to help them maintain their dignity. However, we go beyond the extension of material assistance. We offer personalized counseling to our clients in order to enable them to return to full or even partial functioning in the community and the working world. Some of the women who receive Carmei Ha'ir's assistance serve simultaneously as volunteers in our organization. In this manner, they feel that they are contributing to the community and that they are worthy of respect and esteem. These volunteers have a much better chance of ultimately finding gainful employment.

Carmei Ha'ir Open Restaurant: 72 Agripas St. • Jerusalem, Israel
Carmei Ha'ir Israel Mailing Address: P.O. Box 6084 • Jerusalem, Israel • 91060
Carmei Ha'ir USA Address: 1356 E. 10th St. • Brooklyn, N.Y., USA • 11230
Tel: +972 2 500 4222 • Fax: +972 2 500 4220 • info@carmeihair.org.il • www.carmeihair.org.il

TABLE OF CONTENTS
SURVIVORS

We honor all of you by donating
to the soup kitchen Carmei Ha'ir!

To make a donation to Carmei Ha'ir send your check to:
Carmei Ha'ir USA
1356 E. 10th St.
Brooklyn, NY USA 11230

RECIPE INDEX

APPETIZERS

• •

SALADS

BREADS

• •

SOUPS

KUGELS

• •

MAIN DISHES

• •

SIDE DISHES

CAKES

• •

COOKIES, PIES, AND OTHER DESSERTS

PASSOVER RECIPES

Vegan Kosher Substitutions

DAIRY: Soy, rice, almond or nut milk can replace **cow's milk** in any recipe. Soy, rice and almond milks are available in a variety of flavors including plain, vanilla, chocolate, and strawberry. For **desserts**, try using almond, oat, or coconut milk. For **whipped cream**, try Rich's brand nondairy whipping cream, beaten until stiff peaks form - you can find it at most **Kosher** or specialty baking stores. For **buttermilk**, combine one cup soy milk and one tablespoon vinegar. For **cheese**, brands such as Daiya and Follow Your Heart offer many dairy cheese alternatives and come in flavors such as mozzarella, nacho, Monterey jack, and cheddar flavors. Tofutti brand makes a wide variety of soy cheeses, including nondairy **cream cheese**, as well as vegan **sour cream** and **ice cream**. You can also replace cottage or ricotta cheese with crumbled, seasoned tofu. For **parmesan cheese**, try Soymage vegan parmesan cheese or nutritional yeast flakes. For **mayonnaise** try Follow Your Heart Vegenaise. For **yogurt** try Silk or Whole Soy brand vegan yogurts. For **butter** or **margarine**, a good nondairy vegan substitute is Earth Balance buttery spread.

MEAT: **For beef, turkey, chicken, etc.** the following brands offer many vegan meat substitutes that can be altered for meat in recipes - Amy's Kitchen, Boca, Butler Foods, Cary Brown's, Field Roast, Follow Your Heart, Gardein, Gardenburger, Health is Wealth, Lightlife, Morningstar Farms, Nate's, WhiteWave, Yves.

EGGS: Tofu is great for **egg** substitutions in recipes that call for a lot of **eggs**. To replace one **egg** in a recipe, purée 1/4 cup soft tofu. Some other egg replacement options are: 1 egg = 2 Tbsp. potato starch; 1 egg = 1/4 cup mashed potatoes; 1 egg = 1/4 cup canned pumpkin or squash; 1 egg = 1/4 cup puréed prunes; 1 egg = 2 Tbsp. water + 1 Tbsp. oil + 2 tsp. baking powder; 1 egg = 1 Tbsp. ground flax seed simmered in 3 Tbsp. water; 1 egg white = 1 Tbsp. plain agar powder dissolved in 1 Tbsp. water, whipped, chilled, and whipped again.

GELATIN AND HONEY: Agar-agar and carrageen (Irish moss) can be used in recipes that call for gelatin or honey. Vegan gelatin mixes are also available - in flavored and unflavored.

Elizabeth Silberstein
Teaneck, N.J., U.S.A.
Submitted by her daughter Gisela Zerykier, M.D.

1931, Elizabeth Silberstein, my mother, was born in Vienna, Austria, as were her parents, of Polish descent. Her mother Gisela, was born Kolbuszower, in 1903; her father, Jacques Silberstein, born in 1897, and her sister, Margareta, born November 8, 1925.

In her own words, her story, through letters she sent me.

Elizabeth and her daughter Gisela

"In Vienna, I loved the veranda where all my toys and your plants were, mom, and where I even drew on the walls, painted with a roller of that picture of a stag and a deer in the woods, repeated thousands of times. I colored them, drew flowers, little hearts, and you never said anything to me; I was so proud to walk around with my doll pram, but I also liked the shoe –box with an attached string which I pulled with a little doll inside, I could do everything. I didn't want to eat, I wasn't hungry, and papa was saying to me, "you will remember one day this food, you'll see, you will miss it"...Yes papa, I was hungry, very hungry, and at those times I remembered the good food prepared by my mother who was saying "leave her, she'll eat later", and I could go spit the piece of meat that I was chewing on for a long while. What a time! The whole family happy at the table. In the night, from the room where I was sleeping with my sister, I would often go to my mom's bed; she'd make room and take me in her arms, and I'd sleep there until the morning, it was so good. Nobody will ever take that away from me...

You wanted my address in Vienna? Goetehoff, Schutaustrasse, No 3, second floor. You could see in the street on one side & the park and benches with trees on the other side of the windows. It was like a park, with houses around and there was also a little bridge that ended in other streets where our family doctor lived. I remember I went in emergency, because I was bleeding profusely from the nose, and it was rose petals I had pushed there, because the rose didn't smell at all. With his mirror on his forehead, he took it off with tweezers; I must have been around 5, because I wasn't yet going to school. I remember the dress in pink angora that I was wearing, knit by my mom, every evening she knit for me and my sister, still in Belgium as a matter of fact, she made for me a magnificent sweater, with the gloves and the scarf the same, with all sorts of wools".

1

1938. Suddenly, my universe went upside down, from the pink life I was living to a gray one, and then, black. My father had to escape quickly; the hunt for the Jews was starting. First, the men. He left the summer of 1938 for Belgium, illegally of course. When we received his telegram to tell us he had arrived well, we packed our valises to join him. For me, the first big catastrophe; my toys had to stay, my baby doll in the pram with little lace curtains, all sky-blue inside and so soft. I was allowed to put the baby-doll in a trunk that was leaving for Brussels; my sister was looking longingly at her piano. My mom had wrapped in the crate for Brussels the Shabbat candles, the Chanukkiah, the Pesach dishes. While leaving, as my papa had already proclaimed, she would repeat "in three months, the most, we are back, Hitler's regime can't hold". She toured the apartment to look at each room. She closed the door with the Yale key and the exodus towards Belgium started. At the station in Vienna, the family was wishing each other that with God's help we would find each other again in Brussels. In the train, my sister was sick, me, sad, and as always, on my mom's lap, my head against her. We ran all night, and we arrived in Colognes. At the hotel my mother explained to me we had to separate to cross the border. I didn't want to understand because I didn't want to leave her. A peasant woman came to get me; one of the boys of the hotel, seeing my distress, made for me a little bag which he filled with candy. We had to part and I left, slept in an attic and the next day we took the train again. The woman had put on me an ugly red kerchief with white spots, and a tattered doll in my arms. At the German border, with false papers, I was to be silent, keep my head lowered on the doll. I had my first big fright.

I arrived in Brussels, papa and my sister were waiting at the station, my poor mother arrived two days later by truck. She had crossed the forest by foot, lost her shoes, and her two legs were bandaged, but I was so happy for us to be reunited. Life got organized slowly; almost the whole family was there. Two of my father's brothers had gone towards Switzerland and were never found again; probably taken back by the guards and their dogs at the border. I got registered at school, first year; I could only write the gothic script and didn't know a word of French. After the first trimester, very proud, I came home and told my family I was put in second year where I was following classes very well. I made myself some friends, I was well liked, invited; my sister had older friends. We lived in a furnished apartment; for Shabbat, there was always additional family or friends. A sister of my mother, widowed, was living with us. A rather large kitchen also stood for living and dining room. We had the radio. When some opera was playing, mom would sing along. She was working in a Jewish grocery store in our street. She prepared cakes & cookies at home; we took them to the bakery to bake in the oven.

1940, May 10th, the Nazis arrive in Belgium and the Belgian police arrest all the German and Austrian Jews. My papa gets a paper from the police; he must be ready by 10:00 AM with food and clothes for 48 hours. My mother runs to do the shopping; at 10:00 a truck stops in front of the house, they shove him in and I see for the first time in my life my mother cry while saying good bye, my papa kissing me hard, telling me to be good, that he'll be back soon. In the afternoon, we have to go to the police too for identity control, and it is there that I see my papa for the last time, behind bars with his brothers and brothers in law.

I wasn't going to school anymore. My poor mom was no longer working, the Jewish stores were closed. She knitted; my sister was taking charge more and more, she was an extraordinary girl; she had learned to fix runs in stockings for a meager living. My mom had lost much weight; she could now wear my sister's clothes. I was wearing my sister's things, and also my mom's. We were getting once in a while some news from my father who was in several camps in France, 25 words through the Red Cross, mom was sending him little packages every 2 or 3 months. My aunt received her convocation and she left, not wanting to be picked up, from fear we would also get taken. We never heard from her again.

2

1942, May 10, someone rings the bell: "Mom, there is a beggar at the door". But it is my Uncle Ernst who jumped from the train to Auschwitz, with others, alas many were shot down. He is dirty, skin and bones, exhausted, haggard. My mom took care of him; he put on my father's clothes and took my aunt's room. After a few days of very sad talking, he told us that papa had typhus, that he tried to escape twice, and begged my mother to place me somewhere else, to hide me. They said for children, no pity, they disappear as soon as they get to the camps. My sister took me to the convent; I cried all the tears of my body. When she came after 2 months to see me, I made such a fuss to go back home that I was punished by the Sisters. My mom cried a lot, and my sister took her away. I was often cold, hungry, and afraid. I was able to go back home once, from Saturday to Sunday night, my sister gave me orders not to pain my mother. I didn't want to go back, cried a lot; my uncle brought me back to reason. Time was passing badly, but it was passing. The sisters would threaten the worst punishments because I was not baptized, and take our food away. My sister was going to come as a novice. First, she had to sew her habit. Three days later, the Gestapo came to arrest everybody at home, I learned it from a lady who was visiting her daughter in the convent, it was her luck that she wasn't home, that horrible night when the Gestapo surrounded the whole block, and arrested all the Jews, house by house. I could not believe it, and I went to the mother superior to ask to go see. I went, and the land-lady told me everything in details. It was horrible because I was on their list, and nobody would tell where I was. I saw hell in front of me…

1943, my family was deported, this is the family's last address: 59, Rue Otlet, Anderlecht. Later, much later, I learned that they went to Malines (Belgium); from there to the concentration camp of Auschwitz.

I returned to the convent, (Orphelinat St. Joseph, Rue des Champs, 129). There were many Jewish children there; I remember very well Arthur, Etienne, and the youngest ones: Norbert, Marcel, Robert and Irene, the youngest one wasn't yet three. I remember so well, because Elise, my cousin, and me, we took care of the little ones with Sister Rose, also a Jew disguised as a nun. I had to work. I cleaned, took care of the boiler in the winter, and cleaned the toilets also, no flush, they were often clogged. Until the deportation of my sister and my mom, I was getting a package every Friday, with bread, cake, jelly, cookies, etc… How they must have deprived themselves to bring me this package every week. We suffered from cold, I was always hungry, no soap. We had boils, scabies, fleas, and bedbugs.

I stayed there until *1946*, when "Association Israelite d'aide aux Victimes de la Guerre", a Jewish organization looking for hidden Jewish children, got us out of there. Then started the hope that someone would come back. I didn't want to be adopted for fear they wouldn't find me.

I was very well in this home for Jewish children, it was in the country, at Profonsart (Limal), directed by a very intelligent woman doctor. All my missing ones, twenty of them I knew and loved very well, are all present to my eyes, as I saw them the last time, young, very young, good looking and in good health. For me, they are missing people; I can never see them as dead. There is much more to tell, that my name was changed, I was baptized, served mass. With the priest, who had no saying there, I got along well enough; he understood the situation and so much other sufferings. I prayed as much as I could, and very hard at the chapel of the convent. It doesn't matter where you pray. I wasn't heard, so today, if it happens that I pray Shabbat or at the synagogue, or in my bed, it is thinking of them that I do, and specially my mother who told me the Shema Yisroel.

Time erases nothing, all is present. But also, life is here, continues with her ups and downs. I got married, and had, thank God, three good children, and so, through their remembrance, they are all always present.

My mom never stopped hoping her family would come back. They were all exterminated in Auschwitz.

She started a life with her orphaned peers, who became each other's family, and her closest friends for the rest of her life.

She wanted to study after the war, but was deemed too weak then, from severe malnutrition. Her request for a permanent visa was judged of "no value" by the Belgian government, who was not in support of her stay in Belgium. She was suffering from severe decalcification, which led to the loss of her teeth, a small stature, a frail build; it was much later in life I realized she always wore dentures. She regained some health, youthfulness, and was a beautiful bride at 21. She had three children, and my father, of Jewish Russian descent, her companion of over 50 years, was at her side always.

As a child, I idealized my mom to no end, found her beautiful and found beauty in her sadness too. She named me Gisela, after her mother. She passed away in July 2004 in Brussels, after a valiant fight at the hospital. Her heart finally gave up.

She loved little ones, she loved the country side, and she loved cows; there is peace about cows in a field. She was a knitter when I was young, and would knit little clothes for our dolls, as we played in the park, and give them to us at holidays; it was understood I wasn't to make a conscious connection! When I was very young, we took sea-side vacations during the summer. These are some of my best memories. My mom wasn't much of a cook; sadly, she didn't find a source of nurturance to match what she had lost. I have no treasured recipe to share here, BUT my mom was a nurturer of little children, and loved all children, regardless of creed or color, and knew what all mothers know, that to bring peace in this world, you go home, love your family, and protect the children. She gave all she had to give, and I became a doctor, which gave her much "naches". I enjoy writing, and so, I "cooked up" a brief essay, and a poem, in lieu of a food recipe.

She loved Israel, embraced its ideal version, a land raised from our ashes, and turned into a lush garden, such a life giving metaphor for the survivors. There she had and has, many friends. She visited yearly, it was her home too.

I have three children of my own, and my younger daughter Sarah has made Israel her home. She, with her husband Yonatan Caras, started this project by envisioning a cookbook to feed the needy of Jerusalem.

My children called my maman "O'ma". In the names of our ancestors, grandparents, & the whole mishpacha, papa & I are so proud of you my dear children, you have brought us all home!

Elizabeth and her sister

Hansel & Gretel revisited.   My Revenge.

Oven & flames,
Revenge, repay.
Children to be fed
Warmed up, and then read,
To fall asleep, in safe enchantment.
My heart, catch fire
And let it run down my blood, dip-drip, pen & brush
SHOW & TELL
How good life
Becomes fodder for deranged ovens.

The flaming sword is for the Angel
But he lends me a quill
As he fans my out-rage,
My thirst for revenge.
Flames of hatred to erase,
Darkness smolders in the night.
My choked fumes of rage,
Choked scream, to the sky?
NO. To the insanely sane,
Show & tell the burning pain,
Expose the heavy black smoke of charred flesh and bones,
As humanity goes to ashes.
I dip my pen in the flaming darkness, and trace
In the sky that arches our joined hearts.
Truth, always in the searching.
Says: "Show & tell".
Un-fairy tales for us to know,
And out of the soot, the cinders, the grubby clay
Remold! Re-fairy the tales
So children won't fear
The forever ovens of the night
Was hatred victorious?
My revenge is to tell,
As I enter evil again,
Armed with a little flicker
Which snickers at insane evil,
And show, in its trembling flame
The persistence of the fairy tale.

I turn to the Angel, give Praise & Thanks,
She answers : "no sweat dear, Anytime."
She lights a small cigar,
Blows out the fragrant smoke,
And hands me my next feather

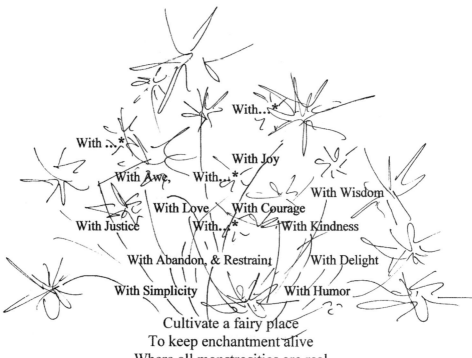

With...*
With ...*
With Joy
With Awe,   With...*
With Wisdom
With Love   With Courage
With Justice   With...*   With Kindness
With Abandon, & Restraint   With Delight
With Simplicity   With Humor

Cultivate a fairy place
To keep enchantment alive
Where all monstrosities are real
And Heroes to match, who win,
After fierce trails, fierce batailles.
Darkness transfigured into light
Voice, sword, pen and brush!
The fighting truth of all
Is always in the making,
The story of it all lives in fairy tales.

Gisela Zerykier MD, child of Elizabeth Silberstein, survivor.

Golda Goldberg Zerykier
Teaneck, N.J, U.S.A.
Submitted by her son Abraham Selig Zerykier M.D.

"My Dear Grandchildren". So begins a letter my mother wrote to my 3 children a short time before she passed away. In this letter she describes her years during the war. She writes of being taken to a labor camp in Czechoslovakia then to Auschwitz and then to Bergen-Belsen, and she gives snippets of her 'life' in these camps. These were stories she never told me and would only hint at when I asked her about those years. Yet, my daughter Sarah had gotten her Bubby to write them down so that they would not be lost. For that my dear Sarahle, I and the rest of the family are so very grateful. At the end of the story about her years in the concentration camps she decided to write another letter to her grandchildren, to leave them with some memories "of my home in a more or less normal time." I guess to show them that there had been some normalcy in her life.

My mother was born Golda Goldberg (Goldja) in Chrzanow, Poland in 1913. She had one sister and five brothers. Her father, known as Reb Selig, was a teacher of Talmud and Polish to boys who did not attend public school. He also was a founder and principal of the Bais Yaakov school for girls in the area. He was a religious intellectual who imbued in his children a love of reading and learning. My mother wrote "I used to observe my parents talking to each other, always a smile on their faces and in their eyes. Once, I heard him saying 'I love you' to her. I was surprised to hear that because religious people did not express themselves like that in front of the children." Her mother, Chana Pearl, was a homemaker. She had a "happy disposition but was very strong-minded." This strong will was passed down to my mother and to my oldest daughter Shuni.

When my mother was 19 years old, her mother passed away. She took upon herself the task of raising and caring for four of her brothers, the youngest being 5 years old. One older brother was already married, and her older sister, who was engaged at that time, got married a few months after their mother died. "After Bruchja [her sister] left home, father said to my brothers 'Now Goldja is your mother, you have to treat her as one'.

This was the end of my youth as it changed my life, my way of thinking. I felt all of sudden a great responsibility for my four brothers. David was 5 years old and Yosek was 7, and to care for their well being, to raise them, to continue in mother's image the way she would want me to, matured me before my time. I promised the children to stay home and never leave them... I also did some charity work and visited sick people."

My mother was arrested on a Friday in September of 1942 while on her way to the bakery to place the cholent in the oven for Shabbos. She was taken, together with many other Jewish girls, to the town square, and from there was transported to a labor camp in Czechoslovakia. "I left my father and two brothers behind, helpless. It was a bitter end of my home life. I left all my dreams behind."

Top Row: Brother Hershel and wife
Bottom Row: Goldja, Reb Selig (father), Bruchia (sister), Yosek (brother)

In the labor camp, my mother was given a job in a factory operating a weaving machine. "The German civilians who worked next to me treated me pretty good. They were afraid to talk to me, but they brought me cigarettes, bread, fruit & the newspaper 'Der Spiegel'. I didn't ask for it. Some of the workers were Chechoslovaks but Nazi followers. I got to know a Pole who lived not far from Chrzanow. He worked in a different department as an engineer, and went home twice a month. I sent letters that he delivered personally, and he brought me back letters and some clothes, for which he was well paid. It was a lifesaver for all of us. About 5 months later he came back with the letters. No one was home; the Germans had deported all the Jews to Auschwitz. Father, Bruchja & Perele [my mother's sister and niece] were gone. I had a nervous break-down. My friend [a camp Doctor] took me to her quarters where I was unconscious for 2 days and nights. I recovered and went back to work. When the Germans came to the factory for an inspection and I was absent, they went to the camp to find out what was wrong. I was in bed, couldn't walk. I knew I'll be sent for extermination. Two days later I went back to work. At the next inspection they went over to the foreman in my work place, talked to him and looked at me. I felt a fire burning in my body. After they left, the foreman came over; he said he told them that I am a good worker and handling the machine very well. He said 'I'm sorry', and left. When I came back to the camp I was called to the camp commandant and told that I will be sent with five others to Auschwitz! This was a few days before Pesach."

"My friend and our Jewish Kapo [an overseer chosen by the Germans] intervened but couldn't change the sentence. We decided to make a Seder & invite the whole staff, including the German head of the camp, 2 other German men and 2 women. We were about 50 people. We took some basic food from the kitchen, like vegetables and eggs. We made borsht, cooked potatoes, and set the table. It looked a little bit like home. I conducted the Seder, explained what it is about, what was done to the Jews at that time. Everybody listened with a serious expression on their faces. I made Kiddush. When I sat down I couldn't keep back the tears from covering my face. I washed and said the bracha [blessing]. Nobody moved. We finished at midnight. The next morning the Jewish Kapo came to me and said they took me off the list, but the other five girls were deported three days later ! Another miracle!"

My mother was eventually sent to Auschwitz, where she survived for 17 months. She described it as "a slaughter house in the open." In reading her letter, more of a memoir, I understand why she found it difficult to talk about her experiences there and what she was witness to.

In 1944, as the American army was marching towards Auschwitz, the inmates were transported to Bergen-Belsen. "About a week before the liberation, the SS hung a white flag on the gate of the camp. Two SS men who knew me from Auschwitz asked me what I will do to them when and if we will be liberated. I looked them right in the eyes and said 'I'll not do a thing to you'."

On April 15, 1945 Bergen-Belsen was liberated by the British army. One of the other inmates suggested that my mother, who could speak English, go and talk to the British. "My friend & I walked out to talk to the liberators. Most of the Germans were already rounded up. They asked me which of them tortured the prisoners. I knew most of them, especially that SS man who asked me what I will do to him, and that woman who punished us so cruelly 2 days before the liberation. I looked at them, they looked at me. Their faces were red, their eyes big. I will never forget that eye contact. I did not point at them. I wanted to show, especially to that murderer from Auschwitz, that the Jews are human. I figured they have their verdict already. I kept my word."

"This is a condensed story of my life and the miracles how I survived. I want to leave these memories to my precious grandchildren with the hope that when you grow up you will join other grandchildren of survivors to keep the memory of the atrocities of the Holocaust alive. It should not be forgotten and never repeated again".

"With All My Love,
Bubby "

My mother knew my father, Sam Zerykier, before the war; her sister was married to my father's brother. My parents were married in Sweden in 1946, where I was born in 1948. Of her six siblings, only the two youngest survived the war, her two brothers whom she had raised after their mother passed away. The youngest, my uncle David, lived close to us both in Sweden and in Brooklyn, NY. The older one, uncle Yosek, settled in Israel and it wasn't until 1958 that my mother was reunited with him.

My mother was an excellent cook, much appreciated by family, friends, and our community at large. My children enjoyed her cakes and cookies... And her famous Gefilte Fish! My wife, like so many others, enjoyed her apple cake! For many years my mother was the specialty cook in a restaurant in Brooklyn that my parents owned together with her youngest brother, David. The restaurant, George's Coffee Shop on Nostrand Ave., was known in the neighborhood for its Jewish fare, and had a faithful clientele. Before each Jewish Holiday, my mother took orders for her gefilte fish from the many customers who had tasted it in the restaurant.
My mother passed away in 1999. My children were 17, 14 and 12 years old at the time. She survived to have a full life, raise me, and delight in her three grandchildren, who were lucky to have been able to spend many good years with their vibrant Bubby. In the end, she was the winner.

I have decided to include two recipes for cakes that she baked on Passover. Had she been given the ingredients, who knows if she wouldn't have baked these in that labor camp in Czechoslovakia when she thought she was going to be shipped out to Auschwitz.

***My mother, Goldja (on left) and
her sister Bruchja in Chrzanow***

Passover Nut Cake
parve

Yosek, Bruchja and Perele

12 Extra Large Eggs separated
1 1/2 cups Sugar
2 Tablespoons Oil
3/4 Cup Cake Meal
2 Tablespoons Potato Starch
3/4 Cup Chopped Walnuts
1 Lemon-Juice and Rind
1 Teaspoon Vanilla Sugar

Directions:
Preheat oven to 350 degrees

1.) Mix dry ingredients together.
2.) Separate eggs, beat whites until stiff.
3.) In yolks add 1 cup sugar and oil, beat until smooth.
4.) Add all dry ingredients and blend well.
5.) Add to stiff egg whites.
Bake in 350 degree oven for 1 hour and 10 minutes.
6.) Use a Bundt Pan that separates.
7.) Hang Bundt Pan upside down on a bottle top to cool.

Passover Jelly Roll

parve

- 12 eggs - Separated
- 1 1/2 cups sugar
- 2 Tablespoons Oil
- 1 Cup Cake Meal
- 2 Tablespoons Potato Starch
- 1 Lemon Juice and Rind
- 1 Teaspoon Vanilla Sugar

Directions:

Preheat oven to 350 degrees

1.) Beat egg whites until stiff with 1/2 cup sugar.
2.) In another bowl mix egg yolks with sugar and oil until smooth.
3.) Add other dry ingredients until well mixed.
4.) Slowly add to the stiffened egg whites.
5.) Separate onto two cookie sheets.
6.) Bake in 350 degree oven for up to one hour.
7.) When cool take dampened linen towel, put either Raspberry of Apricot Preserve on one side of the cake mix, roll into a jelly roll, when finished sprinkle with shredded coconut or powdered sugar.
8.) Jelly roll can also be filled with chocolate or any other fruit filling you prefer.

Sam Zerykier

Teaneck, N.J., U.S.A.

Submitted by his grandchildren, Shuni Zerykier Geis, Sarah Zerykier Caras, and Yonah Zerykier

**Sam Zerykier
in the early 1930's**

Our Zeidy, Sam (Szulem) Zerykier, was born in Dumbrova, Poland in 1914 to Abraham and Liba Zerykier. He was the fifth of six children in a family which included his older brothers Yaakov and Yosef, his older sisters Ethel and Rivka, and his baby sister Sarah.

The Zerykiers were a close and successful family, as our Zeidy's father owned and operated a candy factory. Sadly, Yosef was killed at an early age when he was hit in the head by a rock thrown by some Polish boys, and Abraham passed away when Zeidy was only five years old. Zeidy's mother and older brother, Yaakov, who was only 13 or 14 at the time, were left to run the factory. At one point they hired a man to run the factory for them but soon found out that he was stealing from them so they fired him. Yaakov took over the running of the candy factory.

After a while the candy factory became too difficult, so Zeidy's mother sold it and bought a grocery store. Things went well for a while until the Poles began to boycott all Jewish businesses.

After the Nazis entered Poland all of the Jews were forced to wear yellow armbands. One Shabbos, our Zeidy was all dressed up in a suit, on his way to visit his girlfriend, Anja. Because he wanted to look nice, Zeidy decided not to wear his armband.

He was spotted in the streets by a group of Poles who yelled to a German soldier "That's a Jew!" He was then stopped by the German soldier and forced to join the work brigade, carrying rocks from one area to another. He suggested to the German that the work would be finished faster if he could bring a wheelbarrow that was standing at a short distance from the work site. The German agreed, so Zeidy went to get the wheelbarrow and when he was at a certain distance from the work site Zeidy started to run. The German fired shots at our Zeidy, but he escaped. He did, however, leave his new suit behind.

By 1942 most Jews in Poland were placed in ghettos. Trying to avoid that fate the Zerykier family closed their grocery store, left their apartment and tried to go into hiding. They asked a non-Jewish neighbor to watch the store, telling him that he could eat whatever food he wanted as long as he did not sell or give any of it away to others, since they only expected that they would be gone for a short time.

The family's number one concern was to protect their mother. They took her to a church and begged the priest to take her in and hide her with the other Poles being hidden there, but the priest refused to let her in. As the family was walking away from the church, it was struck by a bomb.

**Wedding photo of
Golda & Sam Zerykier
October 27, 1946**

After a few days of searching unsuccessfully for a place to hide, they decided to go back home. But when they went into the store they found that everything was gone. The Polish family who had been entrusted with caring for the store had stolen everything. Someone told our Zeidy where the man was hiding and when Zeidy went to confront him, the man came at him with an axe and threatened to kill him. Our Zeidy left, with his life still intact but his family's livelihood gone.

Sam at age 91 1/2, Shuni's Bridal Shower, June 2006

Soon after, the Zerykiers were taken and forcibly moved into a ghetto. In the ghetto, there was a Jewish police force controlled by the Nazis. Every day the police would round up about 1,000 Jews and send them to the concentration camps. At this time, the Jews did not yet know what was happening in the camps.

Our Zeidy and his family went through this selection process and he was sent to the camps. His sister, Rivkah, ran away and he was sure she would survive but sadly she did not. She died in our Bubby's arms after the liberation. His youngest sister, Sarah, got married two days before she was taken away. She did not survive either.

Once in the camps, Zeidy was lined up with the other men when a German soldier asked if any of the men were carpenters. Our Zeidy said "'I am a carpenter.' I didn't even know how to hold a hammer in my hand, but I said 'I am a carpenter.'"

And so Zeidy was taken to Brunslov. Throughout the war Zeidy was moved around to various camps and in the end, he was liberated from Bergen-Belsen. He and his brother Jack (Yaakov) were the only survivors from their family. Jack had been married before the war to Bruchja, our Bubby's sister and they had a daughter, Perele. Neither Jack's wife nor his daughter survived the camps.

Soon after the war both Zeidy and his brother were sent by the Red Cross to a Displaced Persons Camp in Sweden. It was here that our Zeidy found our Bubby, and in 1946 they got married. In 1948, our father, Abraham, was born and in 1953 they immigrated to America on a plane that was used to transport soldiers. They settled in Brooklyn, New York, and began to make a new life for themselves.

When asked about the war, Zeidy begins by naming all of his family members, whom they married and the names of their children. It is clear that what was most important to our Zeidy was not the horrors he endured during the war, but the memories of the people who were lost. At many points in his story, our Zeidy talked of survival. He said "I knew if they not gonna kill me, I gonna survive."

Zeidy was the patriarch of our family until January 23, 2008 when, at the age of 93, he passed away. He was a proud man who loved his family and took great joy in being with us. He had an amazing sense of humor, which endeared him to everyone he met. Whenever Zeidy showed us the few pictures he had left of his family, we knew that even though they are not alive today, they and their story will never be forgotten. Although we miss him greatly, we know that he is up in 'shamayim' (heaven), reunited with his family.

13

Zeidy's and Bubby's Apple Cake
(Zeidy would peel the apples)

Dough
3 cups flour
3 tsps baking powder
3/4 cup sugar
3 sticks margarine
  (at room temperature)
3 eggs
1/2 tsp of vanilla

Filling
3 lbs apples
3 Tbsp bread crumbs or matzah meal
1/2 cup sugar
5 tsp strawberry jam (optional)
handful of raisins (optional)

Directions:

Preheat oven to 350 degrees

1.) Combine the flour, baking powder, sugar, margarine, eggs and vanilla to make a dough.
2.) Put in the fridge for an hour.
3.) Divide the dough into two parts with one part having more.
4.) Roll out the bigger portion of dough and place it in an 8x10 pan making sure to cover the bottom and sides of the pan.
5.) Put 1 1/2 Tbsp of bread crumbs or matzoh meal on the dough.
6.) Peel and thinly slice the apples.
7.) Line the pan with half of the apples.
8.) Sprinkle 1/4 cup of sugar on the apples. You can put raisins in at this point if you like.
9.) Put in the rest of the apples.
10.) Sprinkle 1/4 cup of sugar on these apples.
11.) Put 1 1/2 Tbsp of bread crumbs or matzoh meal over the apples. You can now add the strawberry jam on top if you like.
12.) Roll out the other portion of dough and put it on top of the apples making sure not to leave any space between the bottom and top dough. You can go around the edge of the cake with a fork to make sure it is sealed and make a nice design, too.
13.) Poke a couple holes in the top of the cake with a fork so the apples can breath.
14.) Bake uncovered for one hour.

Golda and Sam on motor scooter in Sweden

14

Anna Steinberger
Houston, TX, U.S.A.
Submitted by Anna Steinberger, PhD.

It was a rainy night of September 4, 1939 with almost unreal silence, a silence after many hours of intense bombing by German planes. It was the fourth night after Hitler's army invaded Poland and was rapidly advancing across the country toward our hometown, Radom. It was the night when my uncle, a country doctor, knocked on our door and told my parents, my brother, Jacob (16 yrs) and me (11 yrs) to quickly get dressed and get on top of the horse-driven buggy. My aunt, their son, and Mom's mother were already seated on the straw covered buggy. And so we left behind our home, belongings, and our prewar life for an unknown future.

After a few days of traveling toward the Eastern boarder under daily air raids and shelling from low flying Messerschmitts, we stopped in Rovno, a small town in the Ukraine. We had no choice! The Germans killed one of our horses and the remaining one became too weak to pull the wagon. Surprisingly, a few days later, we found ourselves occupied by the Soviet army which, by agreement with the Nazi government took over the Polish part of Ukraine and Bialorus. Had our horse given up a few miles earlier, we would have been taken over by the Germans. We were offered Russian citizenship and transported by cattle cars to a collective farm near Stalingrad.

My father and brother had to work in the fields and my Mom in a food processing factory. Not knowing the Russian language I was placed into the first grade (after having already completed six grades before WWII started). Living conditions were poor and we were often hungry and cold, but glad for having escaped the Germans! Mom mostly regretted not having saved any family photographs, particularly those of the children. It seemed my Mom aged ten years during those few months and lost a lot of weight, but she bravely carried on. About one and a half years later we were transferred to Stalingrad where both of my parents worked in a clothing factory (tailoring is what they did before the war). They had to leave before 6 A.M. and return after 7 p.m. carrying a small container of watery soup from the factory kitchen for my brother and me to eat. During this period, Jacob and I attended school a few miles away from home. Things worsened when German forces attacked the Soviet Union on June 22, 1941 and eventually threatened to occupy Stalingrad.

My brother was drafted into the Russian army, while we were once again packed into a cattle train with many other people who also escaped the German invasion, and moved to Alma Ata, the capital city of Kazachstan. My parents worked again in a factory and I attended school. What helped us fight starvation was a little vegetable garden outside the city that Mom attended regularly with some help from me. This little plot of land provided us with some corn and other vegetables to supplement our meager rations of bread and flour. Mom became very imaginative in creating foods that made the flour last longer. We had no idea where Jacob was or if he was even alive. It was only after the war ended, that he was able to locate us through the International Red Cross. Despite fighting on the front lines as an artillery officer, he survived! Our joy was boundless, although we did not actually see him until we returned to Poland in 1946.

15

We remained in Poland just a few months before making our way to a DP Camp in the American occupied sector of Germany. I continued my study of medicine in Frankfurt while my parents were biding time. After a long wait of over three years, the three of us finally immigrated to the USA! My Mom's sister who lived in New York helped my parents with a job and later in opening a store of ladies coats. I worked in a medical laboratory for one year. My brother chose to remain in Poland until 1964, when he joined us in the USA.

I am happy to say, that despite the uprooting, the dangers and difficulties endured during the war, my parents succeeded in creating a comfortable life in this country. They lived long enough (around 91 yrs) to celebrate my marriage (to a survivor whom I met in Alma Ata), the birth of two granddaughters, my graduation from Wayne State University with a PhD degree followed by a successful research career, their own 60th wedding anniversary and also the birth of a great grandson. I will always remember their courage, love and hope for a better tomorrow. Ultimately, they not only survived the war, they won the war!!

Cabbage Rolls

meat

1 Large Cabbage
1 1/2 ground beef
1/2 cup uncooked rice
   (preferably the quick cooking type)
1 large onion
2-8 oz. cans tomato paste
Olive Oil

This used to be my favorite dish when I was growing up in prewar POLAND. I am referring to my Mom's prize recipe for "CABBAGE ROLLS". Whenever I took a sniff of the wonderful aroma coming from the kitchen, I knew that we are having cabbage rolls for dinner that evening. What a treat!! I would like to share that feeling with you.

Preparation:

1.) Freeze cabbage IN A SEALED PLASTIC BAG 2-3 days prior to use. When ready to use, defrost the cabbage (overnight in the refrigerator or ~1 hr. in warm water) then separate individual leaves.
2.) Cut onion into small squares and fry in oil until light brown.
3.) Add tomato paste plus 1-2 cups of water and boil for 1-2 min. to blend.
4.) Add your favorite spices (garlic, salt, pepper, cilantro, etc).
5.) Mix meat with the rice and spices to taste.
6.) Roll each cabbage leaf with some meat/rice mixture and arrange in an oven dish in a single or multiple layers.
7.) Pour the tomato sauce to cover the rolls.
8.) Bake covered at 350F for ~1.5 hr.

16

KEEPS WELL FROZEN OR FOR SEVERAL DAYS REFRIGERATED... ***ENJOY!!***

Ann Eisenberg
West Bloomfield, MI, U.S.A.
Submitted by Carole Master

We were eight siblings, five girls and three boys, and my parents. We were born in Sviget, Romania. When the war broke out in 1942 they took my two brothers and my father to forced labor. In April, right after Passover they took all the Jews and my whole family to the ghetto. We were in the ghetto together until May, then they put us in a cattle car and the train took us to the unknown.

After three days and nights we found ourselves in Auschwitz. Men and women were separated, and then the selection took place. We were sent either to the right or to the left. The people who went to the left went to the crematorium. My sister and I were sent to the right, while my mother, three sisters and my little brother went to the left...which was death.

My sister Rose and I were sent to march through the gate, we were shaved, and stripped of our clothing then sent to the cold showers. Everybody got a piece of soap with the word "Jew".

I was in Auschwitz for six weeks. I carried dirt in a buggy from here to there and then had to break rocks into small pieces. We were sent to an oil refinery factory that was bombed out, and we had to clean and help rebuild it. Then it was bombed again. We were taken to another town, Somarda, Germany. This was an ammunition factory and we stayed there for six months.

When the allies were approaching, that was when they took us on the never ending death march. If you couldn't walk they beat you to death. No food, no water for six weeks. Thank God my sister was able to help me along in the snow.

One morning the Russians occupied that part of Germany so we went back to Romania. We found only one brother and an empty house which the Russians took over.

I, Ann Eisenberg survived because God wanted living witnesses......

Anne (standing) and her sister

17

My Dough
dairy

5 cups flour
1 lb. butter
3/4 pint sour cream
3 egg yolks
1 whole egg
3 tsps. baking powder
1/4 cup sugar

You can make Ruggala, Poppy Seed Cake, Apple Cake and whatever you wish.

Directions:

1.) Work it out together and refrigerate overnight.
2.) Bake whatever you want, and smear it with egg whites.
3.) Bake 1 hr. 350 degrees.
   ENJOY!

Poppy seed Roll
dairy

Directions:

1.) Mix poppy seed 1 can, and 1 1/2 tbsp. honey & 1 small can crushed pineapple.
2.) Smear with 2 beaten egg whites.
3.) Bake on a cookie sheet.
4.) Bake at 350 degrees.
5.) Roll out 1 sheet of dough...

Ruggala
dairy

Directions:

1.) Roll out dough.
2.) Cut in 3" long strips.
3.) Filling:
   - Apricot Jam, ground walnuts, sprinkle sugar & cinnamon
4.) Roll it up and cut into 3" pieces.
5.) Smear with 2 beaten egg whites.
6.) Bake at 350 degrees.

Apple Filling
dairy

5 apples peeled and sliced
1 cup sugar
1 tbsp. cinnamon
2 tbsp. potato starch or cornstarch

Directions:

1.) Divide dough in half.
2.) Roll half dough for bottom layer.
3.) Add filling.
4.) Cover with the same size dough.
5.) Smear with 2 beaten egg whites.
6.) Bake at 350 degrees for 1 hour.

Rachel Pirak
Springfield, N.J., U.S.A.
Submitted by her daughter-in-law Myra Pirak

She was born and raised in Koselovo, a small town in Czechoslovakia. In 1944, she and her siblings and parents were rounded up and transported to Auschwitz. They arrived in May, 1944 on the first day of Shavuot. Her mother and her sister's four year old daughter were separated and told they were going to the "showers" - they were gassed. Her mother was forty-six years old. My mother-in-law was 18 years old at the time she arrived at Auschwitz, the youngest of eight children.

They were taken as slave laborers and sent to work in a munitions factory. The conditions were deplorable and my mother-in-law became malnourished and weak. Her sisters force fed her and propped her up every morning when they took attendance. She especially credits one sister (whose 4 year old daughter was killed) with secretly getting hold of an extra potato and secretly boiling it and pouring the water the potato was cooked in (containing the nutrients) down her throat to give her nourishment. As a result of this malnourishment, in her later years my mother-in-law lost all her teeth.

She has a number, A13040, tattooed on her forearm. Five siblings and her father survived the war and were liberated from Auschwitz in May, 1945. They returned to Czechoslovakia. My mother-in-law married in 1946 and had a daughter in 1947. In 1949, they emigrated to Israel where my husband was born in 1953. They left Israel for the US in 1962 because it was so difficult to earn a living there.

My father-in-law started one of the first toy companies in Israel, he also had several patents in hydroponics (growing vegetables without soil). My mother-in-law is a wonderful cook and baker, she worked for 25 years for the Rabbinical College in Morristown, New Jersey as the dairy chef, making breakfast and lunch for 300 students and baking cakes for snacks. She makes a batch of home-made challah every two to three weeks for at least the thirty years that I have been married to her son.

19

Challah

parve

5 lbs flour plus 3 cups as needed
4 ounces of fresh yeast
1 cup of sugar
4 jumbo eggs plus beaten egg for brushing top
2 1/2 sticks margarine (non-dairy)
5 teaspoons salt
5 cups water, divided

Directions:

Preheat oven to 350 degrees

1.) Dissolve yeast in 1 cup lukewarm water.
2.) Add 1 cup flour to yeast mixture.
3.) Set aside and let rise ½ hour.
4.) In a large bowl put flour in, make well in center and add eggs, sugar, salt, margarine, 4 cups of water and yeast mixture.
5.) Knead dough. If dough is sticky and loose add more flour (up to two more cups may be needed).
6.) Let rise at least two hours.
7.) Grease six eight inch round pans.
8.) Braid challah, place into pans and let rise again at least ½ hour.
9.) Brush challah with beaten eggs.
10.) Bake 45 minutes to 1 hour at 350 degrees until golden brown.

Enjoy!

Basha Untracht (Betty Drang) & Leizer (Lester) Drang

Springfield, N.J, U.S.A.
Submitted by their daughter Myra Pirak

Both of my parents came from the same small town in eastern Poland called Zamosc. My father was a friend of my mother's older brothers. At the outset of Hitler's takeover of Poland, they each escaped and crossed the border into Russia. My mother, her parents and siblings ran from place to place, lived in forests and endured many hardships in the five years that they lived and tried to survive in the Ukraine, learning to speak Russian, working in the cotton fields, and surviving malaria. My father spent the war years also in Russia where he was arrested and sent to Siberia from where he escaped and continued to run from place to place and not be caught.

After the war, my mother and her family returned to Poland to try to find other members who may have survived, as did my father to try and locate his mother and sisters, who hid in the cellar of a farm. They were killed by Polish peasants after the war who discovered their location.

They each made their way through Poland, into Germany. They were placed in dp camps and eventually emigrated to the United States to the lower east side of Manhattan, where they met in front of the HIAS (Hebrew Immigrant Aid Society) building each had gone to for assistance. My father recognized my mother as someone from his hometown and they reconnected leading to their marriage in New York in 1953. My father is deceased for five years now, my mother lives across the street from me independently. She frequently speaks to student groups about her Holocaust experiences. She has written her memoirs for our family and she has published writing vignettes about her life in several publications in New Jersey.

21

Kreplach

meat

(my favorite childhood recipe of my mother's)

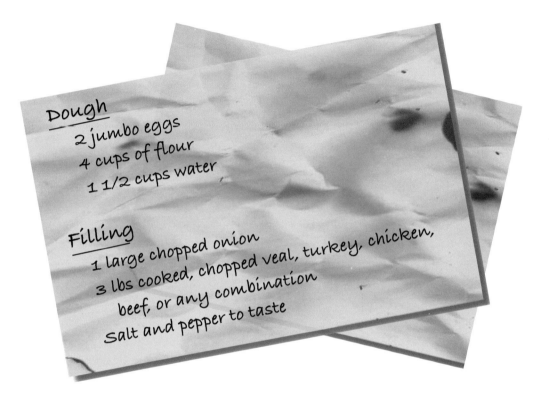

Dough
- 2 jumbo eggs
- 4 cups of flour
- 1 1/2 cups water

Filling
- 1 large chopped onion
- 3 lbs cooked, chopped veal, turkey, chicken, beef, or any combination
- Salt and pepper to taste

Directions:

1.) Combine all ingredients to form a soft dough.
2.) Sauté onion in a small amount of oil until translucent.
3.) Add to meat mixture.
4.) Roll out dough until thin and cut into 2 inch squares.
5.) Add a teaspoon of meat mixture in center of each square and fold into a triangle, pinching edges to stay together.
6.) Cook in a large pot of salted, boiling water for 10-15 minutes until done.
7.) Drain, and cool.

Enjoy!

Betty Drang's Apple Cake

parve

(my father's favorite recipe of hers)

Dough:
- 2 jumbo eggs
- 2 sticks of margarine
- 1/4 cup of oil
- 1/4 cup of orange juice
- 2 full tablespoons of baking powder
- 2 tablespoons or packets of vanilla sugar
- 1 full cup of sugar
- 3 cups flour

Combine all ingredients to make a soft dough. Divide dough into two pieces.

Filling:
- 4 lbs. of Cortland apples, peeled, cored, and sliced thin
- Combine apples with cinnamon, 1/4 cup sugar, 1 tablespoon or
- 1 packet of vanilla sugar, and 1 tablespoon of oil

Mix well.

Directions:
Preheat oven to 375 degrees

Grease 9x13 pan lightly. Place half of dough in pan and pat evenly to 1/4 inch thickness on the bottom and up the sides of the pan. Dust with handful of flour then add apple mixture. Put another handful if flour on top of apples. Roll out remaining dough until 1/4 inch thick and cover top of apples sealing well all around. Top with crushed walnuts, cinnamon, and sugar. Bake at 375 degrees for 45 minutes to one hour until golden brown.

Enjoy!

Carol Wilner
Columbia, MD, U.S.A.

Carol and her granddaughter Emily

I am a child survivor of the Holocaust- a hidden child who survived an impossible situation. I was born in Boryslav, Poland (the Ukraine then) in 1941. It was a time of turmoil and uncertainty. Children, old, and weak were taken away to die. I escaped because of the courage, cooperation and incredible sacrifice of a number of people who made a commitment to try and save me.

The town where I was born was made into a slave concentration camp where only the strongest and fittest were allowed to remain. My father, who had studied in Vienna and was fluent in German, became an interpreter for the Germans. My mother dug ditches.

At first we lived outside the camp, but it became increasingly dangerous. Every day Jews were gathered up and sent to death camps. When I was 18 months old it became evident that I could no longer survive on the outside so I was smuggled into the camp where my father's friends built a secret crawl space for me.

I remained hidden from the time I was 18 months until I was four. I was not allowed to cry, and I remained hidden by myself for endless hours until someone could come down to check on me. At night I was taken down to be with my mother. I never smelled fresh air or felt the sun, and was not able to examine the world the way babies do. I am often asked, and I ask myself, how it was possible for a toddler to survive such confines and to understand that crying meant death. Somehow I understood, and under impossible conditions I remained hidden.

My mother had a baby boy who was not so lucky. He was born in the camp and he was taken away to die on the day he was born because it was impossible to hide two children. My mother had to make the choice.

When I was four we were liberated by the Russians and we lived in Poland for another two years. The conditions were terrible so my father decided to take the risk and have us smuggled over the border into Czechoslovakia, Austria, and finally into a displaced persons camp run by Americans in Germany. We took nothing with us but the clothes on our backs and whatever money my father had managed to save. The three week journey was difficult, arduous, and dangerous. Most of the survivors in the camp were preparing to go to Palestine. Like us, they had lost everything, but when Palestine became Israel it became their refuge and dream.

But then, through the Red Cross, my father managed to find his nephew and niece who had survived and come to America. They sent us papers, and we made the decision to come to America rather than Israel. We arrived in August, 1949 when I was 8 years old.

Chakchooka

parve

1 large eggplant
1 large onion
1/2 green pepper
1/2 red pepper
1/2 yellow pepper
3 large garlic cloves
1 small can chickpeas (reserve some of the liquid)
2 lemons
1 tsp. salt
1/2 tsp. ground pepper
1 tsp. curry powder
1/2 tsp. cinnamon
1/2 tsp. turmeric
6 Tbsp. olive oil

To Prepare:

Wash and dry eggplant. It's best prepared whole on a grill, turning often until skin is charred and pulp tender so that it has a smoky flavor. However you can also prick the eggplant on all sides with a fork, cover with aluminum foil, and bake for an hour at 400 degrees. Remove eggplant when done, and scoop out pulp. Mash in a bowl or food processor, but make sure you retain some body and texture. **Do not** mince.
Add 3 minced garlic cloves, mix well, let stand.
Dice onions and peppers and sauté in olive oil until tender.
Add eggplant mixture and chick peas with some of the liquid.
Add lemon juice of 1 1/2 lemons.
Add seasoning, mix well and cover. Cook over low heat for 30 minutes.
Add more seasoning if you want spicier. Keep tasting.

The dish goes well as a side dish with lamb or broiled fish, or by itself over rice or cold with Pita bread.

"Grema" Etta Hauptman

Columbia, MD, U.S.A.
By her daughter Carol Wilner

Everyone called my mother Grema. It was a name that my youngest daughter made up when she was a baby and couldn't pronounce Grandma. You could say that it's a combination of Grandma and Ima (Hebrew for mother). And the name fits her and became hers, and soon no one remembered her real name, Etta.

She was the bravest woman I ever knew. Even before the war, growing up in a shtetl, she overcame extraordinary hardships and learned how to survive incredible difficulties. In the camp she witnessed and experienced horrors that are hard to imagine, and it was only when she became old that she spoke about them. We did not talk about our experiences.

When my baby brother was born in the camp she had to make the impossible choice about which one of her children to save, knowing that she had to let go of one to give another a chance to live. She lived with that nightmare all of her life, but she was the strong one in the family, carrying all of us with her strength and courage.

She had wanted to go to Israel, but instead we came to the United States. And she made a life here, and raised her children, and made sure that we got an education, and nurtured us in a way that was truly amazing. She was 59 when my father died. She then made the decision to make Aliyah and fulfill her earlier dream.

She moved to Jerusalem, bought an apartment, and started again. She lived in Israel until well into her seventies and then returned to America to be closer to her children and grandchildren.

Grema was everybody's grandmother. She took care of all my friends and they all loved her. At the age of 75 she made one move- to Miami Beach where the sun shone and she could be warm. She loved it there and became the center of a strong social circle, helping to take care of others. She was full of love and joy and good sense.

She had learned to let go of unimportant things in life. She never judged and had little patience for trivial things. She had learned to filter out the unimportant and focus on living and loving her family. Most of all, she wanted her children and grandchildren to be decent human beings. "Be a mensch" she would say.

And oh yes, she loved to dance. In Miami she danced every night until she could dance no more. One of my fondest memories is of her dancing a tango with a stately and courtly gentleman who was one of her many friends.

Etta and her daughter Carol in March, 1948

Gremas Bullanikis Potato Pies

parve

Crust

2 cups all purpose flour
2 tsp. Baking powder
3/4 tsp. salt
1/4 cup margarine (non-dairy)
2 3/4 cups cold water

Potato Filling

4 medium potatoes, peeled and cut into quarters. Boil until soft
1 large onion diced
2 tsp. salt
ground pepper to taste
1/2 can 14.5 ounce sauerkraut (drained)
1 beaten egg for glaze

To Prepare:

Preheat oven to 350

To make the crust:

Sift flour with baking powder and salt into large bowl. Cut the margarine into small pieces and blend with fingertips into the flour so that it becomes the consistency of large crumbs. Add water and mix, gathering the dough into a ball and kneading it for a minute or two, adding a bit of flour as needed to get the right consistency. Cover and refrigerate for 30 minutes.

To make the filler:

While the dough is chilling mash the potatoes. Fry the onions in oil until soft and golden brown. Add onions, sauerkraut and seasoning and mash together until potatoes are smooth and ingredients are well mixed.

Remove dough from refrigerator and knead on a smooth surface that is coated with flour. The dough should be soft and pliant. Pinch off a chunk of dough about the size of a large egg and with a rolling pin coated with flour, roll out into a circle about the size of a saucer. Roll it as thin as possible without falling apart. Place mound of potato filler in the center and trim the dough with a knife so that it is even (about 1/2 inch all around). Pinch the dough around the potato so that it covers the sides evenly but leaves the center open (like a tart). Using a small brush, glaze with a beaten egg.

Place on a cookie sheet and bake at 350 degrees for approximately 45-50 minutes or until the dough is golden brown.

For dairy, serve warm with sour cream. Makes 6 pies.

Erwin Diwald
Milwaukee, WI, U.S.A.
Submitted by his daughter, Frances Diwald Mendelsohn

Born in 1907, my father, Erwin Diwald was a lawyer in Vienna who was an expert in Canon law. He built a successful practice by being able to obtain annulments for Catholics—the only way a divorce could be obtained in that very Catholic country. His legal career ended shortly after Hitler's invasion of Austria. My mother, Selma Gehler Diwald, was a pharmacist who took over the operation of her uncle's pharmacy near the Stefanskirche after he was taken to Dachau. Her own father, Victor Gehler, was also taken to Dachau but after several months my grandmother, Maria Keitsch Gehler, bribed the SS and was able to obtain his release in late 1938. They immediately went to Haifa in what was then Palestine where they lived until their deaths in the early 1950s.

After the arrest and incarceration of my grandfather, my parents knew they had to get out but had no one who could sponsor them to come to the US. My aunt, Paula Diwald Grunfeld, having escaped to Paris because the Gestapo was looking to take her into custody because of her anti-government activities, was instrumental in saving their lives. Fluent in six languages, she quickly found a job selling petit point purses in an exclusive Parisian store. To supplement her income, she gave sightseeing tours of Paris to visitors—mostly from the US. In this way she met a couple from Chicago who agreed to sponsor my parents. After several unsuccessful attempts to leave Austria, my parents finally made it to France in mid-1938. They lived in Chateau Thierry until their visas were finally obtained in the summer of 1939. The delay was two-fold. My mother had been born in Galicia, which by WWII, was a part of Poland; the US quota for Polish-born people was very low. They also discovered that an anti-Semitic Foreign Service officer at the US Consulate in Paris had lied about the existence of their visas for several months.

They left Europe on August 29, 1939 on the Champlain, a French ocean liner. On September 1, the war broke out and the rest of the voyage was made under radio silence. When they arrived in New York, they were offered temporary housing by HIAS. They went to Chicago to thank their sponsors and eventually ended up 100 miles to the North in Milwaukee. My mother worked in a drug store but not as a pharmacist because she did not have the state license. She died of cancer in 1996. My father became a successful tire salesman. He never felt he could take the many years to learn US law and take the Bar exam here. During the War, he built propellers for our B-17 bombers. He opened his own tire store in the later 1950s and retired in 1970. He was moved to an assisted living facility in Los Angeles near his younger daughter, Susan in 2006 and died in late 2008.

Before Hitler took over Austria, my parents lived the good life, complete with a live-in maid. Therefore cooking was not something they did. Before her marriage, my mother had taken some cooking classes and Marillen Torte was one of the desserts she learn to make. It became one of her most popular dishes, always admired—and devoured—by their many friends in Milwaukee.

Marillen Torte (Apricot Torte)

dairy

1 15 oz. can of unpeeled Apricot halves, drained on paper towels
1/2 lb unsalted Butter
1 scant cup Sugar
3 large Eggs or 4 medium
2 cups sifted Flour
1/2 tsp Baking Powder

Directions:
Preheat oven to 350 Degrees

1.) Cream butter and sugar.
2.) Mix in eggs, flour and baking powder
   (mix powder and flour together first).
3.) Pour into greased (butter) spring form.
4.) Place apricots on top.
5.) Bake 350 Degrees for 1 hour.
6.) Let cool.
In the Viennese tradition, the torte can be served with whipped cream

Erwin and Selma Diwald, 1938

**Erwin and Selma's
55th wedding anniversary
with grandsons Dan,
Steve, and Mike, 1992**

29

Ellen Rosanski Katz Wolf
New York, NY, U.S.A.
Submitted by her daughter-in-law Jackie Katz

Frankfurt, Germany

At fourteen, Ellen Wolf should have been giggling over boys and discussing the latest fashions with her older sister. But this was 1939, and Hitler was solidifying his reign of terror. Life was never to be the same again. From December 2, 1938 to the outbreak of World War II, in September 1939, roughly 10,000 children between the ages of 2 and 17 fled to Great Britain on the Kindertransport. None were accompanied by their parents. In fact, many were never to see their parents again. My mother-in-law, Ellen Wolf, was one of those children.

With jewels sewn in the hem of her coat, Ellen was sent to stay with relatives in England. Her sister, Ruth, was too old to qualify as a child on the train. Attempts to secure her employment as a nanny for the younger children traveling on the train were unsuccessful. Ellen had to make the trip alone. Ellen arrived in England to live with relatives she had never met. Everything was foreign to her, everything except Judaism.

While her life was filled with strangers, she didn't speak their language, the locale was unfamiliar, and the national customs disparate. But she could take comfort in the predictability of the rituals of her religion, especially in the laws of kashrut. It was the food that became the connecting point for her. In a time of utter chaos and loss, the laws of Judaism were the rock upon which a new life was to be built.

The sisters were eventually reunited in America. Ruth had migrated from Seattle to Chicago to New York. Each married and they lived most of their adult life together in a two-apartment home in Queens. Food and the preparing of it remain very important to my mother-in-law. It is still her means of connecting. At every Seder, for each of her children, grandchildren, nieces and nephews there is that favorite dish that Ellen makes just for him or her. And while there are many different dishes, this recipe for Matzoh Cake is a universal favorite. Dishes may come and go but the Matzoh Cake is a staple.

During the war, when Jews were forbidden to celebrate Passover, Seders were held in secret. Preparations had to be simple and fast. At the last Seder that Ellen was to attend in Germany, Matzoh cake was served.

" Throughout history, the will of the Jewish people to survive has been tested. From December, 1938 through November, 1939 about ten thousand Jewish children fled Nazi Germany on trains known as "Kindertransports.' My grandma, Ellen Rosanski Wolf, was one of those children. She is my personal link to the survival of the Jews against the greatest of odds. Without her and thousands like her, many of us wouldn't be here today. So, I am dedicating my bar mitzvah in honor of all the children who survived that terrible time to keep the light of the Jewish people from being extinguished forever."

Evan Katz Bar Mitzvah speech
December, 2003

This simple recipe made the trip with Ellen from Germany. Like Ellen, it too survived.

I believe that this cake is symbolic of the children on those trains. The matzoh in it represents the haste with which the children fled from Nazi Germany and the sweetness of the chocolate represents the childhood of which they were deprived.

We serve this cake every Passover as our reminder. *Enjoy this at your Seder and never forget.*

Ellen Wolf's Matzoh Layer Cake

dairy

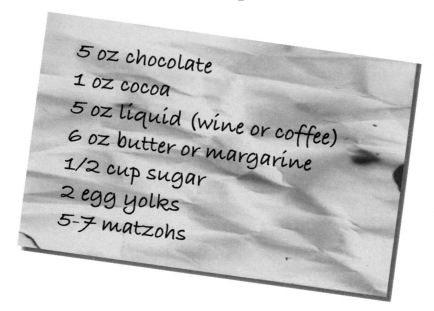

5 oz chocolate
1 oz cocoa
5 oz liquid (wine or coffee)
6 oz butter or margarine
1/2 cup sugar
2 egg yolks
5-7 matzohs

Directions:

1.) Melt and cool chocolate and cocoa.
2.) Beat egg yolks with butter and sugar.
3.) Mix chocolate and cocoa into the beaten butter mix to form a spread.
4.) Brush matzoh with coffee or wine.
5.) Spread layer of chocolate spread mix.
6.) Add next matzoh to the top and repeat.
7.) Continue until all chocolate spread mix is used.

Poppy Seed Dressing
parve
by Jackie Katz

1/2 cup sugar
1 tsp dry mustard
1/3 cup cider vinegar
1 1/2 tsp minced onion
1 cup oil
1 1/2 tsp poppy seeds

Mix in blender. Great with any salad with chopped fruit.

Special Brisket
meat
by Jackie Katz

Brisket
Italian dressing
1 cup BBQ sauce
1 can cranberry relish

Directions:
Preheat oven to 300 degrees

- Marinate brisket in Italian dressing for a couple hours or over night.
- Wrap in foil and bake in pan for 2 1/2 hours at 300*.
- Open foil and bake and additional 1/2 half hour at 300*.
- Remove meat from foil and refrigerate with juices overnight.
- Combine pan juices, 1 cup BarBQ sauce and 1 can cranberry relish in saucepan.
- Slice meat against grain.
- Pour gravy over sliced meat and reheat at 300* for 1 hour.

Voila!

Abram Roitman

Bryn Mawr, PA, U.S.A.

Submitted by his daughter Rita Roitman

A few days after the war broke out, Abram and his brother fled Warsaw with thousands of young people and headed east on foot towards Russia. Within days, they encountered air attacks from the German Luftwaffe, devastation in the cities, and the advance of the Russian army. They turned back to the relative calm of Zolkiewka, the village where he grew up. Within weeks Poland was de facto a divided country.

With the hope of help from their oldest brother (not knowing that he had been executed in the purge by Stalin) Abe, Yitzchak and his brother's fiancée chose between the perceived lesser of two evils and went to the Russian side to a labor camp near Kiev, but after 6 weeks were shipped to a forced labor camp in the much less forgiving Siberia. Only the young, strong and resourceful (Abram excelling in the latter) survived 2 years of horrible flies in the short summer and the lack of much food or clothing in the harsh, long winter.

Abe's charm and love of song proved valuable in securing sustenance. Released after 2 years, the survivors traveled by train and foot to the warmest accessible climate, Tashkent / Uzbekhistan, where open-air living in a park was tolerable. Joining cohorts, he found bits of work that led him to a sugar factory.

Charm and smoozing again provided connections that launched a successful dual career as a factory worker and conspiring sugar smuggler for sale on the black market, and survival for the next 2 years until the end of the war. It was only during this time, that those survivors began to learn of the extent of the horrors that particularly befell those caught under the hand of Hitler and collaborators. Ironically, his foray into socialism and that of his brother before him provided a path for his survival as a Jew.

Abram and wife, Eva

33

Eva Roitman
Bryn Mawr, PA, U.S.A.
Submitted by her daughter Rita Roitman

Eva was 15 when war broke out in Poland. Her family dead, she was helped by neighbors to get to her teacher in a larger city. She had grown up in a mixed Jewish and Catholic town and was known for being an incredible student. Her teacher and best friend helped her prepare for the role that saved her life. She passed as a retarded Catholic servant girl. Despite losing all of her family, she survived, but believed that she would never have a family again.

Later in life, she was able to marry and have children and grandchildren, returning to her Jewish roots. She relished her role as mother and grandmother, believing that her children and grandchildren made all of her suffering worthwhile. Her determination to survive numerous illnesses throughout the rest of her life was incredible to witness.

Rita and her parents tagged and waiting for transit to Canada

Eva's Latkes
dairy

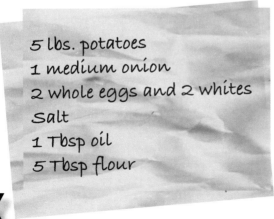

5 lbs. potatoes
1 medium onion
2 whole eggs and 2 whites
salt
1 Tbsp oil
5 Tbsp flour

Directions:

1.) Hand grate onion and potatoes.
2.) Spoon out liquid.
3.) Add eggs, salt and flour.
4.) Fry slowly in vegetable oil.
5.) Eat with sour cream.

34

Friedel Perschel
Johannesburg, South Africa
Submitted by her niece Marion Gordon

*Marion and her mother Frances en route
to South Africa to their new life.*

My Aunt Friedel and her son David lived in East Berlin. During the worst days of the Nazi era they were hidden by various friends, some non-Jewish. I was never told how her husband was caught or what happened to him.

Through the Jewish agency we managed to trace her after the war. We arranged through friends to have her flown to South Africa for a visit. She stayed with us for about two months and we listened to her stories of how they survived on boiled potatoes, lived in dark, sunless rooms and had very little physical or mental stimulation. She always told us that people can survive hardships, and their physical wounds will heal but the mental scars stay with them forever.

Friedel's son David

Friedel's nieces Margot and Marion

35

Friedel Perschel's Winter Meat Stew

meat

This recipe belonged to my aunt Friedel, my mother, and her family.

Directions:

Please note the quantities of all ingredients depend on how many people you want to serve.

1.) In a large pot fill half full with cold water, add 1 whole peeled onion & salt.
2.) Add soup meat, short rib & bones and boil until tender.
3.) In another pot boil green beans-cut in half, until tender.
4.) In another pot peel and boil potatoes until soft.
5.) Melt 2 tablespoons non-dairy margarine and 2 tablespoons flour.
6.) Make a Roux. Dilute with liquid from the beans and the meat stock.
7.) When Roux is thickish consistency add 1 cup vinegar and ½ cup sugar.
8.) Stir until well mixed. It must be sweet and sour.
    Taste and adjust until the taste is pleasing.
9.) Now to this sauce add the meat (less the bones) the beans and the
    halved potatoes.
10.) Stir and allow to cook slowly for ½ hour.

To serve place the pot on the table and allow all to help themselves!

Lynda's famous South African Brisket

(Marion's daughter)
meat

1 large brisket
1 package onion soup
1 can Coca Cola
1/4 c. Worcestershire sauce- Vegan
1/3 c. Grand Marnier Liquor
2 packages dried fruit (prunes, apricot, peaches, apples)
1 oz. flour
1 oz. margarine
1/3 c. hot water
salt and pepper

Directions:
Preheat oven to 325 degrees

1.) Place brisket in roasting pan.
2.) Pour coke and Worcestershire sauce over it.
3.) Sprinkle onion soup on top.
4.) Cover tightly with foil and bake at 325 degrees for approximately 3 to 4 hours until soft.
5.) Take brisket out of oven and let cool on a tray.
6.) When cool, slice into 1/4 inch slices.

Sauce:

1.) Skim fat off the gravy that is left from the cooked brisket.
2.) Pour gravy into a saucepan and add the dried fruit and cook until soft, about 15 minutes.
3.) Add Grand Marnier and cook 5 minutes longer.

Serving: Place sliced brisket on platter. Surround with dried fruit. Thicken sauce with flour, margarine and hot water (mixed together). Season. Pour some sauce over brisket and serve the rest on the side.

South African Asparagus Tart

by Lynda Gluck (great niece)

dairy

- Puff pastry sheets or refrigerator croissant dough
- 2 cans drained asparagus cuts
- 1 medium chopped onion
- 8 thinly sliced mushrooms
- Lemon pepper
- Garlic salt
- 12 oz. heavy cream
- 2 extra large eggs
- Shredded Cheddar and Mozzarella Cheese- Kosher

Directions:
Preheat oven to 375 degrees

1.) Line 13x9 inch Pyrex dish with puff pastry dough.
2.) Saute chopped onion and sliced mushrooms in butter.
3.) Season with lemon pepper and garlic salt. - spread over the pastry.
4.) Place drained asparagus cuts over this.
5.) Now whisk together 12 oz. whipping cream and 2 eggs.
6.) Pour over asparagus.
7.) Season again.
8.) Sprinkle grated cheese on top. Dot with butter.
9.) Bake at 375 degrees for 30 minutes until golden brown.

Good with fish meal.

South African Shabbat Whole Roaster Chicken

by Lynda Gluck (Marion's daughter)

meat

whole roasting chicken with pop up
washed and patted dry

1 can halved apricots with juice

1 package onion soup mix

1/2 jar chutney

Directions:

Preheat oven to 375 degrees

1.) Put chicken in a roasting pan or in a cooking bag in a roasting pan to cook quicker.
2.) Pour juice from apricot can over chicken and inside of chicken.
3.) Pour chutney over chicken and rub all over chicken.
4.) Pour onion soup dry mix on top.
5.) Bake for 2-3 hours covered @ 375 or temp. suggested on roaster package.
6.) Last half hour uncover and put apricots on the top and let roast until chicken is finish.
7.) Remove chicken. Thicken gravy with 1 oz. of flour, 1 oz. of margarine and hot water mixed together.

Serve with chicken.

Geitel Gervic
Winnepeg, Canada
Submitted by Rita Roitman

Greitel was in Poland when the war broke out. She was the mother of three boys- two of whom were twins. She was forced to live though the horror of witnessing the murder of her children and husband. She was kept alive through the generosity of a farmer who had dug a shallow pit in his barn where he hid Jews. She lived in that pit for a year, and never got over the guilt of surviving when her family had not. She became "mother" and "grandmother" to all of the survivors around her and their children.

She was a warm and generous soul, and she cooked without recipes. My mother and I would gather around her as she cooked, guessing at the measurements so that we could duplicate her fabulous cooking. Greitel became the grandmother I did not have, and I spent summers in Winnipeg, Canada watching her tend to her glorious garden and cook fabulous meals using ingredients grown in her garden.

40

Greitel's Honey Cake
parve

6 large not jumbo eggs
1 cup buckwheat honey
1 cup oil
1 cup sugar
1 cup hot water
   (mix with honey, add 1 tsp baking soda and 1 tsp instant coffee)
3 cups flour sifted with 2 tsp baking powder

Directions:

Preheat oven to 250 Degrees

1.) Separate eggs- into whites add a pinch of salt before beating, then gradually add sugar (saving a bit for yolks).
2.) Beat the yolks, add oil, mixture of honey and water.
3.) Then add whites and at the end add the flour.
4.) Mix together gently.
5.) Bake for 2 hours at 250.   (If your oven is colder then bake at 300.)

Henny (Levenberg) Goldberg
Woodmere, NY, U.S.A.
Submitted by Pearl Ratz

Henny Levenberg was born in Lebow, Latvia on December 31, 1928. She was 12 years old when the war broke out. She was the youngest of three daughters. Her father was a businessman in the building trade. Her mother was a housewife who raised three daughters. When the war broke out Henny worked for the railroad under her parents care.

In July of 1944 she was separated from her parents, who were gassed in Auschwitz. She was sent to Stutthof labor camp, where she remained until she was liberated by the British on May 5, 1945. She was taken to Sweden to recover from TB. There she met her husband of 44 years, David Goldberg. Today she is the mother of 3 children and the grandmother of 10. She makes the best mandel bread in the whole world.

Henny Goldberg

Wedding of Henny and David Goldberg
October 22, 1949

Bubby's Cookies

parve

3 cups of flour
3 sticks of margarine
3 tsp. of baking powder
1 cup of sugar
3 eggs
1 tbsp. of vanilla

Directions:

Preheat oven to 350 degrees

1.) Soften margarine at room temperature for approx. 1 hour before mixing ingredients.
2.) Mix all ingredients together.
3.) Put in refrigerator for one hour.
4.) Roll out on very well floured surface.
5.) Cut into desired shapes.
6.) Bake at 350 degrees for 30 -35 minutes or until golden brown.

Bubby's Famous Mandel Bread

parve

Directions:

Preheat oven to 350 degrees

1.) Mix all ingredients together.
2.) Using floured hands make 2 long loaves 3/4 inch high by 1 1/2 inches wide.
3.) Place on a cookie sheet covered with aluminum foil.
4.) Bake until lightly brown. About 20 -25 minutes.
5.) Remove cookies from oven and carefully cut the loaves into 1/2 inch slices diagonally while still hot and lay them on their sides.
6.) Place back into oven and cook another 10 minutes, check not to over brown!
7.) Let cool and enjoy.

3/4 cup sugar
2 eggs
2 tsp baking powder
1 pinch of salt
1/4 cup orange juice
3/4 cup oil
3 cups flour
6 oz. chocolate chips

Make sure not to leave any leftovers because they are delicious!

43

Jacques Fein
Columbia, MD, U.S.A.

I, Jacques Fein (Karpic) was born in 1938 in Paris, and my sister Annette was born in 1940. Our parents were Rojza Karpic (nee Tascynowicz) and Szmul Karpic, who were born in Poland in the 1910's. After the start of WWII, around 1942 we were placed in hiding in Vers-Galant near Paris. A French Jewish organization, Ouvres de Secouurs aux Enfants (OSE) helped in this effort. Unfortunately many thousands were killed in the war. Our father was deported to Pithiviers and then murdered at Auschwitz in 1942 and our mother was deported to Drancy and then murdered at Auschwitz in 1943. Many members of our family in France were also deported to Auschwitz. Several cousins and aunts and uncles survived.

We were hidden with a Catholic family in Vers-Galant (outside of Paris) until 1946; when a French organization, Ouevres de Secours aux Enfants (OSE), placed us in orphanages, called "homes" with other children. We left France in 1948 and were adopted by an American family, Harry and Rose Fein, now deceased.

I arrived in the US at age 10 and went through the "normal, usual " phases of an American Jew - school, college, worked in computer software, marriage, moved to Columbia, MD in 1970, had two children Rachel & Matthew, divorced in 1974; remarried in 1986 to Judee Iliff with step-daughter Laura; and still live in Columbia. In June 2005 I became a grandfather with Sam, who was named after my father.

I have been heavily involved with Holocaust related organizations and the Jewish community, including president of the Jewish Federation of Howard County in 1995-1997. My involvement is based on two points. First, I was lucky to have survived, while many thousands of children and millions more were murdered. I received help among others from the UJA money in the 1940's. So for me, it is payback time. Second, as Jews we are responsible for each other, and that is the focus of this life of mine.

**Fein Family
(Jacques front center), 1939**

**Jacques and sister with
daughter of family that
hid them**

Jacques and his grandson

44

French Toast

parve

(Why the name French Toast I do not know)

2-3 eggs
* NOTE: you can substitute Cholesterol free eggs
2-3 slices any bread you wish
* Challah works great

I was a toddler in France so I never really cooked then, but I love French toast.

Directions:

1.) Using 2 or 3 eggs; break, mix and add seasoning as you wish.
2.) Use any bread you wish 2 or 3 slices -- Challah works great.
3.) Mix them happily & gingerly with the eggs.
4.) Prepare a pan with some margarine or PAM or the like and cook the toast on medium high heat.
5.) Remember to turn the toast.
6.) Cook till brown or as you like .
(remember to ask your diner how they would like the toast)

I like my French toast well done with salt but that is the person's choice.

Arlette Silberfeld Baron

Baltimore, MD, U.S.A.
As told to Joanne Caras

Arlette's mother

Arlette's father

I was born in Paris in 1939. My mother was Hungarian and my father was Polish. My parents owned a small jewelry store in Paris where friends and neighbors gathered for tea and conversation.

When the war broke out in France my father joined the French army in the foreign battalion. He was captured by the Nazis and taken to a prison camp in Germany, where he was kept alive only because he was able to repair watches and clocks for the German soldiers.

Soon after I was born people began to come to the jewelry store warning that the Nazis were starting to round up Jews in Paris. My mother sent my older sister Rene to live in a convent. I was just a baby so my mother hid me in a country farmhouse outside of Paris until the war was over. Food was very scarce so we ate mostly what we could pick from the trees in the forest. By the time I was three I would go out in the forest and fill burlap bags with chestnuts, which my mother would roast or boil. When we could no longer find any chestnuts we brought home the only other thing we could find, large mushrooms.

My mother was not sure if they were poisonous so she tried them before she let me eat any. Once they were proven to be safe they became a great source for stews and other recipes.
When the war ended, my mother and I returned to Paris and we were reunited with my sister. Since we had not heard from my father for a few years we assumed that he was dead. Then one day we were returning from the market when all of the neighbors shouted "There is a surprise for you in your house!" It was my father, whom I did not know, alive and well!

Today Arlette lives in Baltimore. She has five children, including Rabbi Hillel Baron, and more than twenty grandchildren.

Arlette Baron (left) with husband and children, 2002

Arlette Baron's Fruit Cake

parve

3/4 cup Sugar
1 Tbsp Baking Soda
1/2 cup Egg Whites
1/2 cup Oil
2 Tbsp Vanilla
2 cups flour

Arlette and her older sister

Directions:

Preheat oven to 350 degrees

1.) Mix all ingredients together except for flour.
2.) Add flour and mix again.
3.) Pour into a 9x13 pan sprayed with vegetable spray.
   "It doesn't have to be perfectly patted down!"
4.) Spread one can of your choice fruit pie filling on top.
5.) (Optional 1 cup walnuts on top.)
6.) Bake at 350 degrees for 40-45 min. until the outer edges look brown.

*Rabbi Hillel Baron (on left) with President Bush as
he prepared to make the White House Kitchen Kosher*

Lentil and Beet Soup
parve

1 lb lentils
2 qt water
2 Tbsp oil
1 pkg. Goodmans onion soup mix
2 Tbsp garlic powder
2 beets peeled and quartered
1 butternut squash peeled and seeds removed
  and cut into very large chunks

Directions:

1.) Add together lentils, water, and oil in a 4 quart pan with a heavy bottom.
2.) Add rest of ingredients, and bring to a boil.
3.) Simmer 40 minutes until a knife slices through the vegetables.

Variation: add spices or other vegetables

**Arlette Baron's son, daughter-in-law, and grandchildren
Rabbi Hillel and Morah Chanie Baron and children**

Leah Friedman
Baltimore, MD, U.S.A.
As told to Joanne Caras

I grew up in Germany with seven brothers and seven sisters. When I was 18 years old my family was told to gather all of our possessions because we were being "relocated." We had no idea at the time that our destination was Auschwitz.

When we first arrived at Auschwitz we were met by people singing and dancing, totally unaware of what was going to happen to them. My mother asked me to hold my baby sister, only 2 months old. A German soldier told me to place my baby sister on the ground and he crushed the helpless little baby to death. My two older sisters and I were separated from the rest of the family and taken to a barracks where our heads were shaved. We didn't even have time to say goodbye to the rest of our family. We later learned that going to the left was to the ovens and to the right was to live. Three of us went to the right. The rest of our family went to the left. A German soldier said to us and the other young girls in their barracks, "Do you smell that burning smoke? That is your parents!" Two other times we were able to escape the gas chambers by "the will of Hashem." Each time we were fortunate enough to be in the right line at the right time.

One week later we were taken to the ghetto in Krakow, Poland, where we were given jobs carrying heavy wood and stones up and down hills with guard dogs following us. When the work was done we were taken back to Auschwitz. We had very little to eat. Several times the Germans came and took away the weaker girls from the group. Each time we were lucky to be in the stronger group, because the weak ones were killed. Throughout the ordeal I was able to stay with my sisters. Twice I thought that we would die. One time a small piece of saved bread was the only thing that kept us alive, and another time we were given the skin of a potato and a piece of black bread when all hope was lost. Barely alive, the three of us girls were forced to work hard and to run until we could hardly walk. At one point my sister began to cry saying that she could not run any more. We were certain that she would be taken away to die, but to our surprise and joy a German soldier saved her. And from that one saved life there now are 35 great grandchildren!

Leah Friedman

Our next stop was Bergen-Belsen, 75 girls in one room. There were no beds, only a bare floor. Every day a few of the girls would die of weakness or starvation. Shortly after we arrived at Bergen-Belsen the war ended. The first time we realized the war was over was when we saw British airplanes dropping fruit and vegetables for us to eat.

A few days later the British soldiers came in and took us to a hospital. We were given food and clothes, and beds to sleep on. Some how, some way, the three of us had survived what millions of others, including the rest of our family, had not.

After the war I was given another gift from Hashem. I learned that another sister had also survived, leaving four remaining from our original family of seventeen.

49

About a year after we were liberated I was going to visit my sister for Shabbat. At the train station I ran into the son of a Rabbi who had taught Torah to my family years before. My mother had always told us to "Be nice to the Rabbi because he has a son who could some day be my son-in-law." Five months later my mother's premonition came true. Without one penny we married, and we built a life together in America that produced three children, twelve grandchildren, and twelve great grandchildren.

Every Jewish woman should be married to such a wonderful man as I had for fifty years.

◇◇

Broccoli Noodle Kugel
parve

2 pkgs frozen broccoli defrosted
1 stick margarine
2 med onions
6 eggs beaten
1 can sliced water chestnuts
1 cup Coffee Rich
1 foil pack onion soup mix
16 oz. medium wide noodles cooked and drained

Directions:
Preheat oven to 350 degrees
1.) Sauté onion in margarine.
2.) Mix all ingredients.
3.) Pour into greased pan 9x13.
4.) Preheat oven to 350 degrees.
5.) Bake for 45 minutes.

Honey Cookies
parve

6 jumbo eggs
1 1/4 cup sugar
16 oz honey
1 tsp baking powder
1 tsp baking soda
1/2 tsp cinnamon
1/2 tsp all-spice
7 cups flour

Directions:
Preheat oven to 350 degrees
1.) Mix in mixer.
2.) Refrigerate for 2 hrs.
3.) Drop by tsp on lined wax paper baking sheet 2 in. apart.
4.) Bake 350 degrees for 12-15 min.

Potato Kugel
parve

3 lbs potatoes peeled and cut into small pieces
  (if you do it the day before put in refrig. covered in water)
2 Large onions slices
1/2 Tbsp salt
1/2 cup oil
4 jumbo eggs (lightly beaten)
1/2 tsp pepper (optional)

Directions:

Preheat oven to 350 degrees

1.) In food processor mix onions & potatoes together, just pulsing enough to chop.
2.) Mix in the rest of the ingredients by hand.
3.) Spray 9x13 pan with vegetable oil.
4.) Pour in the mix.
5.) Bake 1 1/2 hours at 350 degrees.

Leah Friedman's Strawberry Ice Cream
parve

Great for passover

3 egg whites
1 cup sugar
1 Tbsp lemon juice
1 Tsp vanilla sugar
pint of strawberries (washed tops and trimmed)

Directions:

1.) Mix egg whites and sugar.
2.) Add lemon juice and vanilla sugar.
3.) Add strawberries one at a time on low speed until well blended. Gradually make mixer speed higher.
4.) Mix until light and fluffy about 10 minutes.
5.) Pour into 9 x 13 in.
6.) Freeze.

51

Lillian Berliner
Beechhurst, NY, U.S.A.

My name is Lillian Berliner and I was deported with my family from Hungary in 1944. My mother and I survived Auschwitz, labor camp in Bremen and Bergen Belsen. We were liberated by the British troops on April 15, 1945.

Most of my family was deported from Hungary and the majority perished in the Auschwitz gas chambers. Miraculously, my mother (in her early 40's) and I (a teenager) survived Auschwitz, Bremen and Bergen-Belsen together. We were never separated.

We were starved in Auschwitz and to alleviate our numerous hunger pangs, we invented frequent "dream meals" ranging between coffee klatches, luncheons, informal and formal dinner parties.

Last picture of the Herskovits Family (Elisabeth and Albert seated, with daughter Lili), taken in the Spring of 1944, before deportation.

We planned our menus carefully for hours and in great detail. Our favorite dishes and desserts took priority and were frequently repeated. The table settings, the color of dishes, tablecloths, napkins, flowers for each occasion and the seating arrangements were also discussed.

This may sound delusional I know, but during these meal planning sessions, we were briefly transported to a normal world, a world that was so far from our miserable reality. We actually tasted the dishes we prepared and our hunger pangs disappeared during the hours of planning. We could hardly wait for the next planning session.

There was no need or time to plan "dream meals" in Bremen (labor camp) thanks to the kindness of an old, Danish retired seaman, who gave us his daily sandwich and to a French prisoner of war, who shared his Red Cross packages with us. In Bergen-Belsen, we were too sick and weak to even dream.

The two recipes I have included, one for an appetizer and one for dessert, were always on our menus and were native to my home-town of Kolozsvar (also known as Cluj), Hungary, on the Romanian border in Transylvania.

Liptauer - Cheese Spread

dairy

8 oz. whipped cream cheese
4 oz. margarine
1 1/2 tbsp. minced onion
2 squirts anchovy paste (not too much since salty)
paprika- to redden the spread

Directions:
1.) Mix well.
2.) Refrigerate.
3.) Serve with crackers or bread.

Palacsinta (Crepes)

dairy

3 eggs
1 1/4 cups flour
1 cup milk
1 tsp sugar
pinch of salt
1 cup club soda
margarine or butter

Directions:
1.) Mix eggs, flour, milk, sugar and salt.
2.) Make a smooth pancake dough.
3.) Let dough rest for 1-2 hours.
4.) Stir in Club Soda at the last moment, just before cooking the pancakes.
5.) Heat an eight inch frying pan.
6.) When the pan is hot, add 1/4 tbsp. margarine or butter.
7.) Let it melt and cover the bottom of the pan. Pour a ladle of the batter into the pan.
8.) Gently tipping and twisting, so it covers the whole pan.
9.) When the top bubbles, turn the pancake over and cook for another 4-5 seconds.
10.) Remove the cooked pancake into a large plate.

Fillings for pancake:
Apricot Jam or Farmer cheese mixed with an egg yolk, sugar and raisin mixture. Roll the filled pancake and then fry lightly to heat before serving.

53

Anna Baron Torn
Columbia, MD, U.S.A.
Submitted by her daughter Chaya Schapiro

At the age of 4 years old the Germans invaded Poland. Anna was born in the village of Bilgoray to Michael and Rivka Baron, the 3rd of 4 children. A local non-Jewish villager insisted to her father to leave Poland immediately and go into the vast land of Russia. Her father took them and they hid in a hut somewhere on the Volga River. They barely ate anything for many years. A younger brother was born while they survived in Russia. After the war they traveled throughout Europe until Israel became a state.

They moved to Israel and Anna started her schooling and eventually was drafted into the Israeli army. She thought she had enough of war, but while at the base her unit was ambushed and the 1956 Sinai War began. After this war she moved to the USA and started a family. Anna has 4 children and 11 grandchildren, she lives in Columbia, MD. Her husband, Louis Torn, also a survivor is living in a nursing home in Rockville, MD.

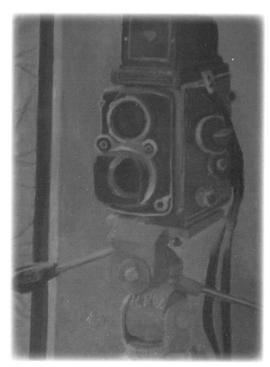

A painting by Chaya Schapiro of her father's camera. He was in the Holocaust as well and when he eventually came to the U.S.A., he became a photographer and this painting is a metaphor of his life.

Gazpacho (cold soup)

parve

Submitted by her daughter Gail Torn Binyamin

1/2 medium onion, peeled and coarsely chopped
1 small cucumber, peeled, pared, seeded
    and coarsely chopped
1/2 tsp Worchestershire sauce
1 clove garlic minced
1 drop hot pepper sauce
1/8 tsp cayenne pepper
1/4 tsp black pepper
2 Tbsp olive oil
1 large tomato, finely diced
2 Tbsp minced chives or scallion tops
1 lemon, cut in 6 wedges
4 cups Tomato Juice

Directions:

1.) Put 2 cups of tomato juice and all other ingredients except diced tomato, chives, and lemon wedges in the blender.
2.) Puree.
3.) Slowly add the remaining 2 cups of tomato juice to pureed mixture.
4.) Add chopped tomato. Chill.

Serve icy cold in individual bowls garnished with chopped chives and lemon wedges.

Yield: 6 servings. Serving Size: 1 cup

Naomi Rosenfeld

Baltimore, MD, U.S.A.

As told to Joanne Caras

Editor's Note: *On the nights of November 9 and 10, 1938 rampaging mobs throughout Germany and the newly acquired territories of Austria and Sudetenland freely attacked Jews in the street, in their homes and at their places of work and worship. At least 96 Jews were killed and hundreds more injured, more than 1,000 synagogues were burned (and possibly as many as 2,000), almost 7,500 Jewish businesses were destroyed, cemeteries and schools were vandalized, and 30,000 Jews were arrested and sent to concentration camps. This night would forever be known as Kristallnacht.*

I was twelve years old. That day I was called to the butcher to pick up some salami. We hadn't had any meat for a long time so my family was happy to have the salami.

Suddenly I heard screaming and banging outside the butcher shop. The butcher pushed me out the back door, salami in hand, and said "Don't look back!" I heard the shattering of glass and the breaking of windows. I went out into the back alley and ran home. I saw the words "JEWS" written on the building.

On the way home I passed the Synagogue. The building was on fire and the Torah Scrolls and prayer books had been taken out of the Synagogue and thrown on the ground where people were deliberately walking all over them.

When I got home I screamed to my family that something terrible was happening. Then I blacked out.

I knew that we had to leave but my mother wanted to stay. We finally left on the last train at 11 o'clock at night, and all we were allowed to bring were the clothes on our backs. The train went to Italy. My nine year old brother, my mother, and I left together. When we stopped at the last station in Germany a soldier yelled "Juden come out here!" We went out and he made us all undress to show that we were not taking anything with us. We were then put back on the train and we escaped to Italy.

Naomi Lissauer
Berlin, 1937

Naomi and brother Yitzcak

56

Parve Cheesecake

parve

No one will believe it's parve!

2 containers plain tofutti cream cheese
   (leave out of refrigerator to soften)
1 egg
1 cup sugar
1 tsp. vanilla
1 ready made graham cracker pie crust
1 can cherry pie filling

Directions:

Preheat oven to 350 degrees

1.) Mix all ingredients except cherry pie filling.
2.) Pour into pie crust.
3.) Bake at 350 for 30 minutes until a little brown.
4.) Let cool.
5.) Add cherry pie around the edge of the crust.

Enjoy!

Diane I. Goldberg

Nyack, NY, U.S.A.

I was born in Charleroi Belgium. I was brought up and did part of my schooling in Gilly, a small town of 24,000 people. My family was observant but my sister Isabelle and I had to go to school on Shabath because it was the law of the land. The Jewish education was only given on Sundays. We lived a happy and easy life - my father having a business of tools and industrial machineries, my mother and her brother Shimon having a small business of fabrics.

Like everyone in Belgium, on May 10, 1940 we saw our world shifting into a war by the invasion of the Germans....for a few days we thought that everything would be OK...But when my parents made a fair assessment of the situation, we loaded the car... my father and mother...my Uncle Shimon and Aunt Henny, my sister Isabelle and I, plus my young cousin Mendele. And we went all the way to the South of France with our "uberbed." Unfortunately, for a reason too long to explain here, we made it back to Gilly in December 1940. From there on, we were trapped. Things were rough for the first two years but we made it being quiet....Food was not in abundance but again, we made it. The big catastrophe came in 1942 when the German edicts hit us one after the other; the obligation of registering as Jews, wearing the Star of David, not going to school after the age of 16, curfew and at the culmination, the infamous "displacement of the Jews."

The orders of "displacement" came and they were just for my sister and I....My parents were never going to send their precious princesses away on their own and they started looking for a way out...At that time, the Germans said they would protect families whose head would volunteer for work at the "Mur de l'Atlantique"....So one day, without telling us what he was doing, and without saying "good bye," my father went to give himself up....When he saw the huge door at the armory closing behind him....he realized that it was a trap and thinking fast and with a huge "chutzpa" got himself out of it. That option of being out, we were happy to hear Queen Elizabeth of Belgium saying that she would intervene to help her Belgian citizens....but we were not Belgian....My parents were Polish...so were we. Having been born in Belgium, I could become Belgian at 16, which I was not yet...My sister Isabelle was born in France...she had no option...except....if we marry Belgian men.....

So start the search for two men who were patriotic...would not "blackmail" us and not ask for their "rights" as husbands. Two neighbors accepted to help us. We got lots of help also from the administration to speed up those "weddings" and when we were "married" we had to go to the German authorities to present our brand new identity card - at that time it was green for Belgian, yellow for foreigners - so we had our blessed green cards and the employee very conveniently forgot to put the red stamp JEW on it. As we came out of the courthouse and ready to go to the German authorities, a friend who was in charge of watching out at the German headquarters ran to my father and told him not to send us...the last two girls who got there to show their new green cards did not come out...... and never came back They were two very close friends.

So start the search for a hiding place. Most of our Belgian friends were very sympathetic but rightly so, scared...it was dangerous....The only one who did not hesitate a second was the Raoul Herremans family, who not only accepted to hide us, but in order to keep us safe and sleeping in a bed, sent two of their children to an orphanage......A month later, my parents got their "orders" and came to join us at the Herremans.

***The Goldberg Family -
Aron, Diane, Isabelle
and Brucha, 1940***

58

My father and Raoul were already friends but my mother and Yvonne had to get to know one another - and friends they became until they died. One year passed and the orphanage knowing that Aline and Raoul, Jr. were there for other reasons asked the parents to take them back needing their rooms for Jewish kids in hiding. I then had to leave my parents to go to a village where a family needed a "nanny"....what they really needed was a maid.... The head of that family was working for the Germans at the military airport of Florennes and my stay there was a nightmare of fear. I was able to go back to live with my parents again when a letter of denunciation was intercepted at the post office advising the German authorities that the Herremans household was hiding "Russians."

Having been alerted by the Underground, we all went to an apartment at the cinema Casino in Chatelet where the owner, refusing to play German movies, had closed the cinema and rented the apartments to Jewish people. We had to run away from that hiding place when the Americans started bombing the major railroad network a block away from the cinema. So not to be killed by the bombings of our Liberators, we went to another hiding place in Chatelet. This is where we had the joy of being liberated by the American troupes. Our joy did not last very long, soon we found out that Six Million of our Blood Relatives did not make it - and my Uncle Shimon was amongst them.....This is when I lost my memory for two years......

Aline Herremans and Diane visiting Isabelle in the "home."

Lazy Diane's Easy Cake

dairy

Topping
One 8 oz pack of cream cheese
(or 2 if you like your guests)
2 eggs (or 3 see remark above)
1/2 cup of powdered sugar
(or more to taste)
Look in your refrigerator for left over sour cream or yogurt

Ingredients for Base
1 pack of cake mix (I like lemon) for base. If you like lemon too, add some lemon juice and lemon zest.
1/2 a cup of nuts (any you like) finely chopped
1 stick of melted butter (or whatever you are using for shortening)
1 egg lightly beaten

Directions:
Preheat oven to 350 degrees. Line a 9x12 baking pan with parchment or waxed paper and put in the base ingredients, lightly mixed. It should have the consistency of loose crumbs. Then mix the ingredients for topping and pour over the base. Depending on your oven.....should bake for 50 to 60 minutes. You know the routine...take it out of the baking pan.....let it cool over wire rack...peel off the paper and cut into squares.

Tsimmes

dairy

Submitted by Ronna Caras

This is an updated version of an old tradition with new flavors that make it very international. It's also very easy to make.

3 lbs butternut squash (preferably 1 large squash)
2 sweet potatoes- peeled, cooked and mashed
6 large carrots- peeled cooked and mashed
Salt and freshly ground black pepper
3/4 cup (1 1/2 stick) unsalted butter
1 Tbsp finely chopped dried sage leaves
2 Tbsp granulated sugar
1/4 cup balsamic vinegar
1/2 cup maple syrup
2 tsp Chinese 5 powder
(this adds a ton of delicious flavor so do not skip!)
Hazelnut biscotti or other crunchy cookie such as
pecan sandies, crumbled, for garnish

Directions:

Preheat the oven to 400 degrees F.

Peel the squash with a vegetable peeler. Halve lengthwise, discard the seeds, then cut into ½ -inch dice. Place in a large bowl and season with salt and pepper.

Heat ½ cup butter in a medium skillet over medium-high heat. When the butter ceases to foam and has turned a light brown, pull the pan off the heat and immediately add the sage, sugar, vinegar (stand back so as not to get splattered), maple syrup and 5 spice powder. Mix well and let simmer over medium-low heat for 1 to 2 minutes to meld the flavors.

Pour the vinegar mixture over the squash and toss well, then transfer to a heavy rimmed baking sheet or baking dish large enough to hold the squash in a single layer. Place in the oven and roast, tossing at least once, until very tender and caramelized, about 30 minutes. Set aside until cool enough to handle but still warm, so the liquids are runny. Lower oven temperature to 350.

Mash the warm squash. Add in mashed sweet potato and mashed carrots with another ¼ cup of butter. Mix together keeping it as smooth or as chunky as you prefer.

Spoon mixture into buttered 5 quart casserole. Top with crushed cookies. Bake in 350° oven for 40-60 minutes until very browned. You can also refrigerate for up to 5 days, or freeze for up to 2 months.

Joanne Caras' Challah

parve

3 packages Yeast
3/4 cup warm water
1 Tbsp sugar
5/8 cup oil
3/4 cup honey- plus honey for glaze
3 eggs lightly beaten at room temperature
1 cup warm water
1 tsp vanilla

Dry Ingredients
- 1 tsp salt
- 2 1/2 tsp. baking powder
- 1 tsp cinnamon
- 8-9 cups flour

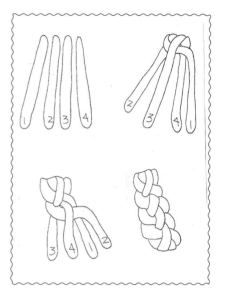

Directions:
Preheat oven to 350 degrees

1.) Combine yeast, warm water and sugar until yeast dissolves.
2.) Allow to sit for ten minutes until it rises.
3.) Add oil, honey, eggs, water, and vanilla to the yeast in a large bowl
4.) Mix dry ingredients together and add to wet ingredients with spoon.
5.) Mix well.
6.) Knead with minimal amount of flour for 10 minutes until dough is smooth as a baby's tooshy!
7.) Put in greased bowl, flip over, and cover with damp towel.
8.) Allow to rise until double in bulk.
9.) Punch down and allow to rise again.
10.) Divide dough into three portions.
11.) Braid the bread per illustration.
12.) Place on greased baking sheets, allow to rise again in a warm spot.
13.) Bake at 350 degrees for 35-40 minutes.
14.) When you take it out of the oven brush honey all over the top for a beautiful, shiny challah.

Vivian's Brownies

by Vivian Caras, cousin
dairy

2 eggs
1 cup sugar
1 cup flour
2 squares melted
 unsweetened chocolate
1/4 lb butter
1 tsp vanilla

Directions:
Preheat oven to 325 degrees
1.) Grease an 8x8 inch pan.
2.) Melt butter with chocolate.
3.) Add eggs and vanilla.
4.) Add sugar and cream the mixture.
5.) Add flour and mix well.
6.) Pour in pan and bake 20 minutes.

Salmon Loaf

by Vivian Caras
dairy

1 tall can red salmon
1 small grated onion
1 medium grated carrot
2 eggs
1/2 tsp. baking powder
1 cup crushed Ritz crackers
1 cup milk
Crushed cornflakes

Directions:
Preheat oven to 325 degrees
1.) Heat milk and margarine together.
2.) Mix all ingredients together except
 cornflakes in a large bowl.
3.) Bake in a 8x8 inch lightly greased pan.
4.) Top with crushed cornflakes
 crumbs before baking.
5.) Bake at 325 for 45 minutes.

Hawaiian Chicken

by Vivian Caras
meat

1 1/2 to 2 lbs. chicken,
 cut up or 8 thighs and breasts
8 oz. apricot preserves
8 oz. Russian dressing
1 pkg. dry instant onion soup mix
Pineapple chunks

Directions:
Preheat oven to 350 degrees
1.) Mix together the preserves,
 Russian dressing and dry
 soup mix.
2.) Pour over chicken and bake
 for 50 minutes or until tender.
3.) Garnish with the pineapple chunks.

Joseph Tauber
Baltimore, MD, U.S.A.
Submitted by his daughters Sara Coe and Marlene Sussman

Our father, Joseph Tauber met our mother Regina Zylberberg when she was about 14 years old. He fell in love with her when he heard her singing a lullaby to her young cousin. They were childhood sweethearts. They married in January 1940 right after Germany invaded Poland in Sept. 1939. Initially they were in the ghetto. In 1944, on a long, brutal walk to Tomashow, they were separated. Regina was sent to Auschwitz and Joseph was sent to Dachau. They endured unspeakable horrors. They lost most of their family members including their parents, most of their brothers and sisters and their baby, Hadassah Tauber who was only 3 years old.

Miraculously, on July 13, 1945 Regina and Joseph found each other each again after they were liberated. In 1948, Regina gave birth to another daughter, Sara Rose in a Displaced Person's Camp in Stuttgart, Germany. They moved to America in 1949 and settled in Baltimore. They had another daughter, Esther Marlene in 1955.

Joseph and Regina were always grateful to G-d for finding each other again and giving them other children. Regina was a nurturing person, and used love in all she did for others. Feeding her family with her delicious food was just one of her many expressions of love.

If there is such a thing as soul mates, Regina and Joseph were soul mates. We were so blessed to have them as parents and role models. Our children were blessed as well to have the most loving and caring Bubby and Zayde. Their memory and remarkable strength and kindness will be in all of our hearts forever.

Joseph and Regina's two daughters,
Marlene Sussman and Sara Coe

63

Regina Tauber's Honey Cake

parve

3/4 cup Crisco
1 cup brown sugar
1 cup white sugar
4 eggs
1 cup honey
1 cup black coffee
3 tsp baking powder
1 tsp baking soda
4 1/2 cups flour
1/2 tsp salt
1/2 tsp ginger
3/4 tsp cloves
1 tsp cinnamon
1 tsp vanilla
juice of 1/2 orange

Directions:
Preheat oven for 350 degrees

1.) Mix all the above ingredients.
2.) Bake at 350 degrees for 1 hour.

Regina Tauber
Baltimore, MD, U.S.A.
Submitted by her grandchildren Danielle Carter, Seth Coe, Sharon Sussman, Marissa Sussman

Regina Tauber was our beautiful and kind Bubby. She always expressed her love to all of us unconditionally. One of the special ways she showed her love was through her cooking. She loved watching us eat her wonderful food. We know her food was so special because the extra ingredient in all of her recipes was love.

Regina Zylberberg married our Zayde, Joseph Tauber, in the beginning of the war January 6, 1940. They were childhood sweethearts and loved each other for many years. They suffered profoundly and lost their baby Haddassah Tauber in 1943. They were separated from each other. Our Bubby was sent to Auschwitz, and our Zayde was sent to Dachau. Miraculously they found each other again after the war. They had another daughter, Sara, in a displaced person's camp in Stuttgart, Germany. They came to the United States in 1949 when Sara was a year old. They had their second daughter, Marlene in 1955.

Both our Bubby and Zayde were never bitter, because they were grateful to have found each other again and thankful to G-d for giving them their two daughters (our mothers). We learned from them the most important values of kindness and gratitude. We were so blessed to have them. We not only remember them when we eat her wonderful food, but their beautiful memories are always in our hearts.

Joseph and Regina Tauber

Joseph and Regina's greatest blessings---
Seth Coe-Sullivan, Danielle Carter, Marissa
Sussman and Sharon Sussman

Regina Tauber's Kugel

dairy

Bubby's Kugel

12 oz. medium noodles
3/4 oz. stick margarine
1 1/2 lb. cottage cheese
6 eggs
3 tsp. lemon extract
3/4 cup sugar

Directions:

Preheat oven for 450 degrees

1.) Boil and drain noodles.
2.) Combine rest of ingredients.
3) Top with cinnamon, sugar and margarine.
4.) Bake at 450 degrees for 15 minutes.
5.) Reduce to 350 for 30 minutes.

Regina Weisz Wolovits
Cleveland, OH, U.S.A.
Submitted by her daughter Gail Hochman

My mother was born on September 10, 1924 in Velky Kapusany, Czechoslovakia. She is the youngest of 11 children. Her parents were hard working people who did their best to care for their children. In the fall of 1938, the Hungarians occupied my mother's town. Life became one horror after another. Every day, men from the Jewish community would disappear, and no one could learn what had happened to them. In March 1944, the Germans entered my grandparent's town. Along with the Germans came the infamous "yellow star" edict. My mother was placed in a ghetto with her sister-in-law, her two nephews and her parents in a tiny outdoor space, no more than 8x8. There they remained for six difficult weeks, sleeping on mud, with little food, unbearable conditions, and constant beatings.

After being forcibly removed from the ghetto, they arrived in Auschwitz after a four-day journey. My mother received a pair of mismatched leather shoes and a blue dress. She was assigned to a wooden bunk bed, along with nine other women and girls.

Regina Weisz before the War

On that very same day, the day before the Shavuot holiday, my mother was separated from my grandmother by Dr. Mengele. She would never see her parents, sister-in-law or nephews ever again.

The next day they were ordered to stand in appel, line-up. Some girls were chosen to go to the gas chambers. My aunt, who was with my mother at this point, was deteriorating quickly, and was selected to go to the death line. Immediately she was surrounded by a human chain. My mother tried to pull her out, but, then, she heard a click in her back - a gun. The nazi soldier gave my mother the option of going with my aunt or returning to the line. She chose the latter.

The food they received there consisted of erasatz coffee in the morning and a slice of bread. For supper they received soup, little more than water. After many months of much horror, my mother was transferred to Trachenberg. Here she dug a lot of trenches for the soldiers. If the work was not up to par, the girls were beaten. The weather was horrible. In Trachtenberg, as in Auschwitz, all the inmates received was a daily bowl of soup. My mother's stay in Trachenberg would prove short lived, however, as from there my mother and others were forcibly marched to a new concentration camp.

They walked for three straight weeks, and finally arrived in Camp Gross Rosen. This was the hell of all hells, according to my mother. But they soon left there as well and traveled on to the infamous Bergen Belsen. Here there were not beds, but plenty of rats. One morning my mother woke up and found a dead rat serving as her pillow. Her daily routine consisted of pulling corpses out of the barracks. She stacked them outside near the barracks six feet high.

There was practically no food or water in Bergen Belsen. At one point my mother became feverish and incoherent, and developed typhus. By some miracle, she started to move and her friend pulled her so she could walk. After that, she was afraid to lie down for fear she would never rise again.

In April, 1945, the English liberated the camp. My mother went to Sweden for a year to recuperate after the war. She came to America in 1946. She met my late father a few years afterwards, and got married in 1952. She had two daughters, my sister Miriam and me, Gail. Today she is the proud grandmother of eight, and great grandmother of five, kenanyahora! My father passed away two years ago and my mother, although missing him very much, is managing on her own, still making her soups for the grandchildren - and those great potatoes!!!

One of the family's favorite recipes is the paprikash potatoes. My mother has been making paprikash potatoes for as long as I can remember. As I was growing up in Cleveland, most of my friend's parents were American. I had the privilege of having European parents and the added benefit of experiencing and tasting all the great foods that my mother prepared from the recipes that she learned from her home in Europe. When I make this special potato recipe, I think how proud I am at the legacy she has given us.

Regina Weisz surrounded by her family

Grammy's Paprikash Potatoes

parve

6-8 potatoes
Onion
2-3 Tbsp oil
Salt
Pepper
Paprika

Directions:

1.) Cut up about 6-8 potatoes after peeling them.
2,) Place in a pot.
3.) Put an onion or two diced on top of this.
4.) Add a bit of oil (maybe about 2-3 tablespoons).
5.) Add, salt, pepper and lots of paprika.
6.) Then add water.
   Add enough not to cover, less than that (otherwise they will be too watery).
   You have to play around a bit.
   The potatoes will eventually break up and be creamy and yummy!!!

Enjoy!!!

Ruth Steinfeld
Houston, TX, U.S.A.

Ruth Steinfeld

I was only seven when my dear mother sent my sister and I away from the Concentration Camp Gurs. It was located on the Southwest side of France near the Spanish Border. This was in 1941. We were then protected by an underground agency called OSE. (Oeuvre de Secour aux enfant) Agency for the rescue of children.

My parents died in Auschwitz on Sept 9, 1942.

I was married in USA in 1954. I wanted to be a good Jewish wife and part of that meant my cooking.

I had no idea even how to make a good soup. I do not remember exactly what my mother looked like, but I remembered the smell of her chicken soup. I worked on it till I felt I had my Mom in my kitchen.

That is the closest to my Mom Anna Krell's good tasting soup. My three daughters, their husband and my seven Grandchildren all agree. "It is the best"

Anna Krell's Chicken Soup
meat

1 chicken hen
2 bunches parsley
2 large onions
1 stalk celery
Salt
Pepper

Directions:
1.) Always use a hen.
2.) Use a lot of parsley.
3.) Add celery and onion.
4.) Let it cook for about two hrs. on a medium flame.
5.) Add salt and pepper to taste.
   *Always use a chicken hen not a fryer.

Ruth Swider

Waukesha, WI, U.S.A.

Submitted by her daughter Cantor Marsha Gelbart Fensin

Ruth Swider (Gelbart) was born in Warsaw, Poland approximately 1913 -1916. She was a sickly infant and, because it was not known whether or not she would live, no birth certificate was ever made. Her parents were Rivka Laya and Sjaya Pesach Swider. She was one of four siblings, Wolf, Leon, Mina and herself. Only Ruth and Mina survived the Holocaust. Leon was also reported to have survived but nobody knows of his whereabouts.

Ruth survived the Warsaw Ghetto, Majdanek, a death camp, Skarzysko-Kamienna, a work camp and Stochowa, a slave labor camp, where she met and married Simon Gelbart after their liberation. Ruth and Simon found that they could not return to their homes, and so they immigrated to Palestine, where their daughter, Marsha, was born. They were in Israel when the state of Israel was founded. The Gelbarts, after beginning to find other members of their families who had survived, then emigrated to Canada, where Simon, a tailor, and Ruth, an accomplished seamstress, had a dry cleaning/tailoring business.

Simon died at age forty three and is buried in Canada. Ruth moved to the United States to be with her sister Mina and her family in New Jersey. She and Marsha became naturalized citizens. When Marsha was sixteen they moved to Daytona Beach, Florida, where Ruth lived for more than forty years.

Following a fall in 2002, Ruth began to live with her daughter, first in Iowa and then with Marsha and her husband Lee in Waukesha, Wisconsin, where she resides today. Ruth has always felt compassion for those less fortunate, devoting many hours to volunteer work at her temple in Daytona and a hospital in Ormond Beach as a Pink Lady. She never said "no" to anyone requesting help, always having extra money to give to those less fortunate, especially children's causes.

In fact, her kindness was such that, after years of selflessly helping out a disabled World War I veteran with no family, when he passed away, he left Ruth his house and his car. Ruth's greatest pleasures now are her beloved grandchildren, Scott and Lori (and their respective spouses) and her adorable, wonderful great grandson Alex, who is the apple of her eye.

Ruth passed away in Waukesha Wisconsin on August 30, 2006 at the age of 92.

71

Ruth Swider's Cholent

meat

1/2 lb. fatty marrow bones
1 C. uncooked barley
1 C. large white kidney beans
Salt and Pepper
4 to 5 whole potatoes (peeled)
2 or 3 cloves garlic (cut in half)
1 onion (cut in pieces or sliced)

Directions:

Preheat oven to 250 degrees

1.) Put all the ingredients into a large pot and cover with water.
2.) Bring to a boil.
3.) Remove from heat and cover with an airtight lid or as my mother did, wrap the top of the pot plus the cover with brown paper or butcher paper or even newspaper works for her, so that none of the steam can escape.
4.) Bake at 250 degrees or cook over the smallest possible flame overnight. (You can also use a slow cooker or pressure cooker if it has a very low temperature.)

Ruth Swider's Eastern European Meat Loaf

meat

1 lb. ground beef or turkey
Approx. 3/8 C Matzo Meal
1 egg, beaten
1 tsp. salt
1/4 tsp. pepper
1 onion, chopped.
Cooking oil and water as needed

Directions:

1.) Mix together ground meat, matzo meal, beaten egg, salt and pepper.
  * If the mixture seems too firm, add a little water.
  * If it is too loose, add a little more matzo meal.
2.) Form into a large patty.
3.) Divide the onion into two portions.
4.) Brown 1/2 of the onion in a little oil in a large frying pan and place the meatloaf patty down to brown with the onion.
5.) Use medium heat so as not to burn the meat.
6.) After approximately 15 minutes, turn the meat loaf over and brown other side with rest of the onions and cook until done, adding water as needed so as not to burn the meat.

72

Sara Stolniki
Windsor, CT, U.S.A.

August 1942. Left to right-
Gutki Stolnicki (22 years old),
Sarah Stolnicki (10 years old)

My name is Seena Schwarz, nee Sara Stolniki. My parents, Ginendel and Judel Stolnicki escaped from the pogroms in Poland during the 20's with their daughter (my sister) and little brother (who passed away in 1930). They came to Antwerp, Belgium, not realizing that they were actually jumping out of the frying pan into the fire less than 20 years later.

I was born in Antwerp in 1931 and was 8 years old when the Nazis entered Belgium. It was in 1942 when the "final solution" came into being. For us September of 1942 was the explosion. I was almost 11 years old and my parents sent me into hiding in an orphanage, where I remained for only 1 month. During that month, my dad was grabbed off the street and shipped off to Auschwitz, where he perished. We had wonderful friends who were involved with the "underground" forces. They found hiding places for my mom and sister. Our home now belonged to the Nazis. It was lucky that I was not at home or we would all have been deported. Our friends, the Jospa's found a hiding place for me in a convent in Brussels. These nuns hid 14 Jewish girls. The neighborhood priest took in the boys.

At 11 I was one of the older ones. There were 2 babies. The nuns and Mother Superior (we called her soeur maman) were angels. My sister came there also. She was everyone's surrogate mother, teacher, and confidante. Of course, we learned catechism, sang hymns in the beautiful little chapel and prayed to Jesus to save all the children. Four of us were baptized, our parents hoping that not being Jewish would save us. Four of us left the convent every morning to go to school. One day, while we were at school the Nazis rang the bell at the convent. We had been betrayed. Because four of us were missing they decided to return the following day and get us all. If a child was missing the nuns would pay with their lives.

After we returned from school my sister (who was not on their list for some reason) braided her hair to look like me, gave me some money for trolley fare and sent me out the door. She was ready to sacrifice her life to save mine. I took the trolley and went to where my mom was hidden as a maid for a gentile family. In the meantime, soeur maman was frantically looking for help to save the children from certain death. She somehow managed to contact a group of underground people. They were young men and women 16 and 17 years old and they decided to help them. During the night, they broke into the convent, tied and gagged the nuns (who did not put up a fight), and cut the telephone wires. They carried the hysterical children including my sister and fled by foot.

They found hiding places for all and all survived. I neglected to tell you that my name now was Simone Brisbois and my sister was Renee. We are in contact with some of these girls and they remember holding on to my sister's skirt while all this was going on. Of course I could not stay with my mom. A cousin, a very brave young woman, found a place for me in another convent in the south of the country, a little town called Durbuy. My sister came there also. This convent was a place for abandoned children and also a school for the area children. I found a few other Jewish children hidden there. We remained there until the "liberation" in the fall of 1944. I was almost 13. My mom was hiding in another village.

73

Bubbie Ginendel's Gefilte Fish
parve

10 lbs. carp (whole)
1 1/2 lbs. Cod fillet
6 eggs.
1 cup bread crumbs (or Matzoh meal for Passover)
About 1 1/2 lb carrots
3 large onions
Salt and pepper to taste
Water

Directions:

Have the carp cleaned, scaled, filleted, and skinned. Take home every part, mostly for the bones and the heads. This is very important because the liquid will not gel without bones. Remove the eyes form the fish (you can throw them away).

1.) In meat grinder (not a food processor) grind the carp, cod, 2 large carrots, and large onion TWICE.
2.) Add the eggs, crumbs, salt & pepper, and a small amount water and mix thoroughly. Use your hands to mix.
3.) Add enough water until the consistency is such that you can form balls (pretty much like meat balls). Shape the fish into balls, the size is up to you.
4.) In 2 large pots pour about 2 inches of water, add 2 sliced carrots and 1 sliced onion to each pot, salt & pepper and bring to a boil.
5.) Gently drop the bones and heads into the liquid, cover tightly and boil on a low setting for about 20-30 minutes until they have begun to look cooked.
6.) Making sure that the liquid is boiling, drop in the fish balls one at a time in one layer.
7.) Shake the pots to keep from sticking.
8.) Cover tightly.
9.) Cook until the balls feel firm to the touch before adding the next layer, otherwise they will all stick together.
10.) Taste the liquid for spices. Add salt & pepper if needed.
11.) Cover tightly and cook on low setting for one hour.
12.) Shake the pot and taste once in a while during that period.
13.) When done, uncover partly and let stand to rest and cool slightly.
    * Do not remove from the pot for one hour or else they will fall apart.
14.) Remove the balls with a spoon and place on a couple of platters.
15.) Decorate with carrot slices and pour a little liquid over them to keep the moist.
16.) Cover in plastic wrap and refrigerate.
17.) Remove the bones with a slotted spoon and put aside.
18.) Pour the remaining liquid in 1 or 2 small bowls and refrigerate.
19.) This will gel and is delicious with challah.

Gutki's and my favorite part of this operation is to sit down when nobody else is in the kitchen we attack the bones, chew them and polish off all the flesh that is left on them. The heads are especially scrumptious. It is a Jewish feast that requires manual dexterity, somehow resembles eating lobster, but better. It brings back nostalgia at its best!

I must confess that I made changes to "Americanize" the recipe. My mom used to cut the whole fish into steaks, scoop the flesh out of each piece and reshape the mixture into the individual slices. Also she chopped with a cleaver, not an electric meat grinder. That's progress, I guess.

About 15 years ago. Left to right: Gutki Miliband (Née Stolnicki), Seena Schwarz (Née Sarah Stolnicki)

Seena Schwarz (Née Sarah Stolnicki)
April 1, 2007

Shary and Leon Kabiljo
Baltimore, MD, U.S.A.
Submitted by her daughters Linda Cohen and Sylvia Rothschild

"What a perfect day for a wedding," thought Leon as he gazed out of his window on this calm spring morning, as nervous as any groom would be on the day of his wedding. Suddenly, he heard a special bulletin on the radio: "April 6, 1941, Belgrade, Yugoslavia was bombed early this morning by the Nazis. War has begun and the Germans are taking over. All Jews will be prosecuted but the first to be taken will be men."

Leon just stood petrified, unable to believe what he had just heard. Immediately he went to the house of his fiancé, Shary where they had only a quiet ceremony in place of the wedding they had once planned.

"Oh dear G-d! The Nazis are here! You must run to the attic!" As fast as his legs could carry him, he ran to the dark, isolated room and hid as best he could. Shary was questioned about where her husband was, but as calmly as possible, she told them that he had returned to his hometown. In disbelief of her reply, they commenced their hunt.

Leon lay in the dark still room, in a frenzy of fear, as he heard the approaching men searching for him. "Siegfried, Frans! Search this dark attic!" Leon's thoughts went only to G-d, as the Nazi troops did their duty. In his quest to find him, Frans accidentally struck a painting of a rabbi, which hung on the wall, and the reverent picture fell to cover a trembling figure. He was ever so grateful, but for how long could this hiding go on? How many other times would he be as fortunate as this? There had to be a solution- some way to escape!

In the cluttered, disordered, and confused turmoil of the train station, Leon and his four closest friends had acquired new passports with intentions of escaping to the Italian occupied zone in Yugoslavia. There, Jews were not arrested and taken to concentration camps. Temporarily, they would be safe. They began to further their plans as Leon spoke in a whisper. "We will split up on the train. Each must try to get into a separate car in order to make our scheme less conspicuous. Stay as calm as possible and most important, have faith in G-d."

Suddenly the train stopped at a nearby station as they approached their destination. In the back of his mind, Leon was almost certain the Nazis were searching the train for Jews. "This waiting is terrible. What's all that commotion outside?" As he glanced out of his window he saw all four of his friends among a group of Jews being taken by the Nazis.

Leon sat terrified as he expected the Nazis to take him as well. "Where's your passport?" they inquired when they finally had reached him. Trying his hardest not to reveal his true identity he handed them his passport.

"Why are you going there?"
"I work for the government but I have my vacation now."

For a moment they just stared at him. "Where's your picture?"

"I was in such a hurry I didn't have time to get one." Leon could feel his heart pounding but something gave him the courage to appear calm. After what seemed like forever, they went on, supposedly without suspicions.

There were no words to describe the way he felt as the Nazis passed him by. He never knew exactly what happened to his friends. It could have been their dialect that gave them away. Leon spoke the Yugoslavian language fluently without any trace of a Jewish accent. Maybe they were so frightened that it became obvious to the Nazis. No matter what gave them away, Leon began to realize his four companions were marching to their death.

At last he arrived and the first thing he did was to write Shary and tell her of this horrifying experience and to ask her to come to him as soon as possible. She had the morbid task of telling the wives of the four men that their husbands were to be killed.

Shary dressed as a Turkish woman and went as the daughter of her father's close friend who wasn't Jewish. Luckily her trip went smoothly and she finally met up with her husband.

Together they continued to struggle to survive. Finally in the Italian occupied area of Yugoslavia, they joined the Partisans, a resistance group. So many friends were killed because of their lack of experience as a soldier. Remember, they were the store owners, the farmers, the doctors and teachers of the town. Finally, English soldiers came and took a group on a small boat to Italy. Although their life was still tough, now at least they were in a refugee camp. The hiding was over.

At long last maybe their prayers were answered. A notice arrived informing them that Franklin Roosevelt announced that 1,000 European refugees would be permitted to enter the United States. Once again, they truly believed God was watching out for them as they were

among those chosen. Excitedly, they boarded the ship with hopes of starting a new life.

Together they looked at their native land for the last time, with everything and everyone left behind them. This scene which remains in their memory to this day, was allowed to grow dimmer and dimmer.

Shary Kabiljo's Cheese Pie

(Great for a diary brunch, lunch or light dinner.)

Submitted by her daughters: Linda Cohen of Franklin, MI and Sylvia Rothschild of Baltimore, MD

1 large cottage cheese (24 ounces) (Fat free or low fat may be used.)
1 package of cream cheese (8 ounces) (May use low fat, if desired.)
2-3 eggs
Sprinkle of flour (about 2 T.)
*Optional: Add 1 package of frozen spinach or fresh spinach.
  (If too thick, add a little milk.)
1 Package of long frozen Phyllo (or fillo) dough sheets
  (Thaw in refrigerator overnight before using for this recipe.)
Melted butter- ½ to 1 stick (Margarine or oil may be used.)

Directions:

Preheat oven to 400 degrees

1.) Combine one large cottage cheese and one large cream cheese with eggs.
2.) Mix with mixer or spoon until well blended.
3.) Add spinach, if desired.
4.) Sprinkle flour into the mixture to thicken a little and mix again.
5.) Microwave butter until melted.
6.) Carefully unroll Phyllo sheets on a smooth dry surface and set 4 or 5 sheets on wax paper and/or cheesecloth.
7.) Brush each of 4 or 5 sheets with melted butter. (Keep the unused dough covered **with** plastic wrap and a damp towel **while not in use**, so it doesn't dry out.)
8.) Brush edges first to prevent cracking. Be sure to brush the last sheet with melted butter.
9.) Put cheese mixture across the entire length of the 4 buttered sheets (one on top of the other) in a 3" strip.
10.) Put the filling on the lower third of the sheets (closest to you) so it is easier to roll.
11.) The cheese mixture should not touch the edges.
12.) Roll up once or twice and then fold in the edges
13.) Continue rolling to the end and gently place seam side down on an ungreased cookie sheet.
14.) Repeat steps 7 to 13, until all the cheese mixture is used.
15.) Bake at 400 degrees for 10 minutes.
16.) Then turn down to 350 degrees and bake for about 40 minutes or until Phyllo dough is lightly browned. ***Serve warm and crispy!***

78

Shoshana Greenwald
Jerusalem, Israel
Submitted by Devorah Feder

My Grandmother, Shoshana Greenwald, of Monsey, NY was a young girl when the Second World War broke out and she was always on the run. Her father, R' Wolf Frey, worked with Raoul Wallenberg saving Jewish lives. When speaking of the holocaust my grandmother barely speaks of all the atrocities she experienced. Instead, she tells us stories about her remarkable parents and their unwavering faith in G-d. My grandmother instilled in every one of her children and grandchildren a sense of gratitude for all the blessings G-d has given us and a sense of pride for being His chosen nation.

My grandmother always reminds us how lucky we are and how special our ancestors were.

This is her special recipe for turkey soup which we all enjoy!

Turkey Soup
meat

6 turkey necks
2 turkey drumsticks (legs)
1 onion
1 celery root
1 sweet potato
2 carrots
3 cloves garlic
2 zucchinis
1 green pepper
2 parsnips
salt and pepper

Directions:
Preheat oven to 350 degrees

1.) Fill a 8 Qt. soup pot 1/2 full with water, bring to a boil.
2.) Peel all vegetables (if you like to serve the soup with the vegetables you can slice them before putting them in the soup, however, if you would like a clear broth place all vegetables in a wrap n boil mesh bag)
3.) Put them into the pot once the water is boiling.
4.) Make the flame lower and cook for 5 hours.
5.) After 5 hours let soup cool before placing it in the fridge.

* If you would like to freeze this soup, it does freeze well.
  To freeze, remove all vegetables and turkey and freeze only liquid broth.

79

Caesar Salad Dressing
parve

1/2 cup oil
1/2 cup mayo
1 tbsp mustard
1 fresh clove garlic

Directions:

Pour all ingredients into a blender
and blend until smooth.

Serves 4

Delicious Duck Sauce
parve

4 cups water
4 tbsp cornstarch
2 tbsp lemon juice
4 tbsp apricot jam
2 tbsp brown sugar
4 tbsp ketchup
1 tsp poultry seasoning

Directions:

- Pour all ingredients into a saucepan, bring to a boil.
- Stir over low heat for 5 minutes.

* When cooled this sauce goes nicely with a roast or over chicken.

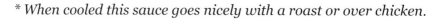

Ambrosia

parve

10 oz. Rich's Whip
12 oz. frozen strawberries
11 oz. can of mandarin oranges
1 can pineapple chunked or crushed

Directions:

- Combine all ingredients and chill before serving
  * *Works great as an appetizer or as dessert.*

Shoshana Greenwald enjoying quality time with her great grandson, avraham shmuel binyamin feder who is named after her great grandfather the ksav sofer of pressburg.

Honey Cake

parve

1 1/2 cups sugar
4 eggs
1 cup oil
1 cup honey
2 tsp baking powder
2 1/2 cups flour
1 cup cool tea
1 tsp baking soda

Directions:

Preheat oven to 350 degrees

1.) Grease a 9 x 13 pan and set aside.
2.) Mix all ingredients together well and pour into prepared pan.
3.) Bake at 350 for 45 minutes to 1 hour.

Easy and Delicious Rugelach

parve or dairy

Dough:
  5 1/2 cups flour
  4 sticks of margarine (parve or dairy
  1 10 oz dessert whip (parve or dairy)
  1/2 cup sugar
Filling:
  1 cup sugar
  6 tsp cocoa
  2 tsp cinnamon

Directions:

Preheat oven to 350 degrees

1.) Prepare 2 greased or parchment paper lined cookie sheets and set aside.
2.) Mix all dough ingredients to form dough.
3.) Divide into 3 separate balls.
4.) Refrigerate for easier handling.
5.) Mix all ingredients for filling together and set aside.
6.) Once the dough is chilled, take each ball and roll out into a circle about 8 or 10 inches in diameter.
7.) Brush lightly with oil and sprinkle with prepared filling.
8.) Cut into 16 triangles.
9.) Take each triangle and roll up from the outer edge toward the middle.
10.) Place each triangle on prepared cookie sheet and sprinkle lightly with some filling.
11.) Bake at 350 degrees for 10 to 15 minutes.

Decadent Dairy Chocolate Cake

For Pesach

1 lb chopped semi sweet chocolate
2 sticks of butter
8 eggs

Directions:

Preheat oven to 325 degrees

1.) Grease an 8 inch parchment lined spring form pan and set aside.
2.) Melt the chocolate and butter over low heat.
3.) Beat the eggs for 5 minutes, then fold half of the egg mixture with melted chocolate and butter, then add the other half.
4.) Pour into the prepared pan and bake at 325 for 45 minutes.

Serves 10

Sol Filler
Auckland, New Zealand
Submitted by his wife Ruth Filler

Sol Filler

My late husband Sol Filler was born in a small town in Galicia, Poland, in 1922. He was the oldest son of Gedalye and Runia Filler, who worked hard in their bakery making Challahs, pastries, bread, rolls, and all sorts of beautiful yeast delicacies for the people of Brzozow and the surrounding towns and villages.

In 1938 the Germans invaded Poland and in no time were occupying every part of the country, which spelled disaster and dread for the Jewish people, who were murdered and tortured, starved and beaten on a daily basis.

Sol's brothers and others from the small "Stetl" had already left to flee over the border into Russia. He would have also gone, but an order came out that the bakery was to produce hundreds of loaves of bread for the occupying Germans. Sol's father was unable to cope on his own, so Sol decided to remain and help.

Thus he was caught in the Nazi net, and a short time later he was transported, together with many other young men from their town, to a nearby work camp, then to the ghetto in Krakow. Finally he and his younger brother were taken to Auschwitz, where they were slave laborers in the coal mines.

After many years in captivity they were forced to go on a death march, in which many people perished. Five months later they were liberated and made it to Czechoslovakia. After their liberation they discovered that they were the only ones from their family who had survived.

After the war they were taken to a displaced persons camp in Germany and ultimately received visas to go to Australia, which is where I met him in 1951. We were married in Auckland, New Zealand in 1952.

We were blessed with two beautiful daughters, the elder one achieving fame as a comedienne/actress/singer, Deb Filler, based in Canada. She has performed in many countries. Our other daughter Esther married and has three children, all of whom live in Auckland.

Sadly, Sol passed away in 1999, but in his memory, and to honour him, I am submitting the following recipe for your cookery book.

Filler Family - from top left: Deb Filler (daughter), Ron Haver (grandson), Ruth Filler, Arron Haver (son-in-law), Esther Haver (daughter), Sol Filler, Daniella Haver (granddaughter), and Samara Haver (granddaughter)

Marinated Herring in Cream

dairy

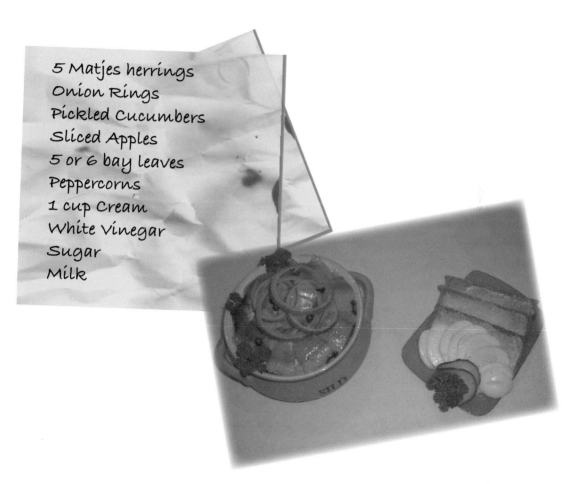

5 Matjes herrings
Onion Rings
Pickled Cucumbers
Sliced Apples
5 or 6 bay leaves
Peppercorns
1 cup Cream
White Vinegar
Sugar
Milk

Directions:

1.) Cut herrings into bite sized pieces.
2.) Put in flat dish, layered with thin onion rings, pickled cucumbers, finely sliced apples, 5-6 bay leaves, pepper corns.
3.) Dilute 1 cup of cream with white vinegar, sugar, and a small amount of milk.
4.) Pour over herring, cover and let marinade for a day in the refrigerator.
5.) Eat with fresh challah or brown bread- delicious!

Hazel Nut Cake

parve

350 g hazel nuts (other nuts can be used),
　　　coarsely ground.
10 eggs, separated (this recipe can be halved quite easily).
350 g fine sugar
1/8 tsp salt, 1 tbsp rum, (or rum essence)
1 tbsp. coarse matzo meal,
　　　(fine white dry bread crumbs can be substituted).

Directions:

1.) Cream sugar and egg yolks, add ground nuts, salt and rum, , fold in stiffly-beaten egg whites, together with matzo meal or bread crumbs.
2.) Line spring form with baking paper, bake 40 - 50 minutes in moderate oven.
3.) When cool, fill with cream, either flavoured with instant coffee or drinking chocolate granules.

Delicious!

Note: This can be used for Passover.

New Zealand Cheesecake

dairy

Filling:

- Five 250 g (8 oz.) packets of Philadelphia cream cheese .
- Place in beater with 1 3/4 cups of sugar, 3 tbsp. all-purpose flour, 1 1/2 tsp. each of grated lemon and orange peel, 1/4 tsp. vanilla essence.

Beat till smooth.

- Add 5 eggs, one at a time, and then 2 egg yolks, plus 1/4 cup of heavy cream.

Place in prepared tin.

(This recipe can be halved.)

Preheat oven to 500 degrees
Line the base of a large spring form cake tin with ready-rolled sweet pastry, (can be bought frozen from supermarket), prick with fork, and bake until pale brown (around 25 minutes, medium heat).

When cool, line sides of tin with more of the same pastry, straighten top with pastry wheel to look decorative.

In very hot oven, (500 F), bake for 10 minutes, reduce oven temperature to 250, bake for another 1 hour.
Serve either plain, or with boysenberry or pineapple topping (glaze). Even lovely with fresh strawberry or raspberry topping.

Enjoy.

87

Deb Filler's Challah Recipe

parve

This makes 2 loaves, one which can be frozen till ready to bake.

- 2 free range/ organic eggs
- 1 three pkg. yeast (or 2 tsp.)
- 4 TBS light veg. oil
- 2 3/4 cups warm water
- 1 cup sugar
- 4 tsp. salt
- 7 - 8 cups flour
- poppy seeds
- 1 egg yolk beaten with 1 tsp. water

Directions:

Preheat oven to 400 degrees

1.) Dissolve one teaspoon of sugar in the warm water in a large mixing bowl, which has been rinsed with hot water.
2.) Sprinkle the yeast on top and let stand 10 minutes.
3.) Stir to dissolve and add oil, sugar, salt, eggs and beat well.
4.) Add three cups of flour at a time until all flour is mixed. Dough should be sticky.
5.) Cover dough and let rest for 10 minutes.
6.) Turn out onto a floured board and knead for 10 minutes, adding flour as needed.
7.) Place dough back in a greased bowl and cover with a damp cloth in warm place until double in bulk, about 2 hours.
8.) Punch down, divide dough in two.
   * If not baking both loaves, either refrigerate or freeze second batch until ready to use.
Note: when using the second loaf, allow to come to room temperature until continuing with following.
9.)   Allow loaf to rise again for 45 minutes.
10.) Punch down, divide dough into three equal parts.
11.) Shape into tubular shapes by hand.
14.) Braid loaf together ensuring that the ends are secured and tucked under.
15.) Place on a lightly greased baking sheet.
16.) Cover with a damp cloth and let rise in a warm place until double about 45 minutes.
17.) Brush with beaten egg yolk and sprinkle with poppy seeds.
18.) Bake at 400 for 30 minutes, until deep golden brown.

- To store yeast dough, grease top well and cover with wax paper and then a damp cloth.
- Make sure cloth stays damp. Will keep five days in fridge. Freezes well.
- Best place to raise yeast is on top of stove.

Lemon Cream (Citronen Creme)

dairy

Juice of 4 - 5 juicy lemons.
6 eggs, separated.
1 large Tbs. sugar.
2 heaped tsp. Gelatin or
  one packet of unflavored Gelatin
    * Kosher Gelatin is hard to find.
Hot water.
1/2 pt. Whipping cream, whipped, with sugar added.

Directions:

1.) Beat egg whites until stiff, put aside.
2.) Beat egg yolks with sugar until pale and creamy, add the lemon juice.
3.) Add the gelatin (which has been dissolved in 1/4 cup of boiling water).
4.) Add beaten egg whites, folding it in, and then fold in the beaten cream.
5.) Leave to set in refrigerator (covered).

The same recipe can be used with drinking chocolate, or 1/2 cup of coffee, or cocoa melted in warm milk (all with extra sugar added), instead of lemons.

Sonia Krivavnik Finkelstein
Houston, TX, U.S.A.
Submitted by her daughter Edith Finkelstein Hamer

Sonia Krivavnik Finkelstein survived the Holocaust by receiving visa number 7 from Mr. Chiune Sugihara on July 24, 1940 in Kaunas, Lithuania. Mr. Sugihara was a righteous gentile working in the Japanese Embassy in the summer of 1940. He handwrote over 2000 visas saving many lives. These visas gave their owners permission to travel over Russia and enter Japan. The visas were not exactly against Japanese law but rather Mr. Sugihara stretched and stretched and stretched the laws of his country so that he could help as many people as possible.

It is submitted by her daughter, Edith Finkelstein Hamer, listed as a child on the same visa. It was a favorite childhood recipe and probably handed down from her grandmother who perished in the Holocaust.

◇◇◇

Mom's Lithuanian Cookies
dairy

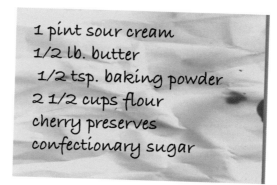

1 pint sour cream
1/2 lb. butter
1/2 tsp. baking powder
2 1/2 cups flour
cherry preserves
confectionary sugar

Directions:
Preheat oven for 375 degrees

1.) Combine first three ingredients and add enough flour so that you can roll the dough.
2.) Cool overnight.
3.) Cut cookies with the top of a glass (or cookie cutter) after rolling and folding the dough.
4.) Add a cherry from cherry preserves in the middle of each cookie.
5.) Bake 375 degrees for about 15 minutes.
6.) Cool and coat with a mixture of confectionary sugar and water mixture.

Tauba Luft Klausner
Menro Park, CA, U.S.A.
As told by her son David Klausner

In short, my mother was born in Hrubieszow, Poland in 1917, and escaped with her family to Russia in 1942, where they lost their mother in 1944, exited in 1945-6 to Germany, and one half came to New York in 1949, and the other half to Argentina the same year.

Brisket
1995 recipe of Gloria Mish

meat

Luft Family (clockwise) Si, Joe, Jacob Klausner, Tauba [Luft] Klausner, David Klausner, Wolf Luft

1 (3 to 4 lb) brisket
black pepper
garlic powder
1 tsp minced garlic
1 envelope onion soup mix
1 (10 ounce) can mushroom gravy
2 beef bouillon cubes, mashed
3/4 cup ketchup
1 (6 ounce) package fresh baby carrots
4 potatoes peeled and quartered
1 lb mushrooms, sliced

Directions:
Preheat oven on broil. (350 degrees)

1.) In small bowl, mix together onion soup mix, mushroom gravy, bouillon cubes and ketchup.
2.) Season brisket with pepper and garlic.
3.) Place brisket on baking sheet and sear 5 minutes on both sides.
4.) Remove brisket from oven and transfer brisket to a roasting pan.
5.) Reduce temperature to 350 degrees.
6.) Pour bowl contents over brisket and cover.
7.) Roast on bake 2-1/2 to 3 hours, or until tender.
8.) After 1 hour add carrots, potatoes and mushrooms.
9.) Slice against grain and serve with gravy.

Hi latke cravers!

parve

3 or 4 large baking potatoes
    (I used 4 large Russets)
1/2 to 3/4 cup finely grated onion
    (I used 3/4 to 1 cup)
3 large eggs, beaten
2 teaspoons salt
    (I used Kosher salt)
Freshly ground white pepper to taste
    (I used 1/4 to 1/2 tsp.)
1/2 teaspoon baking powder
2 to 4 tablespoons matzo meal or flour
plus matzo meal or flour as needed
    (I used 2 tbs. matzo meal only)
Vegetable oil for frying.

Directions:

Grate the potatoes, half finely and half medium-fine. (I only did medium-fine strands) into a large mixing bowl. (I put them in a strainer to drain before I hand squeezed them in bunches into a separate bowl.) You should have about 4 cups grated potatoes. Cover them with (cold tap) water and let soak for at least 15 minutes or up to 1 hour to remove the excess starch. Rinse the potatoes and drain well, squeezing them with your hands to remove excess moisture (very important).

Combine the grated potatoes in a mixing bowl with onion, beaten eggs, salt, pepper, baking powder and 2 tablespoons matzo meal. (I combined all ingredients together then mixed with grated potatoes at the last minute right before the oil was hot enough to begin frying so they wouldn't get too soggy.) Add more matzo meal if too much liquid accumulates in the bottom of the bowl. (I didn't do this; instead, I squeezed liquid out as needed as I shaped each patty.)

Pour the oil into a large frying pan to a depth of 1/8 to ½ inch, and heat. When the oil is hot but not smoking, gently drop the potato batter by the large spoonful into the hot oil, pressing down on them lightly with the back of the spoon to form thin pancakes about 2 ½ inches in diameter, keeping the latkes about an inch apart. Fry the latkes until they are light golden on one side, then turn and cook them until light golden on the other side. Remove them to a paper towel-lined platter to drain, blotting off the excess oil as they cool. (I had 2 frying pans going at once which is faster and reduces sogginess.)

Repeat until all the batter is used up, adding a bit more matzo meal or flour to the mixture as more liquid starts to collect in the bowl, and squeezing out the extra liquid. (I never added more matzo meal but kept squeezing out liquid.) Skim the surface of the oil to remove any floating potato bits, which can burn and give the oil and off-flavor. Discard the oil and use fresh oil as needed. (I discarded the oil after every batch of 4 potatoes.)

When the latkes are cooked and cooled, transfer them in a single layer to baking sheets. Place the baking sheets in the freezer and freeze until the latkes are hard. Transfer the frozen latkes to freezer storage bags. They can be kept for up to 2 weeks.

When ready to serve, preheat the oven to 425 to 450 degrees. (Important to use this hot of an oven.) Arrange the frozen latkes on baking sheets, in a single layer without crowding. Bake for about 15 – 20 minutes, turning once, until golden brown. Drain briefly on a paper towel-lined platter. Serve hot. Serves 4 (about 14 to 16 small latkes).
* **Served with apple sauce, jam and/or sour cream.**
* **Best when served freshly made and hot.**

Cholent (stew)

meat

1/2 cup of large lima beans (optional)
1/2 cup of barley (optional)
1 package kishka
2 potatoes (medium)
1 carrot
1 onion (medium)
1 28 oz. can of crushed tomatoes
2 lbs stew meat, or sausage, or turkey, or mixed.
1 tbsp paprika
1 tbsp pepper
2 tbsp salt
3 tbsp garlic powder

Directions:
1.) Soak beans overnight.
2.) Drain.
3.) Cut potatoes (you don't have to skin them, just scrape and wash them), carrot, onion.
4.) Put everything into a crock pot (or such).
(I like to put potatoes in first, some of the spices next, then the optional beans, then more spice, then the can of tomatoes, then meat, etc.).
5.) Put kishka in the middle (make sure to puncture the skin/case).
6.) Fill to the top with water.
7.) Cover and cook on low for at least 12 hours.
8.) No need to mix it.
* If you want a vegetarian version of this, just leave out the meat.
It still works out fine. You can also substitute other meats.

93

Chocolate Strudel

parve

3 cups of regular flour
3 Eggs
3 level tsp baking powder
3 tsp vanilla extract
3/4 cup of corn oil
3/4 cup of sugar
bitter cocoa
cinnamon
raisins
crushed back walnuts, almonds, pecans

Directions:

Preheat oven to 350 degrees

- Mix and fold the flour, baking powder, 3/4 cup sugar, 3 eggs, vanilla and 3/4 cup of oil in a mixing bowl.
- Knead the mixture (add water as necessary to knead) and separate it into two equal parts.
- Flour a surface, spread out the dough, and roll a pie flat approximately 1/4 inch or less thin.
- Do not make it thinner than 1/8 inch as it will not hold together when rolled up.
- Mix the bitter cocoa with sugar and cinnamon in a cup until it is sweet enough for your taste.
- Spread the mixture on the dough and firm it down with the back of a spoon.
- Remove extra mixture and save it for the other dough.
- Spread raisins and nuts on top as you like.
- Roll the pie flat up from one edge, and when completely rolled up, flatten the ends to seal them.
- Oil (or PAM) a baking dish, and place the two strudels in it.
- Bake the strudel for about 30 minutes, baste it with an egg yolk and sugar during its last ten minutes of baking.

94

Crispy Spiced Potatoes

parve

1 ½ pounds white or red boiling potatoes
3 tablespoons vegetable or olive oil
1 teaspoon paprika
½ teaspoon onion powder
½ teaspoon garlic powder
½ teaspoon salt (or rosemary for lower salt content)
½ teaspoon black pepper
pinch of cayenne (red pepper)
nonstick vegetable spray

Directions:
Preheat oven to 400 degrees

- Scrub potatoes, but do not peel.
- Cut each potato in half, and then cut each half into 4 wedges.
  (If potatoes are very small, cut each half into 2 wedges.)
- Place potato wedges into a pot and cover with water.
- Cover pot, bring to a boil, and cook potatoes for 10 minutes.
- While potatoes are cooking, combine oil and seasonings in a large bowl.
- When potatoes are finished cooking, drain them and toss while still warm
  with seasoning mixture. (Potatoes can be prepared up to this point several
  hours in advance, and left at room temperature.)
- Prepare a baking sheet with nonstick vegetable spray.
- Arrange potatoes in a single layer, and bake at 400 degrees for 20 minutes,
  until golden brown.

Serve immediately.

95

Yvonne Braunsberg Wagner

Miami Beach, FL, U.S.A.

Yvonne was born in Berlin, Germany in 1929. At the age of 9, Yvonne and her two sisters left Germany under the Kindertransport program. Her cousins in England had made arrangements to send them to a British Boarding School in the country to be safe. The girls never saw their family again as they all perished in the Holocaust. Yvonne became a children's nurse in England. She met her husband, Peter, at a Jewish Youth Group in London where Peter was studying at the University of London.

Peter and Yvonne moved to the United States in 1953 and lived in New York until 1960. Peter received a one year job offer in Washington, D.C. and they moved and settled in Bethesda with their three children, Elizabeth and Charles and Wayne. Yvonne managed a real estate business, was President of her Temple and of her B'nai Brith Woman's chapter. She is very active today in many charitable organizations in Washington D.C. and Miami Beach.

Spinach and Cottage Cheese Soufflé

dairy

low salt, low fat recipe

2 pkg. frozen chopped spinach defrosted and drained
12 oz cottage cheese
1 large chopped onion sauteed
4 eggs beaten or egg beaters
8 oz low salt cheddar, grated- Kosher
Nutmeg and Garlic Powder

Directions:
Preheat oven to 350 degrees

1.) Combine all ingredients.
2.) Bake in greased casserole 40 min. at 350 degrees.

* Can be used as a side dish or main course.

Sophie (Zosia) Billys (Bialystok)
Millie (Milanka) Selinger
Cleveland, OH, U.S.A.
Submitted by Millie Selinger

Henrik (Henry), 1939

Sophie (Zosia), 1939

I was 11 months old when the war broke out in Poland. I was born in Lodz on Sept. 21, 1938. My parents were returning from their summer house to the city when Kosciuszko's statue was blown up in the square. That, my mother said, was the start of the war in Poland. Once the Jews were rounded up to the ghetto, my mother and father decided that saving the baby was their only concern. So my mother put her armband into her pocket and bought a cross at the jewelry store. From that day on her mission was to acquire gentile papers so my parents could parade as Polish Greek Catholics. Eventually she succeeded and we lived as non-Jews during and after the war.

After the war ended they decided they preferred to return to Judaism. They found Poland's circumstances remained detrimental to Jews. So in 1947 they decided to escape to Germany. There, at the age of 8 1/2 I learned that I was Jewish. In 1948 we came to the United States under the quota system and were sponsored by my father's uncle's employer from Cleveland, Ohio. We settled there and enjoyed a life of freedom.

My parents are 94 and 96 (in June of '06) years old, respectively.

Millie (Milanka) at age 9, passport photo taken in Germany, bound for the USA, 1948

Millie (Milanka) at age 4 with her mom Sophie (Zosia) in Poland, 1942

Bigos

meat

2 lbs. sauerkraut with liquid
2 lbs. cabbage, cut up or shredded
1 lg. onion sauteed
1-2 lbs sliced and sauteed sausage (may use cut-up
    pieces of leftover meat: beef, lamb, turkey, etc...).
10 prunes
10 or more dried mushrooms soaked
    for 1/2 hr in water to soften, sliced
liquid from soaked mushrooms
salt and pepper
Bullion cube or powder
    diluted in 1c water
bay leaf

Directions:

Preheat oven to 300 degrees

1.) Place all ingredients in large pot or baking dish.
2.) Bake at 300 for 4-5 hrs or more, turning once an hour.
3.) Sprinkle brown sugar at end if it is too tart.
4.) Best if re-baked the next day.
5.) May be frozen.

Sophie (Zosia) and Henry dancing

Millie (Milanka) with her mom Sophie (Zosia), in Germany after the war, 1947

Millie (Milanka) and her family

R. Gabriel S. Silten
Pomona, CA, U.S.A.

I was born in Berlin, Germany. My parents, Ilse and Fritz, immigrated with me to Amsterdam, Holland, and we were caught there when the war started. In 1943 we were deported to Westerbork, a Concentration Camp in Holland. Six months later we were deported to Theresienstadt in Czechoslovakia. We were there for a year and a half before the camp was liberated by the Russians in May, 1945. We then returned to Amsterdam where I grew up.

We somehow survived together, although my grandparents, great-aunts, great-uncles and their descendants, and all of my aunts, uncles, and cousins were murdered.

Gabriel Silten, 1990's

Rote Gruetze (Red Fruit Pudding)

- Sour red cherries
- Red currant berries
- Raspberries

parve

**Ilse Silten
(mother of Gabriel), 1977**

Directions:

1.) If cherries have pits, boil all together and mix well.
2.) Later press through sieve to remove pits and stems.
3.) If the cherries are pitted boil them separately and put later into the other mix so that the cherries remain whole.
4.) After mixing, add sugar to taste and thicken mixture with cornstarch dissolved in water on the flame.
5.) When thickened to pudding consistency, pour into bowl and refrigerate.

* Can be eaten as dessert with vanilla sauce, cream, or whipped cream.

(American Version)

1 package frozen raspberries
1/2 package water
Cherries, prepared as stated above
Add sugar to taste
Add a little lemon juice
Approx. 1 tablespoon cornstarch

Directions:

1.) Prepare cherries.
2.) Boil raspberries with water and sugar a short time.
3.) Add cherries.
4.) Dissolve cornstarch in water and thicken mixture to pudding consistency.
5.) Pour in bowl. Cool, refrigerate.

* Can be eaten as dessert with vanilla sauce, cream, or whipped cream.

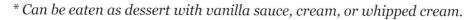

99

Ruth Kohn Colten Bloch
Baltimore, MD, U.S.A.

Erna (Berger) Colten

I was born in Zagreb, Croatia May 24th, 1937. My mother was born Erna Berger in 1909 and became Erna Kohn when she married my father. It is very hard for me to recollect the true facts of all that happened, as I was only five years old at the time. It was then that Hitler came into our town of Glina, Yugoslavia, now known as Croatia. Still there are some moments that are very clear in my mind.

When Hitler invaded our little town we were thrown into jail by the Croatian sympathizers. They took possession of our home and my father's business. I still recall my grandmother sitting in this huge jail cell where we were all cramped together including my mother, father Irvin Colten, and brother Robert Colten.

One of the Croatian sympathizers came to my father and asked that he give over his two children. My father refused and told them that they can have his home and his business but not his children. It was then that they released us and let us go home under their watchful eyes. We were told to collect a minimal amount of our belongings; then they put us on the last fishing boat out of town. In another words, we paid our way out. Later we found out, that, if my father had chosen to give us up, they would have taken us out in the backyard and shot us. Their feeling was that if you were not true to your children you would not be true to them. This all occurred around 1944, which was already very late in the War.

Somehow we landed in the mountains between Italy and Yugoslavia. Partisans were hiding us until they put us on a ship to South Italy in a town called "Taranto." We lived there until we moved further north to Milano. We stayed in Italy until October 1949 when a cousin of my mother's, Jesse Newman, who lived in New York, sponsored us to the USA. We arrived to our new life on October 11th 1949. When we arrived in New York anti-Semitism was rampant so my mother's cousin suggested that we change our name. So our last name was changed legally from Kohn to Colten. From Ruth Kohn I became Ruth Colten. We were very lucky to have escaped. My mother's family: 2 brothers, father etc.- 33 members in all, lost their lives. Some were killed in a concentration camp called "Jacenovac."

An uncle Egon Berger (another of my mothers' brother) managed to escape and later wrote a book about his experiences. I have the book; it is written in Croatian and full of grotesque pictures. It was published in 1964. It was used at the trial of one of the Croatian Nazi sympathizers. He was locked up at the end of that trial. My mother had still another brother "Leon" and he managed to escape as well. Both uncles lived to a ripe old age. One ended up in New York with us and the other stayed back in Yugoslavia and lived under Tito's rule until his late 70's.

This is about all I can recall or what I remember from what my mother and father told me. My mother never wanted to talk about it.

Of all of us my mother was the most traumatized from the Holocaust. Mom passed away May 2000 at the age of 91.

In Fond Memory of my mother Erna (Berger) Kohn.

*Ruth Bloch (12 yrs),
Robert Colten (16 yrs),
John Berger (cousin),
Danny Berger (cousin)
coming to USA
October, 1949*

100

Pecan Torte
dairy

1 Cup Sugar
7 eggs, separated
1 Tbsp Instant Coffee Powder
2 Tbsp Powdered Cocoa
1/2 lb grated Pecans

Erna (Berger) Colten, 1993

Directions:
Preheat oven to 350 degrees
1.) Beat together sugar and yolks until thick and lemon colored.
2.) Beat whites until stiff.
3.) Mix pecans, coffee powder, cocoa powder together and fold in whites and yolks alternately.
4.) Bake in (2) 9" round layer pans lined with wax paper.
5.) Bake at 350 for 20 minutes. Cool.

For filling and frosting:

Directions:
1.) Cook marshmallows and coffee together in top of double boiler until marshmallows are melted.
2.) Cool.
3.) Fold in heavy cream, whipped stiff.
4.) Spread between cooled layers and on top and sides of cake.
Refrigerate until ready to serve.

1/2 lb marshmallows
3 Tbsp strong coffee
1/2 pint heavy cream

First Row (left to right): Heidi Bloch Hiller (Ruth's daughter), Erna Colten (her 90th birthday) Lisa Bloch Lisberger (Ruth's daughter). Second Row (left to right): Merele Colten McClure (Ruth's brother's wife), Susan Berger married to Danny Berger (Ruth's first cousin), Bernie Lisberger (Ruth's son-in-law), John Berger (Ruth's first cousin), Ruth Bloch. 1999

Rose and Hyman Salzberg
Framingham, MA, U.S.A.
Submitted by their granddaughter Marcia Rothenberg

Grandma Rosie and Grandpa Hymie left their families and Poland separately before WWII. Hymie stowed away on a ship, and Rosie found a long lost relative in Texas.

Both of their families that they left were killed in their villages in Poland. When Rosie and Hymie left Poland they were both 17 years old, and Rosie's parents wanted a better life for her in the U.S. Rosie knew of her family in Galveston, Texas and she sailed there and hated it. They were very cruel to her, so by herself she made it to NYC and met up with Hymie, who she knew from her town in Poland. Hymie used to tutor Rosie's younger brothers.

She was a seamstress; he took whatever job he could find, working for a cleaner, driving a truck, selling honey eventually in the Catskills. They married on a rooftop in NYC, with no relatives with them. They wanted to marry under the stars. They had four children, one of whom is my mother. When WWII broke out, they would not allow a newspaper into their home, they were so terrified of what was going on in Europe.

Hymie had sent his parents money to leave Poland, and it was later discovered that his father had saved the money under a floorboard in the house and never used it. Many letters were sent to both families in Poland, but they never heard a word until one day, a cousin living in Israel, told them they were taken from their homes and the entire village was wiped out.

Right then, Rosie and Hymie stopped what they were doing and sat Shiva for the people they loved.

Working hard, they made a success of their lives and stayed with one another until Hymie's death. Grandma Rosie loved to cook. I still remember the smells coming from the kitchen and how warm and safe she made us all feel. She never spoke of her family that died, or of how she felt leaving Poland so many years ago.

Rosie

Rosie with 3 of her 4 children

Hyman

Grandma Rosie's Cookies

parve

1/2 dozen eggs
1 1/4 c. sugar
1 1/2 jigger rum
juice of one lemon
2 t. vanilla
8 t. baking powder
12 oz. oil
9 c. flour (measure unsifted)
1 t. salt

Directions:

Preheat oven to 350 degrees

1.) Beat eggs, add sugar gradually while continuing to beat eggs, add all liquid ingredients and beat.
2.) Sift flour with baking powder and add to egg mixture, work in until hand comes out clean.
3.) Put in refrigerator for 1/2 day or overnight.
4.) Roll out to 1/4 inch thickness and cut.
5.) Bake for 10 mins.

Grandma Rosie's Gefilte Fish
parve

2 pounds white fish
2 pounds pike
4 eggs
3 onions
2 carrots
Salt and pepper to taste
1 t. sugar

Directions:

1.) Fillet fish (remove skin and bones) or if possible, have it done at store.
2.) Chop fish for about 5 mins. until broken into small pieces.
   * If you have meat grinder, put fish and one onion through grinder and eliminate some chopping and grating the onion.
3.) Beat eggs slightly and add to fish together with grated onion and seasonings.
4.) You can start with 1 t. salt and 1/2 t. pepper, in addition to sugar, then taste after chopping fish mixture which should be well seasoned.
   * *The secret of good gefilte fish is in the chopping- the longer the better in order to give fish a good texture.*
5.) To cook: slice carrots and 2 onions and place in pot with 2 or 3 glasses of water.
6.) Bring to a boil, and then add fish which has been shaped into large balls.
7.) Wet your hands when making fish balls and they won't stick to hands.
8.) Cook slowly for a couple of hours.

Honey Cake

parve

1 lb. honey
6 eggs
2 glasses (cups) sugar
3/4 glass (cup) oil
1/2 glass (cup) coffee
1/2 glass (cup) seltzer
2 t. baking soda
1 t. baking powder
4 1/2 glasses (cups) flour
1 orange (squeeze juice)
1 lemon   "   "
1 t. cinnamon
1 small glass (shot glass) whiskey
1/2 cup raisins
1/2 cup chopped nuts

Directions:

Preheat oven to 350 degrees

1.) Start mixing eggs, honey, and sugar first for 20 mins.
   (Rosie didn't use an electric mixer, so for 20 mins. She mixed by hand.
      If using a mixer, beat until well mixed.)
2.) Sift the flour and baking powder.
3.) Mix in everything and beat for 20 mins. except the lemon juice, orange juice, and nuts.
4.) Then put all in after 20 mins. of mixing.
5.) Put oil in 10x16 inch pan and bake at 350 degrees for 1 1/4 hour.

Henna Master
Montreal, Quebec, Canada
Submitted by her daughter-in-law Carole Master

Ma and Pa, Henna and Ralph Master, from Poland entering Montreal, Quebec, Canada

My father-in-law Ralph came to Montreal, Quebec, Canada in 1936, and my mother-in- law followed in 1938. Both were born and grew up in Lublin, Poland. The Pa, as we called him, had two sisters that never made it out, his Dad died at an early age and his mother perished in the camps with his two sisters. His brothers Moshe got out earlier and Maurice followed later after escaping Poland through Portugal, Belgium and ultimately England.

My ma had 2 brothers who never made it along with her folks. Her sister Golda survived the camps. Golda came home with numbers on her arm telling how she had to watch her husband and son being burnt alive, while she was tied up.

My father in law's brother Moshe who was a reverend and cantor in Montreal, brought my Pa over to be a choirmaster...Their name was Gelibter, and somehow Master remained as that's what the officials heard...My Ma was allowed to come because my Pa was going to marry her...and "THE MASTER FAMILY" came to be.

My late mother-in-law Henna Master was a wonderful cook. Even her husband helped her, another survivor, to make Shabbat every Friday night even in a Montreal blizzard. I learned all my Mamaluchun from her, a little Yiddish, and about family.

She had riches in her baby's smiles...if she knew all her children and grandchildren were well and happy...then she was content. When I married her golden son Eli, I soon after asked her for her recipe for her marvelous cookies, that her kids and friends would anxiously wait for. Well she said all the ingredients, and off I went to bake. I put it all together in a bowl, however the mixture seemed very loose. Then I put the cookies in the oven and when I opened it to check....you guessed it, a giant puddle.

I immediately phoned my Ma, "so" she said, "tell me what you put in", I read her back her recipe and she then said" so where's the flour?" I said you never mentioned flour..."How can you make cookies without flour?" Being that I'd never baked before I didn't know that flour was not necessary to tell because I should know that. Between all the great aromas, tastes, and laughter I became a great cook... and I'd like to share what my grandchildren love me to make.

"Nana's Kugel"

dairy

6 brown farm eggs
1 1/4 cup sugar
1 tsp salt
1/2 tsp cinnamon
1 1/2 butter sticks regular salted butter
(Optional) 1 small can crushed
            pineapple/and raisins
1 tbsp vanilla extract
24 oz creamed small curd cottage cheese
        (preferably Breakstone)
1 pint sour cream
1 8 oz pkg cream cheese

2 pkgs. wide Kosher noodles

Directions:

Preheat oven to 350 degrees

1.) Boil 2 packages of wide kosher egg noodles, drain and set aside.
2.) Grease the large Pyrex baking dish.
3.) Combine all ingredients, and add cooked noodles in a large mixing bowl until ready to pour into a larger dish than 9x13.
4.) Dot with butter and sprinkle with cinnamon and sugar.
5.) Finally bake at 350 degrees, for 1 1/2 hours.
6.) Check the bottom of the glass baking dish, for the kugel to be brownish.
7.) Let cool before cutting.
    ENJOY!

Ma's Famous Cookies

dairy

2/3 c. oil
1 cup sugar
2 eggs
2 tsp. vanilla
2 1/2 cups flour
1 tsp. baking soda
2 tsp. cream of tartar
1/2 tsp. salt
jam like rasp. or straw. or apricot, etc. if desired

Directions:
Preheat oven to 375 degrees

1.) Beat oil with sugar.
2.) Blend in eggs and vanilla.
3.) Stir in dry ingredients.
4.) Drop from a teaspoon onto a lightly greased baking sheet.
5.) Sprinkle with sugar and cinnamon (and or a variety of jams).
6.) Bake at 375 degrees for 10 minutes, or until golden brown.

Ruth Gans Mayer
Solon, OH, U.S.A.
Submitted by her daughter Desiree Mayer Kate
In memory of our loving grandmother from Jori and Ethan Kate

Ruth as a child with her brother Ernest, grandmother Paula Rothschild Gans, and great grandmother Johanna Rothschild

My mother had a very difficult life. As a survivor of five years in a concentration camp, she lost a husband and child, parents, aunts, uncles, cousins and friends. At one point she was chosen for the gas chamber where her mother, Paula Gans, switched places with her, choosing death in order to preserve the life of her daughter.

After surviving years as a young woman in a concentration camp, witnessing the lives of her family and friends cut short, and seeing the annihilation of any semblance of home, my mother could have lived a life of misery and pain. Instead she picked herself up by the bootstraps and started a new life.

When my mother finally came to America to start over, she had many health problems & lost her second husband when she was 39. Although she was educated in pharmacy in Germany, it did her no good here. She worked hard for many, many years, battling language barriers and an education that did not apply to American ways.

In spite of many hardships, she was a very incredible mother. She committed her life to making mine better. She spent every available hour with me, and as a result, we were very close. As a single mom, (not common in 1960) she provided me with a good life, strong values and a solid education. She was able to maintain stability for both herself and me until a nervous breakdown in 1977, at the time of my college graduation. She stayed strong to complete what she felt was her "job," but after this breakdown, she was never the same.

As a result of what she had suffered as a young woman my mom's motto was "cherish the sweet things that life affords to you." I reaped the benefits of this motto growing up. My mother made it a priority to concoct various delicious treats to remind us of all the sweetness of life. The following are a sample of the sweet treats we shared throughout our lives together.

Additionally, later in life my mother remembered a favorite recipe that her grandmother used to make. She was not well and knew her time was limited, so she wanted to be sure I knew how to make the whole matzo-matzo balls, just as her grandmother did. I lost my mom, my best friend and my hero due to the misery she experienced 30 years earlier. My husband and children never had the opportunity to know the strong, wonderful woman my mother was. She had become more of a shell of a person at that point. We all loved her in spite of the changes until her death in 1994.

Ruth shorty after arriving in the U.S.

109

Whole Matzo - matzo balls

parve

6 pieces matzo broken in half
6 Tbsp unsalted parve margarine
1 med. onion chopped
1 tsp salt
1/4 tsp pepper
4 large eggs
8 Tbsp matzo meal

Ruth with her grandchildren Jori Marissa Kate and Ethan Garrett Kate, shortly before her death

Directions:

1.) Place matzo in large bowl and cover with water.
2.) Heat the margarine in frying pan and cook onion until clear.
3.) Add salt and pepper.
4.) Drain matzo and press matzo against strainer to squeeze out all the water you can.
5.) Add drained matzo to pan (it will break in pieces).
6.) Cook about 5 minutes to heat through.
7.) Transfer to bowl and let cool for 15 minutes.
8.) Stir in eggs and a few tablespoons of matzo meal.
9.) Add more matzo meal as necessary to form mixture into balls.
   They should be thick enough to hold their shape but not clumpy.
10.) Refrigerate for 1 hour.
11.) Drop the balls into 5-6 quarts salted boiling water.
   They will sink to the bottom and then rise while they cook.
12.) Turn down simmer, cover and let them cook for about 20-25 minutes.
13.) Using a slotted spoon remove and place them in hot chicken soup.

Makes about 15-16 balls.

Passover Matzo Tort
parve

8 whole matzos
  soaked for 25 seconds in sweet Passover wine

Cream together:
- 1 cup margarine
- 3 oz. chocolate- melted
- 1 egg yolk
- 3/4 cups sugar

Layer matzo and chocolate mixture on top. Repeat all layers and end with chocolate on top. Cool completely and serve in slices.

Apple Crumble
dairy

2 lbs. granny smith apples (cored, peeled, and sliced)
1/4 cup apple cider
3/4 cup all-purpose flour
1/2 cup sugar
3/4 cup packed brown sugar
1/2 tsp. cinnamon
1/2 tsp. grated nutmeg
1/2 cup butter
pinch of salt

Directions:

Preheat oven to 350 degrees
- In a 2-quart casserole, combine apples and cider.
- Mix flour, sugar, brown sugar, cinnamon, nutmeg, and salt in a medium bowl.
- Cut butter till crumbly.
- Spread sugar topping over apples and sprinkle butter crumbles on top.
- Bake 350 degrees for 40-45 minutes.
- Serve with ice cream or whipped cream.

Makes 4-6 servings

Parisian Cream
dairy

1/2 lb. nestle chocolate
1 pint heavy cream

- Boil these ingredients together.
- Refrigerate for 12 hours. Beat until stiff.
- Use to fill cream puff, jelly roll or lady finger lined spring form pan.

Spiced Nuts
parve

1 beaten egg white
1/2 cup sugar
1/4 tsp. salt
1/4 tsp. cinnamon
1/4 tsp. ground cloves
1/4 tsp. allspice
1 cup whole pecans or walnuts

Directions:
Preheat oven to 250 degrees

1.) Mix all ingredients EXCEPT NUTS.
2.) Oil finger and dip each nut individually into mixture.
3.) Place on greased cookie sheet and bake for 1 hour.

Holiday Brisket
meat

6 -7 pound brisket
   (trim excess fat)
5 large onions thinly sliced
8 cloves garlic thinly sliced
Salt & pepper to taste
3 tbsp oil

Directions:
Preheat oven to 325 degrees

- Toss onions and garlic slices in oil to coat.
- Spread in roasting pan.
- Season brisket with salt & pepper.
- Place on top of garlic and onions.
- Cover tightly with foil.
- Bake 3-4 hours at 325 degrees.
- Test for tenderness with fork.
- Let stand 15 minutes before serving.

Nana's Cookie Dough Pie Crust
dairy

1/2 cup unsalted butter
(makes 2 crusts)
1/2 cup sugar
2 egg yolks
2 cups flour

This recipe can be doubled. Once divided into balls can be wrapped and frozen.

Directions:
Preheat oven to 400 degrees

- Combine butter, sugar, and egg yolks.
- Mix in flour till crumbs begin to form.
- Mold with hands and break into 2 equal balls (4 if doubled).
- Press 1 ball in bottom of pie plate.
- Bake 10 minutes at 400 degrees and fill when cooled.
- If desired, bake for 5 minutes then fill with fruit (apple, pear, peach, plum) slices and vanilla pudding and bake till fruit is soft.

Sweet Potato Royal
parve or dairy

1 cup dry apricots
1 cup brown sugar
2 lbs. sweet potatoes
(cooked and peeled)
1/4 cup butter or margarine
1/2 cup slivered almonds

Directions:
Preheat oven to 375 degrees

1.) Soak apricots in 2 cups water for 2 hours.
2.) Cook in liquid with sugar until boiling.
3.) Use glass casserole dish.
4.) Slice potatoes 1/2 inch thick and layer with apricots.
5.) Top with melted butter and almonds.
6.) Bake at 375 degrees for 35 minutes.

Lemon Cream
dairy
(this is a tart dessert)

5 eggs
Juice of 5 lemons
3/4 cups sugar
1 pint whipping cream

Directions:
1.) Beat eggs, juice, and sugar together.
2.) Cook in double boiler until stiff.
3.) Cool.
4.) Beat whipping cream until stiff.
5.) Fold in cooled lemon mixture.
6.) Refrigerate for 12 hours.

Can eat as a dessert by itself or fill lady finger lined.

113

Daniel Carasso

Randallstown, MD, U.S.A.

Submitted by his daughters
Jeannette Katzen and Eileen Metzger

Daniel Carasso was born in Salonika, Greece in 1912. When the Nazis entered Greece in 1942 he was arrested and sent to Auschwitz. He spent three years there imprisoned, digging tunnels for the Germans every day, eating one piece of bread and soup made from the peels of potatoes that the Germans had eaten.

He was finally liberated in 1945. A man of a large frame, he weighed only 100 pounds. When the Americans found him he was unconscious and very close to death.
"When I opened my eyes I saw an American nurse feeding me soup. I don't remember anything from the three days before that."

In 1979 Daniel went back to Auschwitz to face the memories of his past. He started as a tourist but when the Polish tour guide learned of his past she asked him to conduct the tour.

He led the tourists, all Greek gentiles, into the old gas chambers at Auschwitz and described how the Nazis lured their victims into the gas chambers, which they disguised as showers. They even gave each person soap and a towel.

Mrs. Carasso, herself a survivor, remembers her husband's explanation well. "My husband kept talking but they were all crying. And I had to leave because I couldn't listen to it again."

Rena and Daniel, 1945

114

Kaltsonakia
parve

Dough	Filling
1/2 cup oil	2 cups chopped walnuts
1 cup water	3/4 cups sugar
1/2 tsp. salt	1 1/2 tsp. cinnamon
flour	1/2 tsp. cloves
	4-6 unsalted crumbled crackers
	1 1/2 tbsp. honey

Directions:

Preheat oven to 400 degrees

1.) Boil the oil, water, and salt for 5 minutes stirring constantly.

2.) Remove from heat and let it cool off.

3.) Add little by little flour as much as you need for a dough not too soft or too hard either.

4.) Leave aside for ½ to 1 hour.

5.) Mix all of the ingredients for the filling together and if the mixture is too dry add a couple of drops of water.

6.) Take the dough and cut into small pieces about the size of a walnut.

7.) Roll them into small 3 inch circles.

8.) Fill each one with a teaspoon of the filling mixture and fold them up.

9.) Bake in greased pan at 400 degrees for 30-35 minutes or until they get golden brown..

10.) ***Prepare the syrup***
  - 2 cups sugar
  - 1 ¼ cups water
  - Few drops lemon juice

11.) Boil sugar and water for 5-8 minutes.

12.) Remove from heat and add the lemon juice.

13.) As soon as you take them out of the oven poke them on both sides with a fork and dip them into the syrup immediately.

Original recipe in Greek.

Mommy's Ravani

dairy

2 sticks sweet butter
6 eggs
1 cup of flour
1 cup dry cereal (farina)
1 cup sugar
1 cup milk
3 tsp baking power
1 tsp vanilla
1/2 tsp baking soda

Directions:

Preheat oven to 350 degrees

1.) Beat the eggs, and sugar, warm the milk and melt the butter.
2.) Add them to the beaten eggs.
3.) Add the vanilla and slowly add the mixed flour, farina, baking powder and baking soda.
4.) Bake at 350 degrees in a greased pan for 35 minutes or until the top of the pan becomes light brown.

Meanwhile, prepare the syrup.

Syrup

1.) Boil 2 cups of sugar and 1 1/2 cups of water.
2.) Remove from heat.
3.) Add a few drops of lemon juice.
4.) Pour the syrup over the hot ravani.
5.) Let it cool off. Cut in square pieces.
6.) Add immediately the syrup while the ravani is still in the oven.

Bourekitas

meat

Dough

2 cups flour
3 oz. oil
1 pinch of salt

Filling

1/2 lb. ground beef
1 medium onion
1 tbsp. oil
2 medium sized potatoes
1 egg
1/2 tsp. salt
1/4 tsp. pepper

Directions:

Preheat oven to 450 degrees

1.) In a pan put the flour, oil and salt, rubbing for a few seconds with your hands.
2.) Add water as much as you need to make dough not too soft or too hard.
3.) Let it stand for 1 hour.
4.) In a frying pan put tablespoon of oil and one chopped onion.
5.) Fry until it gets light brown.
6.) Add the ground beef and cook for 5 minutes on medium heat until all of the blood is absorbed.
7.) Remove from heat, and the salt and pepper, and let it cool off.
8.) Add the 2 eggs and mix it all together.
9.) Take the dough and cut into small walnut sized pieces and with a roller open round sheets (size 4-6 inches).
10.) Fill them with the mixture and fold like half moons.
11.) Press your finger on the sides to enclose the filling and trim it.
12.) Bake on greased cookie sheet for 35-40 minutes at 450 degrees.

Rena Gani Carasso

Randallstown, MD, U.S.A.

Submitted by her daughters
Jeannette Katzen and Eileen Metzger

Rena was born in Preveza Greece in 1915. Preveza was a small Jewish community a few hours from Athens. Her father Solomon was a prosperous textile merchant and her mother Simcha stayed home and raised their five children.

In 1943 the Germans invaded their town and arrested all of the Jews. The entire Gani family was sent to the Birkenau/Auschwitz concentration camp where the parents were immediately sent to the gas chambers.

Rena and her sister Ellie were sent to the women's camp while her three brothers went to the men's camp. The three young men fought valiantly in an uprising at the men's camp but were killed along with all the other rebellious men at their camp. Rena and Ellie survived the women's camp and were liberated by the Americans in 1945. They returned to Greece where nothing remained of their once happy family.

Some of their Christian friends had saved photos, a quilt, and a ring from their family and Rena was tearfully reunited with these only remaining artifacts of her family. Soon Rena moved to Athens where she met and married tall handsome Daniel Carasso, known to his friends as Nico. Since both Rena and Nico had lost most of their friends and relatives in the Holocaust their wedding was small, but still filled with the hope and promise of the future.

In 1951 Rena, Daniel, and their little daughter Jeannette came to America. Their family is honored on the Wall of Honor at Ellis Island.

They later had another daughter Eileen and five beautiful grandchildren. Rena volunteered her time in the gift shop at the Baltimore County Hospital. She always loved to cook, especially Greek recipes such as Baklava and Mousaka.

Jeannette and her dad

Rena and Daniel, 1989

118

Rena Carasso's Kourabiedes

Greek Butter Cookies

dairy

1 pound sweet butter
1 pound chopped almonds
2 egg yolks
2 1/2 cups confectioner sugar
1 tsp vanilla
3-5 cups flour..
(as much as you need for a soft dough)

Directions:

Preheat oven to 350 degrees

1.) Beat the butter for 15 minutes.
2.) Slowly add the two yolks, 1/2 cup confectioner's sugar and a little flour.
3.) Continue to beat adding the almonds and flour until a soft dough is formed.
4.) Use your hands to roll the dough and form them either in crescent or round shapes.
5.) Bake in ungreased pan for 15-25 minutes in a 350 degree oven.
6.) After removing them from the oven, let cool and cover, not a little sprinkle, but cover them with confectioner's sugar.
7.) Each cookie should be placed in its own "baking" cup before served.

Have lots of ice cold milk on hand!

"Because Our Parents Survived"
Jeanette Kasten and Eileen Metzger and their families

119

Marion Weinzweig
Phoenix, AZ, U.S.A.

I was born in Lublin, Poland in the late spring of 1940 or 1941 and was named Mania Sztajnman. My parents moved to Opatow shortly after my birth because all of my father's family lived there. My birth was not recorded with the local authorities so as not to have a record of me. We had to move out of our family house into a horrible ghetto. Although only Yiddish was spoken in our home my family taught me to speak Polish so I would not be able to trip myself up.

About three weeks before all of the Jews in Opatow were herded to Treblinka by the Germans and Ukranians to be murdered, my parents arranged for a Polish farm couple, the Ropelewskis, to take me in until they could come and fetch me. My parents gave their money and furniture to the Ropelewskis.

One day my parents took me to the town square and handed me over to Mrs. Ropelewski, who was being driven by a young carriage driver. It was in September of 1942 and I was approximately 18 months old. They kept me for several weeks, then had their carriage driver leave me at the doorstep of a convent in Klimintow. I was the youngest child there. I was baptized. I have little memory except that I was very hungry all the time, scared, and darkness was all around me. I have recurrent nightmares of running and dead bodies all around. In 1945 the retreating Germans bombed the convent, destroying it completely. Luckily we were able to run out, but we saw all of the carnage left behind. I was then transferred to a convent in Loniow.

My father found me after surviving Auschwitz and Buchenwald. The nuns did not want to release me- I was Catholic. They brought all the girls into the room and told him that he had to pick me out. He had not seen me in 3 ½ years but he picked me. They demanded 5,000 zlots from him, so he had to beg for the money from the Jewish committee. I hated my father because he was Jewish and he was a "Christ Killer". My mother was murdered in Treblinka, and that is why I don't know exactly when I was born. My father did not remember. I was malnour-

Marion with her father Majer Sztajnman, 1942 In Opatow, Poland, just before the town was made "Judenrein" (cleansed of Jews)

ished and had a head full of lice. We went to Lodz and I prayed to Christ every night and ran into every church I saw.

My father found a brother alive in Worth of the Danube near Regensburg in Germany so we went there with great difficulty. We had to sneak across the Russian border to get to the American zone. Had we been caught we would have been shot dead. We spent three years in Germany before our visas came through to go to Canada. At eight years of age I was into my fourth language and third name change and had lived a lifetime and had not yet gone to school.

All of my life I wondered if the real Mania Sztajnman was still in Poland and I was a Polish imposter. At the age of 48 I finally accepted the fact that I was Mania when my granddaughter was born and she had the exact blue eyes and expression as my father.

I now live in Phoenix, Arizona and have three children and four grandchildren.

120

Kishke

meat

One lb. casings
(washed in cold water and scraped free of fat.
Cut casings every 12 inches. Sew one side together.)

For 3 or 4 casings:

1 1/2 cup flour
1/4 cup oatmeal
1 small onion- chopped fine
1 tsp. salt

3/4 cup corn flake crumbs
1 cup ground chicken fat
1/4 tsp. pepper
1 tsp. paprika

This is a wonderful kishke recipe that I make for many holidays.

Directions:
Preheat oven to 350 degrees

1.) Combine ingredients and stir well.
2.) Stuff casings loosely.
3.) Sew up other end and rinse.
4.) In pot of boiling water, boil kishke for 2 hours and freeze.
5.) Bake a kishke directly from the freezer at 350 degrees,
    or add to chicken for roasting.

Anna Rahel Lilienfeld Klestadt

Halifax, Nova Scotia, Canada
Submitted by her granddaughter Linda Jonas Schroeder

Anna was born in Duisburg, Germany in 1886. When she was a young girl she studied piano in Berlin. One day she went to a concert conducted by the famous Gustav Mahler. She stood on her chair at the end of the concert and cheered loudly. Her uncle admonished her that if she ever did that again he would never take her to a concert again! When she grew up Anna taught piano lessons before she married Morris Klestadt.

In 1939 she escaped from Germany two days before the war started and all borders were closed. Shortly after that all of the Jews were arrested and taken to concentration camps. It was a miracle that Anna was able to get out just in time, and it allowed her to live while so many others died.

She first escaped to Holland and after eight months there her visa was granted and she came to the U.S.

When she lived in Hawaii she witnessed the bombing of Pearl Harbor. Later she moved to Ohio and then California where she lived until the age of 96.

Everyone knew her as "Mutti" (mom). She volunteered in a hospital library and worked in a kindergarten. She had two children, three grandchildren, and five great grandchildren.

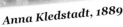

Anna Kledstadt, 1889

Anna, 1896

Anna's Marzipan Chocolate cake
parve

8 egg whites
2 cups ground almonds
2 cups sugar
6 tsp. cocoa

Directions:
Preheat oven to 350 degrees
1.) Beat the egg whites until stiff.
2.) Add 1 cup sugar to 1 cup almonds and sift in cocoa.
3.) Fold in ½ of the beaten egg whites.
4.) Spread into lightly greased 9 inch round cake pan or glass pie dish.
5.) Add the remaining cup of sugar to the almonds and fold in the rest of the egg whites.
6.) Spread over the chocolate mixture in the pan and bake at 350 for 35 minutes.

Linda Schroeder's
Lemon Almond Cake
dairy

6 eggs separated
1/4 cup unsalted butter
1 1/2 cup sugar
1 1/2 cup ground almonds
1 1/2 lemons, juice and grated rind
1 cup flour
3 tsp. baking powder

Directions:
Preheat oven to 350 degrees
1.) Beat the egg whites until stiff, and beat the egg yolks for several minutes.
2.) Melt the butter and add the sugar to it.
3.) Add the ground almonds and lemon to the yolks and add the butter and sugar.
4.) Gradually sift in the flour and baking powder.
5.) Fold in the egg whites.
6.) Spread into lightly greased tube pan (use unsalted margarine).
7.) Bake at 350 degrees for 35 minutes.

123

Vichyssoise
dairy

4 medium onions
2 1/2 cups sliced potatoes
2 cups parve (no chicken broth by Imagine)- to keep Kosher
2 Tbsp chives
1 tsp. butter
Paprika, salt, pepper, curry
1 cup milk
1 cup cream

Directions:
1.) Cook onions and potatoes in
   2 ½ cups water until very tender.
2.) Push through strainer.
3.) Put all other ingredients in the liquid.
4.) Chill.

Flan
dairy

1 1/2 cups sugar
6 eggs
2 cans sweetened condensed milk
   (300 ml or 1 1/4 cups each can)
2 1/2 cups milk

Directions:
Preheat oven to 300 degrees

1.) In a 9-inch pot over low heat, slowly caramelize the sugar until golden brown and thick, stirring often to avoid burning.
2.) When the sugar is ready, beat the eggs, sweetened condensed milk, and milk together, and pour over the sugar.
3.) Place this covered pot into a larger pot in enough water to almost submerge it.
4.) It can be cooked on top of the stove over high heat for an hour, or baked in a 300 degree oven for 2½ hours.
5.) When it is finished, let it cool completely. With a spatula, loosen it from the sides and carefully scrape the bottom of the pot, to ensure a smooth top.
6.) Turn upside down on a platter and spoon the syrup over the top.

Crustless Quiche

dairy

5 eggs, lightly beaten
1/4 cup milk
2 1/2 cups mozzarella cheese, grated
  (Swiss, Gruyere, or cheddar cheese) - Kosher only
veggies of your choice:
  corn, peppers, mushrooms, onions, artichoke hearts,
  broccoli, cauliflower, zucchini, or any combination
Season with basil, tarragon, marjoram
  (garlic goes well with artichoke hearts), or other
  herbs such as celery seed and dill.

Directions:

Preheat oven to 350 degrees

1.) Mix the ingredients and bake 30-35 minutes at 350 degrees, until puffy and golden.
2.) This can be cut into small pieces for appetizers.
    * Cheddar cheese works especially well with corn and/or artichoke hearts, and it is not necessary to add milk.

Anna's Sweet onions on party rye bread

dairy

20 party rye or baguette slices
3 Tbsp parmesan cheese (Kosher)
1 cup mayonnaise
2 sweet onions, very thinly sliced
Paprika

Directions:

1.) Mix mayonnaise with 3 Tbsp grated parmesan cheese.
2.) Spread on party rye bread slices or baguette slices.
3.) Top with thin slice of sweet onions, a layer of grated parmesan cheese, and paprika.
4.) Broil (carefully!) until cheese and onions are crispy. **Enjoy!**

125

Hilda Klesadt and Gerald Jonas
Halifax, Nova Scotia, Canada
Submitted by their daughter Linda Jonas Schroeder

My mother, Hilda Klestadt Jonas, is the daughter of Anna Klestadt (pgs. 122-125). My parents were married in the main synagogue of Duesseldorf, Germany in 1938. Shortly thereafter they escaped from Germany. They were given visas to immigrate to Australia, but after living there for six weeks they came to America. On their way they stopped in Honolulu, and they liked it so much they decided to stay. In Hawaii my father became an accountant and my mother gave harpsichord recitals and was a soloist for the Honolulu symphony.

After witnessing the bombing of Pearl Harbor they left for Ohio with my grandmother and my sister. They settled in San Francisco in 1975.

My father's father, Alfred Jonas was not so fortunate. He was living in the ghetto of Moenchengladbach, Germany in December 1941. He had a visa to leave for the United States but his ship was delayed until December 11th. After Pearl Harbor all German Borders were closed so he could not leave.

He was eventually arrested, taken to Theresienstadt, and then to Auschwitz, where he died.

Hilda and Gerald Jonas

126

Lychee Almond Cake

parve

1 can lychee fruit
3 eggs
1 cup sugar
2 cups ground almonds

Directions:

Preheat oven to 375 degrees

1.) Drain the lychee fruit and cut each into quarters.
2.) Beat the eggs well and continue to beat, adding the sugar.
3.) Thoroughly stir in the almonds and lychee fruit.
4.) Bake at 375 degrees for 40-45 minutes.
5.) Any fruit (apples or pears) can be used.

Chicken with Fruit

meat

Chicken parts, skinned (6-8)
1 1/2 cups orange juice, or enough to cover chicken
1/4 cup brown sugar (optional)
Several apples or pears, cut and peeled

Directions:

Preheat oven to 325 degrees

1.) Bake the chicken in the orange juice and brown sugar for one hour at 325 degrees.
2.) Add the fruit and cook for another hour, or until done.

Leon Levy (born Laizer Lewi)
New York, NY, U.S.A.
Submitted by his son, Dr. Harvey Levy, and his grandchildren, Becca and Ariel Levy

Leon and Lili
60th Anniversary

Born in Dombrowa Gorniza, Poland to a middle-class family selling milk and dairy products, I was sent to the concentration camps at age 17. Both parents and 3 of six siblings were killed by the Nazis. Towards the end of the war, I was transferred from the motor pool to the kitchen in Ludwigsdorf forced labor camp. Through the barbed wire fence, I would sometimes flirt with a pretty girl named Lilka Koniecpolski. One day, I brought her some potato skin shavings I saved from the potatoes I was cutting while working in the kitchen.

I hid them in my trousers until later. I tried to give them to her through the barbed wire fence, but she refused. Returning to the kitchen, I was caught and whipped with 20 lashes on my bare back. After liberation, at age 20, I continued to flirt with this pretty 16 year old. She was not interested in me at all, but only wanted to recreate a semblance of family. With most of our families killed, we both had that same strong need.

On February 3, 1946, we were married near Dachau. We celebrated our 60th wedding anniversary with our two sons, daughters in-law, and four beautiful grandchildren. In this case, persistence paid off, and allowed us both to create our own new family.

Laizer's Polish-French Toast

dairy

1 week old challah bread
2 eggs
1 Tbsp milk
margarine or butter
cinnamon

Directions:
1.) Beat two eggs and one tablespoon milk until thin, then pour onto a flat plate.
2.) Dip both sides of the challah into the beaten egg-milk mixture.
3.) Put margarine or butter onto a very hot frying pan, and drop the dipped challah onto the pan.
4.) Alternate flipping the challah every min. until ready.
5.) You should salivate as you add cinnamon, apple sauce, or your favorite topping.

Lili Levy

New York, NY, U.S.A.

Submitted by her son, Dr. Harvey Levy,
and her grandchildren, Becca and Ariel Levy

I, Lili (Lilka) Koniecpolski, was growing up in Katowicz, Poland with my parents Jacob (who survived) and Regina, and siblings Emanuel (who survived), Helen, Isadore and Anna. At the age of thirteen, I was forcibly taken to a camp in Klettendorf, Germany, where I had to pretend I was sixteen to prevent from being immediately killed as too young to work.

After a while a transport arrived from Holland. I spoke to the man through the barbed wire fence and asked him if he had a comb for lice. Lots of people in the camp had lice and we needed a comb to get rid of it.

The man agreed to give me the comb in exchange for my only slice of bread for the day. Somehow I managed to survive the camp and was liberated in May 1945. Thank God for my survival and my happy and successful family.

Leon and Lili, 1945

Chopped Liver

meat

1 lb chopped chicken liver
1 medium sized onion (raw)
1 small onion (fried)
4 hard boiled eggs
1 teaspoon mayonnaise
1 teaspoon peanut butter
salt and pepper

Mix together and have a good appetite!

129

Liesel Rosenberg

Sarasota, FL, U.S.A.

I lived in Germany until 1938 when I immigrated to Holland with my German father and Dutch mother.

In 1940 the Germans invaded Holland and in 1942 we were forced to wear a yellow star and carry papers with a "J" to indicate that we were Jews.

Soon we were given notice to report for work in Germany. Needless to say I did not trust this order so I decided to find a hiding place.

I lived in an attic hidden by a Dutch Christian family for four long years. I was cold and very hungry most of the time but I was able to avoid transportation to the camps. My parents and grandparents were deported and none of them were able to survive.

Herring Favorite

dairy

1 large can of herring tidbits
1 can of cranberry sauce (whole)
1 pint of soured cream
3 Bermuda onions sliced thin

Directions:

1.) Drain liquid off herring from original jar and dispose of onions.
2.) Marinate 24 hours and then serve on crackers.

Simon Jeruchim
Pomona, NY, U.S.A.

**Simon Jeruchim
Pre-Wartime Photo
Paris, France**

Simon was born in Paris, France. In 1942, in Nazi occupied France, Simon was a 12 year old boy living in a suburb of Paris with his Polish immigrant parents and two siblings, his older sister Alice and younger brother Michael. During that summer Simon's mother was told that all Jews were being rounded up and sent to Concentration Camps. Thus the Jeruchim family escaped arrest by the French police who were collaborating with the Nazis. Compassionate gentile neighbors came to their rescue by sending the children into hiding in separate foster homes around the country side of Normandy, while the parents tried to escape the occupied zone. Unbeknownst to the children the parents were soon arrested and deported to Auschwitz where they perished.

Simon and his siblings spent the war years in farms posing as gentiles, even attending Mass on Sundays. Living conditions were harsh and the farm work was heavy and difficult, but even worse was the loneliness and isolation. There were difficult times for Simon as he missed his family terribly. "At times I closed my eyes and managed to conjure up their presence, clearly seeing my mother and father like I remembered them, reaching for me; and then when I could almost feel their touch my wonderful dream would fade away."

After France was liberated in 1944, Simon and his siblings were reunited and placed into a Jewish orphanage by an uncle who had survived the war. Simon, who was a gifted artist, was asked to paint the Hebrew words of a song on the walls of the orphanage dining room. While painting the letters Simon was reunited with the Jewish roots that had been stolen from him as a child.

"This was the first time I felt some pride in being Jewish, and I wondered whether a mysterious link connected those Hebrew words with my parents' past and the world of their ancestors. In my mind, my awakening toward Judaism had little to do with G-d or religion, but rather the need to come to terms with the Jewish identity I'd worked so hard to keep hidden during the war from others and also from myself."

Simon and his siblings immigrated to the United States in 1949 to live with relatives in Brooklyn, NY. Simon served in the U.S. army during the Korean War. Later he became a successful packaging designer, graphic artist and painter. He is married to Cecile Rojer Jeruchim, also a "Hidden Child" survivor from Belgium. They live in Pomona, NY and are the proud parents of two daughters and six grandchildren.

Editor's Note: *Simon Jeruchim is the noted author of two books "Hidden in France - A Boy's Journey Under the Nazi Occupation," and "Frenchy- A Young Jewish French Immigrant Discovers Love and Arts in America - and War in Korea." Both books are available at Amazon.com and at major book sellers. Simon speaks about being a "hidden child" in schools, synagogues and Holocaust Museums.*

Tomatoes, Onions, and Sardines

dairy

This was my father Samuel Jeruchim's favorite dish and I eat it quite often, as it always brings on the wonderful memories of my childhood with my family.

1.) Slice large tomatoes and arrange slices in a circle in a shallow large dish, leaving the center empty.
2.) Slice sweet onions thinly and arrange them in a circle over the tomatoes, leaving the center empty.
3.) Open a can of boneless, skinless Portuguese sardines in oil, do not rinse.
4.) Gingerly lift sardines out of can and arrange them in the center of the dish.
5) Sprinkle the entire dish with red wine vinegar.
6) Chop parsley and sprinkle over sardines only or over entire dish.
7) Add salt and pepper as needed.
8.) Eat with buttered rye bread.

Cecile Rojer

Pomona, NY, U.S.A.

Cecile and Simon

Cecile was born in Belgium in 1931. She lived in Brussels with her immigrant parents, Abraham and Sheva Rojer, and her two siblings, her older sister Anny and her younger brother Charly.

In 1942-1943, under Nazi occupation, Jews were under severe restrictions as to where they could go and what they could do. They lived in constant fear.

Cecile remembers a particular day in January 1943: *I was sitting at the dining room table eating my lunch which had been prepared by my mother: steak, mashed potatoes-and Belgian endives. I hated Belgian endives! Yet my mother, like most Belgian housewives, prepared and served them several times per week."*

As I was about to finish the meal my gentile girlfriend came to the door asking if I wanted to accompany her to voice lessons. Since Jews were restricted from taking lessons I could only accompany my friend and watch. I asked my mother if I could go.

She responded *"Not before you finish your endives, or I will save them for your dinner." I left with my girlfriend, expecting the endives to be waiting for me when I returned home.*

"While I was away the Nazis came and arrested my parents and they were deported to Auschwitz where they perished. That afternoon was the last time I ever saw my mother. My decision to go with my girlfriend separated me from my mother forever."

"I can hardly remember her face. I can hardly remember her love. Yet today I often eat Belgian endives. Their subtle flavor gently brings me closer to my mother and reminds me of my extraordinary childhood."

Cecile survived by being hidden in a convent in Louvain, Belgium, where she was baptized and stayed until the war ended. Her brother Charles and her sister Anny were also hidden and survived.

After spending the post war years in a series of Jewish orphanages the three children finally immigrated to the United States in 1948 to live with relatives.

Cecile taught ballroom dancing and aerobics at the local JCC-Y. She is the author of "Do You Know My Name?" an educational children's book published by Putnam.

She has been a guest speaker at local high schools where she relates her experiences as a "hidden child" during the Holocaust.

Cecile and her husband, Simon Jeruchim, live in Pomona, NY, where they are the proud parents of two daughters and have six grandchildren

Cecile Rojer Jeruchim
Wartime Childhood Photo
Brussels, Belgium

133

Sauteed Belgian Endives

dairy

3 large white and firm endives
* Do not wash, wipe with paper towel.
1/2 TB sweet butter
1 TB beer (any type)

Directions:

1.) Wipe endives.
2.) Slice in half lengthwise.
3.) Melt butter in frying pan on medium heat.
4.) Sauté endives until brown on all sides.
5.) Lower heat, add beer and cover.
6.) Simmer until endives turn gray and are medium soft.
7.) (Add a little more beer if needed -
   however endives give out a lot of liquid.)

Serve warm (can be reheated in microwave).

Leon Malmed
Pleasanton, CA, U.S.A.

Rachel (Malmed) Epstein
Roslyn, NY, U.S.A.

Leon & his sister Rachel

I was born in France and survived the Holocaust of World War II due to the heroism, sacrifice and kindness of a Christian couple who chose to hide my sister and me when our parents were led away to the death camps.

The heroes of this story are Suzanne and Henri Ribouleau and their two sons, René and Marcel. The Ribouleau family were our neighbors, living a floor below, in our apartment building.

My parents had emigrated from Poland to France, and made a good life for themselves in Compiègne, France; a town located 40 miles north of Paris. They owned a clothing shop and lived in a nice apartment in the center of town. My sister, Rachel, was born in 1932 and I in 1937.

In 1940, I was 3 years old and everything was about to change. France was now occupied by the German army. Jews had to wear a Yellow Star and were no longer allowed to own a business of any kind, thus depriving us of any income. Jews could no longer go to public parks or eat in public places. Jews could no longer go to movie theaters nor were they allowed to own a radio, and on and on. It kept getting worse and worse was yet to come on that horrible Sunday morning, July 19, 1942.

At 5 a.m., two French policemen knocked at the door and asked my parents to accompany them. They did not give any reasons for taking them away and would not let them go back inside the apartment.

"What about our children?" my parents asked hysterically. The cries and questions fell on deaf ears. The policemen had been ordered by the gestapo to arrest only our parents, and that is what they did. The commotion woke up our neighbors from down below. They came to see what the trouble was.

My father explained that they were being taken police headquarters and had no time to make arrangements for us, their children. Thinking that my parents would return in a few hours, Monsieur Ribouleau, a kind man who always had a warm hello whenever we saw him, said to my parents:

Charles, Rachel & Leon, 1943

"Monsieur et Madame Malmed, do not worry, we will take care of your children until you return." I have images of my sister and I crying and clinging to my parents, not wanting to let go of them. Monsieur and Madame Ribouleau kept reassuring my parents not to worry about their children. "They are in good hands with us," they said. Little did we know that was the last time we would ever see our parents again.

So began our new lives as Jewish children hidden by a Christian family. Their lives would be in danger for the next three years.   Incredibly, for the next three years, they paid the rent of our parents apartment, out of their savings, so our parents would have a place to live when they returned!

135

As the hunt for Jews intensified, people who knew about us being hidden would ask: "Monsieur et Madame Ribouleau, why are you doing this? Why are you risking your and your sons' lives?" Their answer was always: "How can we not protect these two children? We have promised their parents that we would take care of them."

These well meaning neighbors made an on the spot vow to virtual strangers not only to care for their children but to protect them from harm. Originally, there was no time to think of the potential consequences of such a decision. It quickly became apparent that it was a life and death decision for them and their two sons. After living with Monsieur and Madame Ribouleau for a few months, I started to call them Maman and Papa although, I never stopped thinking of my own parents, to this day, There were rewards for providing information on people hiding Jews of any age. I vividly recall the time when we had minutes to elude the Germans and the collaborating French Police, who probably had been tipped off of our existence and were on their way to our home with their dreaded black trucks. We ran across the garden, jumped the wall and hid in the fields.

On the same day, our cousin, Charles Malmed, 5 years old who lived in the same town about 5 minutes from our home was picked up by the Germans. He was also hidden by a French Catholic family. He was deported, alone, in the "convoi" 66 January 1944. He probably died in the cattle car on the way to Auschwitz or gassed upon arrival. The war ended in 1945 after 5 long years. Rachel was 13 and I was 8. With great anticipation, we waited for the return of our parents. We thought they had been detained somewhere in Europe. But later we learned that our parents also died in Auschwitz. They left from Drancy in the "convoi" 12 composed of 1,000 deportees, 270 men and 730 women. When they arrived in Auschwitz on July 31, 270 men and 514 women were selected for slave labor. 216 women were gassed immediately. We never found out if our mother died in the transport or in Auschwitz. We never knew either how long did our father survive. It took a long time to accept that we would never see them again At that time, I hated being a Jew, and that feeling lasted for many years. It had brought us so much misery.

A surviving aunt and uncle found us and requested that we go and live with them. My sister and I refused to do so as we did not know these people. After months of legal battles, a judge ordered my sister and me to go and live with our aunt and uncle, total strangers to us. I had come to love the Ribouleau family. They had saved our lives and given us unconditional love. After two years of unhappiness, my uncle and aunt decided to send my sister to an aunt in America. I was 11 years old. Once again, I was separated from my sister whom I loved. She had become a mother to me. I accompanied my sister to the St Quentin, where we lived, train station on a cold December day in 1949. I did not know then that it would be 14 years before we would see each other again.

After months of acrimonious disputes with my uncle and aunt and threats of being sent to an orphanage, they let me go back to Compiègne with the Ribouleau family. I was 12. Finally, I was at peace. At the age of 18, my sister married a nice Jewish boy from Brooklyn. That was 55 years ago. They have two daughters and four grandchildren. I was married in France at the age of 26.

Leon Malmed's Family

My sister and her husband, Izzy came to France. It was a joyous reunion. My brother-in-law convinced my wife and me to immigrate to America. In February of 1964, my pregnant wife, our 18 month old son and I, with a few hundred dollars in our pocket came down the passageway of the SS France in New York harbor. After immigrating to the US, I wrote to papa and maman Ribouleau every other week. In 1979, my sister and I had them awarded the Righteous Status, the highest Honor given by Israel to a non Jew. As long as we live, we will never forget these heroes Henri, Suzanne, René and Marcel Ribouleau who saved us from certain death.

Meat Loaf
meat
from Rachel (Malmed) Epstein

Charles Malmed

Mama and Papa Malmed

Leon and his sister Rachel

2 tbs. oil
1 chopped onion
   saute both till golden brown
1 medium potato and 1 egg
   food processor until smooth
1 pound lean ground meat
1 tbs. tomato paste
1 tbs ketchup
1 tbs soy sauce
1/4 cup chopped parsley
salt and pepper

Papa and Maman Ribouleau
receiving the Righteous
Status from the Israeli
Ambassador in Paris

Rachel's Family

Directions:
Preheat oven to 350 degrees

1.) Mix meat, tomato paste, ketchup, soy sauce,
    parsley, salt and pepper in a large bowl.
2.) Place meat in a foil lined pan and smooth top. (I usually make into 2 small loaves.)
3.) Bake for 45 minutes.
4.) You can broil for about 3 minutes to brown top.
5.) Let stand for a few minutes so it can absorb juices.
    (You can use beef or veal or a mixture.)

Gratin Dauphinois

dairy

from Leon Malmed

potatoes
  * the number is based on the number of servings.
Grated Swiss cheese
salt and pepper
1 egg
1 cup of milk
butter or margarine

Directions:

Preheat oven to 400 degrees

1.) In a rectangular Pyrex pan, spread either butter, oil (no olive oil) or margarine.
2.) Cut potatoes in very thin slices.
3.) Put a layer of sliced potatoes; salt and pepper to taste.
4.) Cover with a layer of grated Swiss cheese.
5.) Add a second layer of sliced potatoes.
6.) Cover with a layer of grated Swiss cheese; salt and pepper to taste.
7.) Beat one egg and one cup of milk and pour over potatoes.
8.) Add thin slices of butter or margarine.
9.) Bake for 1½ hour at 400 degrees.
10.) When the top layer turns brown, cover with aluminum foil to avoid burning.

It's delicious!

Gedempte Fleish - (stew) with apricots

meat

from Rachel (Malmed) Epstein

4 oz dried apricots wash
    & soak for 1/2 hour
2 cups of water
1 onion dry
2 lbs beef shoulder (cut up)
1 tbs oil
1/2 bay leave
1 tbs lemon juice
1 tbs brown sugar
1/2 tbs cinnamon

Directions:

• Brown onion and meat in oil, add remaining ingredients plus apricots and water, cover and cook on low heat for about 2 hours or until meat is tender.

* Freezes well.

138

Reisie Weisz
Vancouver, BC, Canada
Submitted by her daughter Fryda Rachel Fraeme

My mother, Reise Weisz, who is now known as Margaret Fraeme, was born in Ura, Hungary in 1928. She led a comfortable life in a town with few Jews until the Nazis started their systematic degradation of the Jews in Hungary. Her father was taken away and never seen again. In 1944 Reisie was taken to a ghetto along with her mother and five brothers. Two months later they were all taken by cattle car to Auschwitz. When they entered Auschwitz Reisie was sent to the right and all the rest were sent to the left.

Reisie survived Auschwitz for the next few months and then she was sent to a work farm as slave labor. As the end of the war grew nearer she was taken on a death march through the snow. The Jews who survived the march were eventually abandoned by the Nazis who feared capture by the Allies. Reisie miraculously survived and was liberated by the Russians. She spent the next two years recovering in a hospital and that is where she found out that only one of her brothers had survived. He eventually moved to Israel.

After a year in Paris, Reisie found family in Canada and immigrated to Vancouver in 1948. She met her husband in 1950 in shul and they were married in 1950.

Reisie Weiss in front of the T.B. Hospital in 1947

I asked my mother how she was able to survive when so many others perished. She told me that sometimes the only difference between herself and the ones who just gave up and stayed in their bunks until someone came to take them to the crematoriums- was HOPE. My mother never gave up hope that one day she would be rescued and she would be a witness to the atrocities that she and so many others had endured. She was able to envision herself living free with a husband and family some day, and that vision kept her alive.

Reisie Weisz and her grandchildren at her granddaughter's Bat Mitzvah in May of 2006. Husband Jack Fraeme, Jamie Shelnitz, Matthew Shelnitz and Margaret Fraeme (Reisie Weisz)

1985 photo of Reisie Weiss in front of the T.B. Hospital in Hungary, where she spent two years after the war

139

Hungarian Cabbage Rolls

meat

2 small cabbages
4 onions chopped
oil
2 1/2 lb. Ground beef
3 large cloves garlic, minced
2 cups rice uncooked

1 tsp. Salt
1 tsp. Pepper
1 Tbsp. Paprika
30 oz. tomatoes in sauce
32 oz. Bag sauerkraut

Directions:

1.) Remove stem and freeze or boil cabbage to loosen leaves.
2.) Saute 2 onions in oil until soft.
3.) Combine in large bowl: beef, rice, garlic, pepper, salt, paprika, and cooked onions.
4.) Mix together well.
5.) Use 1 tablespoon mixture in each cabbage leaf.
6.) Fold over twice and then roll.
7.) Tuck in end with fingertip.
8.) Place rolls in large pot.
9.) Add 2 more onions, left-over chopped cabbage, tomatoes, sauerkraut and 3 cups water.
10.) Bring to slow boil then simmer covered.

Cook time: 2 hours   Serves: 8

Yaacov Klein Fraemovitz
Vancouver, BC, Canada
Submitted by his daughter Fryda Rachel Fraeme

Yaacov Klein Fraemovitz, now known as Jack Fraeme, was born in Oradea, Romania in 1922. At age 13 he became an apprentice to a tailor. When the war broke out he escaped to Budapest and went into hiding. He was eventually captured and sent to a forced labor camp. He was kept alive because of the skills he had as a tailor.

After the war Yaacov and his only brother were reunited and had to escape from their Russian liberators, who were taking the displaced Jews for forced work in Siberia. They spent the next year in a displaced persons camp in Germany. When an opening occurred for him to move to Canada to help build the railroad he didn't waste any time leaving Europe. He arrived in Vancouver in 1949 and thought it was the most beautiful place he had ever seen. For the first time in a many years he was totally free.

The following year Yaacov sent for his brother, and they have lived next door to each other for 50 years. He met and married his wife Margaret and they now have one daughter and two grandchildren.

*Jack and Margaret's wedding
1950, Vancouver*

Family at a Sedar on a cruise ship

*This bike picture is of
Jack Fraeme after the war
in the resettlement camp*

141

Mandel Bread
"Komishbroit" - Hungarian
parve

2 cups sugar
Pinch of salt
6 eggs
2 tsp vanilla
2 cups oil
6 cups flour
4 tsp baking powder
Fixins (chopped walnuts, or chocolate chips,
        craisins etc.)
Sugar and cinnamon

Directions:
Preheat oven to 350 degrees

1.) In an electric mixer combine the sugar and salt and eggs.
2.) Whip for 3 or 4 minutes.
3.) Add the vanilla.
4.) Then gradually add the oil (save a small amount).
5.) Beat on high till well blended.
6.) Change beaters before adding flour.
7.) Combine the flour and baking soda and slowly add to mixture.
8.) When well blended remove from mixer and divide into 6 equal parts.
9.) Add fixings to each part.
10.) Roll out into long roll at least 12-16 inches long.
11.) Place rolls in oiled jelly pan (will need more than one).
12.) Spread oil on top and sprinkle with sugar and cinnamon.
13.) Bake for 35 minutes at 350 degrees.
14.) Let cool and slice diagonally.
15.) Place pieces on side and bake at 225 degrees for at least 1 hour.

Minna Neuwirth
Brooklyn, NY, U.S.A.
Submitted by her son Cary Feldman

Minna (left) and her sister Sophie not long after they escaped from Europe

In the mid-1930's, Minna Neuwirth was the sixth of seven children living with their parents on the Bismarck Strasse in Cologne, Germany. Her family had emigrated from Poland (near Krakow); in fact, some of her older siblings were born in Poland. Although the wealthier German Jews who had lived in Germany for generations (the Yeccas) were not always that accepting of the working class Galitzianos, the Neuwirths still enjoyed an improved lifestyle and a happy home life. All of this changed as the Nazis rose to power, along the way obliterating any differences between the Yeccas and the Galitzianos, who were treated with equal ruthlessness.

So it was that when things started to get bad for the Jews in Germany, the Neuwirth family realized that the best course—a course that ultimately saved some of their lives--was to get out of Germany; but easier said than done. And where to go? Israel was a fledgling land filled with its own uncertainties. Still, Minna's oldest brother, Shimon, left first for Israel. It was not possible to get into the United States without a proper visa, and you could not get a visa unless someone in the States was willing to sponsor you. Fortunately, the Neuwirths had a first cousin who already was in the US, and he sent the necessary papers for Minna's next oldest brother, Shumuel Aron (Al), who in turn sent for oldest sister Sophie, who in turn sent for next oldest brother David. But fate and the Nazis interrupted this slow but steady plan when, shortly before Krystalnacht, they arrested Minna's father, Chaim, and her only brother still in Germany, Willi. At some point, the family received word through the grapevine that Willi had been shot to death by a guard while working in the kitchen of a prison camp after saying something that the guard did not like, and that their father Chaim had starved to death in another prison camp. Clearly, it was no longer safe on the Bismarck Strasse for Minna, her younger sister, Martha, and their mother, Golda. They packed up what they could, left everything else behind and hid in a smuggler's truck in a daring attempt to sneak into France. They were unsuccessful, but they were able to get into Belgium.

But Belgium was not that safe either, with many Germans and collaborators looking for opportunities to turn in Jews who would be deported to camps. The Neuwirth refugees had to try to get to Nice, France, which at the time was somewhat of a safe haven for German Jews who had taken refuge there. To make matters worse, by then the stress of the times, Golda's arthritis and other ailments left her too sick to travel. She was in a wheelchair and she could not do the walking that one had to do to sneak into France. The new plan was for one of the teenage girls--it turned out to be Martha--to stay in Belgium to take care of Golda; Minna would try to get to Nice herself, and then figure out a way to get Martha and Golda to Nice as well. Minna was able to smuggle into France and eventually made it to Nice. But things were growing worse daily, and it was just not possible to get her sister and her sick mother out of Belgium. So Minna turned her attention to getting out of Europe to the US. With the help of her brother Al in the U.S., and others in Nice, she was able to get on a freighter to begin a difficult journey that took her through Cuba and eventually to the United States.

Potato Pancakes
parve

Potatoes, cooked in many ways, were a staple of the Neuwirth household on the Bismarck Strasse, but potato latkes were a favorite. They continue to be a favorite of the children and grandchildren of the Neuwirths who made it out of Germany. A few of Golda's grandchildren who consider themselves to be latke mavens enjoy a friendly familial rivalry, each claiming to make the best latkes. Here is Minna's recipe recorded years ago by one of the mavens, her son Cary, while watching and helping her whip up a batch.

6 Large Potatoes
2-3 Large Onions
2 Eggs Slightly Beaten
3 Tbsp. Flour
1/4 Tsp. Pepper
1 Tsp. Salt
1/2 Tsp. Baking Powder
Pinch of Uncle Shimons Magic Stuff
(arrowroot)

Shimon, who originally left Germany for Israel, eventually emigrated to the United States, where he became the chef at the Yeshiva University in New York. Unfortunately, he took the secret of his magic stuff to his grave, and there is precious little of it left.

Directions:

1.) Peel, soak, grate potatoes and onions.
2.) Put batter in a strainer to let liquid run off (or let stand and drain).
3.) Stir in eggs and remaining ingredients; spoon into hot well greased pan; brown on both sides; stack, drain on paper towel.
4.) Serve hot with apple sauce, sour cream or sugar.

Note: The secret is the onions. When you think you have put in enough, put in a little more.

Abe Malnik
Dewey Beach, DE, U.S.A.
As told to Joanne Caras

Abe Malnik was born in Kauvnis, Lithuania. When he was 13 the Germans came into Lithuania and set up a ghetto for the Jews. His father was a member of the ghetto fire department and Abe was put to work building the fence around the ghetto.

On October 28, 1942 the Germans rounded up 10,000 Jews from the ghetto and removed them in groups of 100. They told the Jews that they were being taken to be "counted". Each group was taken to a place called the Ninth Fort, where they were executed and burned. Abe and his mother were in the last group of 100, ready to be taken to the Ninth Fort for execution, but his father was able to rescue them because he had saved the life of a friend of a German soldier and the soldier let Abe and his mom escape from the death ride. They were minutes away from death.

When the ghetto was finally emptied Abe spent time in 5 different concentration camps. He and his father were separated from his mother at the first camp and that is where Abe said "goodbye" to her for the very last time. Father and son managed to stay together, and because he was an accomplished barber he was given a job cutting hair for the German guards. He became friendly with the guards and because of that they treated Abe a little better than many of the other Jews. Abe volunteered for every work detail they had because he wanted to stay in good favor with the guards.

At his final camp Abe's father took ill and he was near death. Abe was also very weak and weighed about 75 pounds when they were finally liberated by the Russians. When Abe first saw a Russian tank he kissed it and begged the driver for a piece of bread. After liberation father and son searched in vain to find Abe's mother, but they later learned that she had been killed. They ended up in Poland and Abe joined the Israeli underground, helping Jews to sneak out of Poland to Israel.

After the war Abe learned that his mother had two brothers in America so he set out to come to America. When he arrived here he could not speak one word of English and had only $7.00 in his pocket.

With so little to start, Abe became a successful businessman, a husband for 58 years to his beloved wife Lilly, father to three sons and grandfather of six. He was president of the Holocaust Survivors Association in Washington, DC, starting with seven members and growing it to over 500.

A few years ago Abe and Lilly returned to Lithuania where they distributed money to the local Jewish citizens, started a Soup Kitchen, and bought them an ambulance. Abe is revered in his hometown as a Holocaust Survivor who came home to help those who stayed behind. He and his wife Lilly were part of a team of survivors who traveled to the crematoriums to collect ashes that have been placed in the Holocaust Museum in Washington. Sadly, Abe passed away on April 3, 2007, just prior to the publication of this cookbook.

145

Large Kugel
by Lilly Malnik
dairy

two 12 oz. containers of cottage cheese
one 7 oz. pkg. Farmer Cheese
one pint sour cream
8 oz. cream cheese
2 tsp. vanilla
1 pkg sugar vanilla
1/2 cup sugar
8 eggs
1/4 cup milk
1/2 cup light raisins
1/4 stick melted sweet butter
1 jar apricot preserves
2 pkg. 12 oz. wide noodles

Topping

2 cups corn flake crumbs
2 tsp. vanilla
1/4 cup melted butter
1 cup or more brown sugar

Directions:

Preheat oven to 350 degrees

1.) Cook noodles, drain, add melted butter and stir in a large bowl.
2.) Add other ingredients, stir and put into a well-greased large casserole pan.
3.) Mix topping together and spread on top.
4.) Bake at 350* for 45 to 50 minutes

For a small Kugel cut everything in half.

146

Cooked Tongue Sweet and Sour

by Bubby Ida Malnik
meat

2 T fat or oil
1 onion diced
2 T flour
2 cups tongue stock
1/3 cup white vinegar
1/3 cup honey
1/2 tsp. salt
1/2 tsp. powdered ginger
1/4 cup light raisins
1/4 cup sliced almond blanched
1 lemon sliced thin

Directions:

1.) Add the oil in pan and saute onion till lighted glazed.
2.) Sprinkle flour and brown.
3.) Gradually add the stock, stirring constantly until mixture boils.
4.) Stir in the Vinegar, honey, salt, ginger and raisins.
5.) Cook over low heat for 5 minutes.
6.) Add the almonds and lemons cook 2 more minutes.
7.) Slice cooked tongue and serve with the Sweet and Sour Sauce.

Lilly and Abe Malnik (far right) at their
Grandson Josh's Bar Mitzvah with granddaughter,
son, daughter-in-law and in-laws

Brisket Man's Famous Brisket Recipe

from Lilly Malnik

meat

Garlic powder
Salt and pepper
Paprika
2 onions
1 Tbsp pickling spice
Brisket

Directions:

Preheat oven to 350 degrees

1.) Make a dry rub out of equal parts of the following ingredients: garlic powder, salt, pepper, and paprika.
2.) Rub into brisket.
3.) Slice onions and put on the bottom of the roasting pan.
4.) Oven brown brisket on both sides or in a pan.
5.) Put fat side up in roasting pan.
6.) Add 2 T pickling spice on top of brisket.
7.) Add 1-cup boiling water to brisket and cover with a lid.
8.) Cook until tender.
9.) When cool cut against the grain and serve with gravy.

Gravy

- Flour
- Scrape fat and pickling spice off top.
- Add water, if needed to the gravy drippings.
- Put gravy into blender add flour and heat up.
- Pour over sliced brisket.

148

Lilly Applebaum Malnik

Dewey Beach, DE, U.S.A.

As told to Joanne Caras

Lilly Applebaum Manik

Lilly Applebaum grew up in Antwerpen, Belgium, and at age 13 she moved to Brussels, Belgium with her mother. In the spring of 1940 the Germans entered Brussels. Over the next two years all Jews were forced to wear yellow stars, observe a curfew, and eventually they had to give up their businesses.

In 1942 the Jews were taken from schools and from the streets. Lilly hid in the outskirts of Brussels with her aunt and uncle. Lilly had tonsillitis and she was in the hospital when her brother was taken away. Because she was sick, Lilly's life was saved.

Lilly and her mother continued to hide for two more years. All of their neighbors knew they were Jewish but were willing to protect them by not "denouncing" them to the Germans.

Finally in 1944 Lilly's mother was denounced by a disgruntled former employee. She was arrested and taken away. Lilly stayed with her aunt and uncle but a short time later they too were denounced and arrested.

Lilly was placed on a cattle car with hundreds of other Jews to be taken to Auschwitz. On the cattle car there was no room for people to sit or even stand. People were defecating and vomiting. Lilly slept on top of her aunt and uncle.

At one point a German soldier stuck his rifle through the only small window in the cattle car and starting firing indiscriminately, killing several people and wounding others. When she arrived at Auschwitz, Lilly noticed the smoke coming from one large building. She thought that it was a factory and that she was going there to work. Little did she know that those were the crematoriums. Soon she was sent to Birkenau which was about 6 miles away.

She was tattooed and told "Forget your name. You are now A1543." Twice per day they had what was called "appel". All of the Jews were lined up for roll call and had to stand for 2 to 3 hours in the freezing cold weather. Then, the old and sick were taken away to the crematoriums. They were put on trucks and carted away while an orchestra played classical music to keep them calm.

149

A few months later the Russians came in to Auschwitz. Lilly and the other Jews were taken by the Germans on a "death march" of 4-5 days to Bergen Belsen. Many of the prisoners died along the march but Lilly was determined to live. At one point she looked up at the stars and said "how can this be happening to me? All over the world people are looking at those same stars and they are free. When will I be free?"

After 5 more horrible months in Bergen Belsen Lilly got typhus from a friend who died in her arms. At that point Lilly finally lost her will to live. But miraculously she was finally liberated by the British and Canadians. She weighed only 65 pounds, and was only about one week away from death.

"For five long months in Bergen Belsen I was on the bare floor all the time. No chairs, no benches, no mattress, no blanket. And I felt like an inhuman person, an animal on the ground. I forgot what it meant to sit like a human being, to sit at a table and eat like a person, with a tablecloth, fine china, knife, and fork. I wondered if I would ever be liberated and be a person again. I was only fifteen years old."

Lilly's experience was very similar to that of the Anne Frank. Both were fifteen years old, both were born in Antwerpen, both hid from the Nazis, both were sent to Auschwitz, and both got sick from Typhus. Anne Frank died one week before liberation, but Lilly Applebaum managed to survive.

After two months in the hospital she returned to Brussels hoping to find her aunt alive. She put her name on a wall along with other survivors. Somebody saw her name and got the word to her aunt Sarah, who had also survived.

When Lilly returned to her aunt's home all of the neighbors lined up like a parade. They shouted "Lilly survived!"

Lilly was married for 58 years to her late, beloved husband, Abe, and together they had three sons and six grandchildren.

Lilly Applebaum

Cucumber Salad

parve

2 or 3 English cucumbers (Burpless cucumbers)
1/4 cup sugar
1 tablespoon salt
1/2 cup cold water
1-2 teaspoon chopped dill
vinegar to taste

Directions:

Peel cucumbers, take a fork and with the sharp tongs, run down the sides of the cucumber to make a decorative pattern. Thinly slice on a mandolin. Add a tablespoon of salt and mix well. Transfer cucumbers to a shallow plate and place another plate on top and add weight (something heavy) to press the sliced cucumbers for approximately 20-30 minutes so that the juices come out of the cucumber.

While the cucumbers are being pressed, mix together in a separate bowl the sugar, vinegar, water and dill. Stir well till sugar is dissolved. Taste. Mixture should take on a sweet/sour flavor, preferably on the tart (vinegar) side. After 20-30 minutes of pressing cucumbers, drain water. Rinse salt off the cucumbers and drain well. Combine sugar/vinegar liquid and cucumbers together in a glass bowl and mix thoroughly. Make sure there is enough sugar/vinegar mixture to cover cucumbers. Refrigerate and chill.

Cucumber salad is best when marinated for several hours.
Can keep for 2-3 days.

Bubby's Soup

meat

1/2 lb flanken, with bones (about 2-3 pieces)
2-3 packages vegetable soup mix (Manischewitz)
2 carrots diced
1 large onion diced
2 cloves garlic diced
2 ribs celery diced
2-3 chicken bouillon cubes
16 cups water
2-3 dried shitake mushrooms soaked in water. Cut in pieces
    and reserve liquid to add to soup. (Adds flavor.)
salt and pepper to taste
parsley or dill finely chopped

Optional: To thicken the soup, you can add any of the following: medium potato diced, farfel, alphabet pasta or orzo.

Optional: Add leftover gravy to add flavor

1.) Take meat and place in a large soup pot and cover with water.
2.) Bring to a boil and simmer.
3.) Skim surface of the soup as need for approximately 10 minutes cooking time.
4.) Add vegetable soup mix and simmer for one hour. Add carrots, onions, celery, garlic, and cook another hour.
5.) Stir soup occasionally.
6.) Add chicken bouillon cubes.
7.) Take out flanken and let cool.
8.) When the meat can be handled, cut into small pieces and return to the soup pot.
9.) To finish soup, thicken as needed with ¼ cup orzo or diced potato.
10.) Add package seasoning.
11.) Pour soaked mushroom pieces along with the liquid into the soup.
12.) Salt and pepper to taste.
13.) Garnish soup with fresh chopped parsley or dill.

This soup becomes more favorable the next day. If the soup is too thick, add 1 can of chicken broth. **Enjoy.**

Florence Tabrys

Delray Beach, FL, U.S.A.
Submitted by her daughter Susan Karr

I was born in a small town called Szydlowiec, near Radom in Poland. My family consisted of my parents and six other siblings. The Nazis occupied our town in September, 1939. At that time I was 14 years old.

For three years, we continued to live in our house along with the other people in the town. A fence was not erected and a formal ghetto was not created because the entire Jewish population lived in the center of the town, and was surrounded by the Polish people and the Nazi SS.

We were forced to do various jobs and were fed miserable food rations. We were without any nutrition, calories, or vitamins. My father was a shoemaker and was able to stealthily barter shoes for food with the Polish people—and that's how we were somehow able to survive. I had two older brothers, but since I was the oldest of the girls, it became my duty and obligation to do all of the chores in the house, while I was also forced to work for the Nazis.

In 1942, the Nazi's suddenly gathered the entire Jewish population and segregated us according to our ages and apparent health condition. My parents, grandparents, and younger sisters and brothers were immediately sent to Treblinka, an extermination camp, where they perished. My two older brothers escaped but were later caught and shot.

My younger sister and I were sent to an ammunitions factory where we worked for two years producing shells for bullets. We worked in two shifts, 12 hours each, night and day—and all that was provided was a measly piece of ersatz bread and a bowl of watery soup. All day and night we would dream of food. We would remind ourselves of the simplest things that we ate at home, especially during the holidays. I would think about how I helped my mother prepare the necessary dishes such as gefilte fish, chicken with matzo ball soup, kreplach, stuffed cabbage, and a cholent for shabbat.

As the Russian army got closer and closer, the SS and their collaborators started to transport us from one camp to another—each one worse than the next. At one point we walked dozens of kilometers during the middle of winter in torn or wooden shoes, without any food. We were transported to Bergen Belsen, Burgau, Tirkheim, and we ended up in Dachau where on April 30th we were finally liberated by the American army. Miraculously, I remained with my sister the entire time.

153

After the liberation, we lived in a displaced person's camp for four years. After six weeks at the camp, I met my husband Harry. We got married in Germany and immigrated to the United States. We moved to the Bronx because I had an uncle who sponsored us and his family was living there. I was in the United States for only ten days when I got a job as a seamstress. A couple of years later I gave birth to the first of two lovely daughters. I have two daughters Helen and Susan. They are married. The first has two daughters and the second has two sons.

We lived in New York for many years (Brooklyn, Long Island, and Queens), and had various businesses. We eventually settled in Florida and recently celebrated our 60th wedding anniversary!

Florence Tabrys' Beef Stew

meat

4 lbs. lean beef cut-up into little chunks
1 medium size onion
4 or 5 medium size red potatoes
4 or 5 carrots
3 or 4 stalks celery
A handful of thin spaghetti
1 can of baby peas
Salt and pepper

Directions:

1.) Dice the onion.
2.) Slice the celery and carrots into small pieces.
3.) Place beef, onions and celery into a pot. Add salt and pepper and bring to a boil. Let simmer until meat becomes soft.
4.) Dice potatoes and add to pot.
5.) Add broken spaghetti.
6.) When all ingredients are soft add peas.
7.) Add salt and pepper to taste.

Florence Tabrys'
Mushroom, Eggs, and Onions

(mock chopped liver)
parve

2 boxes of 10-12 oz. mushrooms
8 eggs
3 large onions
Oil, salt

Directions:

1.) Boil the eggs until they are hard-boiled.
2.) Cut the mushrooms and onions into tiny pieces.
3.) Fry the onions in some oil and salt until they are light brown.
4.) Add the mushrooms to the onions and cook until the mushrooms are soft and the onions are dark brown (but not burnt).
5.) Chop the hard boiled eggs (Use as many yolks as desired. 4-6 is preferable.)
6.) Mix all of the ingredients together, add salt or oil to taste.

Rose Meller Price
Columbia, MD, U.S.A.
Submitted by her daughter Luba Fineman

Rose Meller was living in Poland with her family in a small town called Checkocheen. She had four brothers and a sister. When the Nazi army invaded the town she lived in, her family left their home and all of their belongings and escaped into the forest. They walked through fields and farms to get to her married brother's house in another town about 50 kilometers away. It wasn't long before the Nazis got to that town also, and they were rounding up all of the Jews for deportation. Rose managed to escape into hiding. However, word got to her that her mother had been taken hostage and that if she returned her mother would be freed.

Without hesitation Rose returned only to find out that her mother would be sent to a death camp anyway and that she would be sent away to a labor camp in Czechoslovakia.

There for 3 ½ years, under unbearable conditions, Rose was forced to spin the thread that would be used to make uniforms for the Nazi soldiers. Rose remained in the labor camp until Russian soldiers liberated her in 1945.

Then she returned to Poland to see if any of her family had survived. But to her dismay nothing was there for her. Tragically Rose had been the only member of her family to survive. Rose then went to a survivor's facility where she met Morris Price. Shortly after that Rose and Morris married and then decided to leave Poland because of the Pogroms (riots).

They went to Germany and stayed at a displaced person's camp at the American Zone near Munich. Their first child Rebecca was born there in 1946 and another daughter Luba was born two years later in Stuttgart.

In 1949 Rose and Morris made the decision to go to Israel and in 1957 they joined Morris' surviving siblings in America.

My mom, Rose, was an excellent cook. She didn't use recipes. My sister and I would watch her while she cooked and baked, trying to figure out the correct measurements, and we would write them down in order to keep some of her wonderful recipes.

The Price family, Rose, far right

Rose's Apple Cake

parve

5 or 6 granny apples (3 lbs.)
3 cups flour
3 tsp. baking powder
1 cup sugar
2 eggs
1/4 cup orange juice
1 stick margarine or 1/2 cup oil
1 pinch of salt

Directions:

Preheat oven to 350 degrees

1.) Mix all ingredients except apples and knead into dough.
2.) Set aside in refrigerator.
3.) Peel and grate apples and sprinkle with sugar, at least 4 tablespoons (cinnamon optional). Set aside.
4.) Take dough out of refrigerator and divide it into two parts.
5.) Roll out one part of dough and spread it into a greased cake pan (13x9x2).
6.) Spread apples evenly over dough.
7.) Roll out remainder of dough and place it on top to cover apples.
8.) Take a dull knife and draw a brick pattern on dough.
9.) Poke holes with point of knife.
10.) Sprinkle sugar on top.
11.) Preheat oven to 350 and bake for one hour until done.

Rosette Faust Halpern
Silver Spring, MD, U.S.A.
(Rozia Faust)

I was born in Rohatyn, Poland, a town that changed nationality according to political upheaval. I was living in my youth in three countries, not moving an inch out of my house. I was the youngest of a family of six, four grown brothers, and a sister, to a mother in her late forties. I had a lonely childhood; sadly it was followed with a war.

The tragic years during the German occupation robbed me of my parents, some siblings, relatives, and childhood friends. We were humiliated to the point of ultimate degradation, and forced to leave our home to a closed ghetto where every day was designed to annihilate the Jews. Besides epidemic and filth, we were subjected to unbelievable hunger, which forced me to take a dangerous chance and smuggle some food into the ghetto from friendly gentiles.

I was caught, and endured twenty five lashes on my back, which was better than death. I was lucky that the Gestapo was away that day, and the local police were merciful for a price given on my behalf by the Judenraat.

To avoid further investigation about who the gentiles were providing the food, I had to leave the ghetto. With false identification I was placed in the home of a paralyzed Ukrainian woman where I assumed the position of an aide providing complete assistance to her. To avoid discovery I had to watch my behavior. Although I was fluent in the Ukrainian language and dressed accordingly so I would fit the part. The smallest misstep, or an inadvertent remark, would have meant death for me.

Unexpectedly, a distant relative recognized me and, more to protect the people harboring me, I was shipped back to the ghetto just in time for liquidation. I survived, bunker to bunker, hiding place to hiding place, and occasionally helped by friends. Finally I was liberated in 1944 by the Soviet army, the first surviving Jew of only twenty-six survivors out of twelve thousand innocent men, women, and children, all victims of the most heinous crime committed in the history of humanity.

Note: *Details of the history in a forthcoming book.*

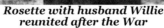
Rosette with husband Willie reunited after the War

158

Stuffed Cabbage
meat

*(Original Recipe of Dvora Faust from Rohatyn, Poland
rescued by Rozia Faust - Rosette Halpern)*

1 lg. head cabbage
1/2 cup raisins
2 lbs. chopped beef
1 lg. sliced onion
1 chopped onion
1 tart apple grated
1/2 cup cooked rice
7 ginger snaps, softened in hot water
1 egg
juice of 1/2 lemon
Salt, pepper, garlic
1 sm. can tomatoes
1 can tomato sauce

*For hors d'oeuvre size- cut cabbage leaf
in half before filling.*

Directions:
Preheat oven to 325 degrees
1.) Soak cabbage in boiling water until limp.
2.) Separate leaves.
3.) Combine beef, chopped onion, rice, egg, and salt, pepper, and garlic to taste- for filling.
4.) Place about 2 tablespoons filling on each cabbage leaf.
5.) Roll up.
6.) In large roaster place any extra cabbage- sliced fine.
7.) Add tomato sauce, raisins, sliced onion, apple, ginger snaps, lemon juice, and tomatoes.
8.) Bring to boil.
9.) Add cabbage rolls.
10.) Bake covered in 325 degree oven for 1 ½ to 2 hours.
11.) For the last 15 minutes remove cover and baste.

Stuffed Veal
meat

*(Original Recipe of Chaya Halpern's
rescued by Rosette Faust Halpern)*

4 lb. breast of veal roast (with bones)
Oil and vinegar
Chopped liver, cooked rice or mashed potatoes for stuffing

Directions:
Preheat oven to 350 degrees
1.) Rinse meat with cold water & place on a wire rack in a large pan
2.) Splash veal with oil and vinegar on the surface including inside the pocket. Stuff the pocket with chopped liver, rice, or mashed potatoes/
3.) Generously sprinkle veal with garlic powder and pickling spice and sweet paprika
4.) Place in a preheated oven 350° and bake until the meat is tender (~2-3 hrs)
   Helpful Hint: Veal shrinks so buy a bigger piece!

Chicken liver stuffing recipe:
Sauté 1 lb. livers in oil with mushrooms, onions, parsley, seasoned to taste with salt, pepper, and paprika for 4 minutes, stirring frequently.

Moishe Perlman
Brooklyn, NY, U.S.A.
Submitted by his granddaughter Rivka Perlman

My two living grandparents are both Holocaust survivors, both originating from Cracow, Poland. They did not know each other before the war, and only met afterwards, in Paris. They both candidly admit that they are alive only through miracles, as are all those who survived, and playfully guilt-trip their grandchildren that they survived for US and so we must do what they want. Here are two of the many, many miracles they experienced:

My grandfather was in the concentration camp, Plaszow, for most of the Holocaust. He pretended to be a mechanic, and would putter around with broken engines all day, praying for them to get fixed. Plaszow did not tattoo their prisoners, they simply had to memorize their numbers. One Yom Kippur, my grandfather gave one of his non-Jewish workers his bread because he was fasting. The worker made him a leather bracelet with his ID number etched into a piece of metal as thanks. Walking to his barracks, tired after a long day, my Zaidy failed to notice a Nazi soldier beating a Jewish inmate with a long piece of barbed wire.

When the soldier whipped the piece of wire back, it hit my grandfather straight in the eye. He was hospitalized for a few days (and after the war finally had to have the eye taken out and replaced with a glass one). One night while still in the infirmary, he went outside after curfew to use the bathroom. A soldier caught him and demanded his ID number. Faced with no other choice, my grandfather slipped off his bracelet and handed it to the soldier. The next day, at roll call, a list of numbers were called to be shot, as a lesson to the rest of the camp. All but one person came forward. The camp ledger was brought out to look up who belonged to this number.... the number did not exist!!

While all this hullabaloo was going on, my Zaidy looked down at his bracelet and realized that his number was comprised of digits that could be read upside down as well as right side up. He had given his bracelet to the soldier upside down, and the soldier dutifully copied down the numbers; the wrong numbers. All the people who had been called up were removed from the camp and shot. Thanks to a piece of leather and some crude metal I am able to have a grandfather. It is a pretty ugly bracelet to look at, yet more precious than any other jewelry our family can own.

**Cesia Lederberger Perlman
with husband,
Moishe Perlman**

160

Salmon Patties
parve

1 large can salmon
2 eggs
1/4 tsp. lemon juice
1/4 tsp. Worcestershire
1/2 cup Italian bread crumbs plus more to roll in
2 Tablespoons mayonnaise or Vegenaise (parve)
1-4 cup grated onion
2 Tablespoons margarine or vegan butter

Directions:

1.) Clean salmon and drain.
2.) Mix all of the ingredients. Roll in extra bread crumbs.
3.) Fry in margarine.
4.) Serve with crackers and mustard.

Matzoh Toffee

dairy

1 box matzoh or 1 sleeve of saltines crackers
3/4 cup of butter (1 1/2 sticks)
3/4 cup sugar
12 ounces chocolate chips or 6 ounces chocolate chips and
6 ounce unwrapped Hershey kisses
Parve- use non dairy chips and margarine or
vegan butter (Earth Balance)
1/2 cup chopped walnuts or pecans

Directions:

Preheat oven to 400 degrees

1.) Line a cookie sheet with aluminum foil.
2.) Line the pan with crackers.
3.) Melt the butter and sugar and bring to a boil.
4.) Stir and keep boiling for 2 minutes.
5.) Pour over the crackers and spread over entire cracker.
6.) Bake for 4-6 minutes.
7.) Keep an eye on this and take out when it has bubbles all over it and lightly golden.
8.) Remove from oven and sprinkle chocolate over the top of the crackers.
9.) Let sit for 2 minutes and spread to cover all crackers.
10.) Sprinkle with nuts.
11.) Freeze and cut or break into pieces.

Addictive

Easy Macaroons
dairy

Directions:
Preheat oven to 350 degrees

14 oz bag of Angel Flake coconut
1 cup sweetened condensed milk
2 tsp. vanilla

1.) Combine all ingredients, mixing well.
2.) Drop from teaspoon, 1 inch apart on well-greased cookie sheet or nonstick aluminium foil.
3.) Bake 350 degrees for 10 to 12 minutes or until lightly browned.
4.) Remove using a spatula.
5.) Melt 1/2 cup chocolate over double boiler and drizzle on top.

Variations:
- For chocolate macaroons delete vanilla and add 2 tsp. melted semi-sweet squares.
- Also can add small chips.

Passover Layered Brownies
dairy

6 ounce cream cheese
4 tablespoon margarine
2/3 cup sugar
2 tablespoon cake meal
2 eggs & 4 eggs
1 tablespoon lemon juice
2 pkgs. Passover brownie mix with the fudge frosting included

Directions:
Preheat oven to 350 degrees

1.) Beat cream cheese, margarine, and sugar.
2.) Then add cake meal, 2 eggs and lemon juice.
3.) Blend and then set aside.
4.) Follow brownie recipe on package using 4 eggs.
5.) Grease 8 inch square pan and alternate chocolate and cream cheese mixture.
6.) Bake at 350 degrees 40 to 45 minutes.
7.) Allow brownies to cool in pan and then frost following the instructions on the package.

Beef with Prunes
meat

4 Tbsp vegetable oil
5 pounds bottom round roast, cut into
   1 1/2 - inch cubes
3 medium onions, chopped
2 tsp sugar
5 carrots, peeled and sliced
1/2 tsp salt
dash of pepper
5 cups water
1/2 cup honey
1 tsp cinnamon
1 cup small pitted prunes
juice of one lemon

Directions:

1.) Heat 2 T oil in deep-sided non-reactive pan over high heat.
2.) Brown meat on all sides. Remove meat and set aside. Wash and dry the pan.
3.) Heat remaining oil over medium heat.
4.) Add the onions and sugar; saute over low heat for 10 minutes, until soft.
5.) Return meat to pan, add carrots, salt pepper and water.
6.) Bring to a boil, reduce heat, cover, and simmer gently 1 hour.
7.) Add honey and cinnamon. Simmer 30 minutes, partially covered.
8.) Add prunes and simmer 30 minutes uncovered or until meat is tender.
9.) Add lemon juice.

Makes 6 to 8 servings.

Cutting the meat into smaller cubes will reduce cooking time.
This dish keeps well for a week in refrigerator and freezes well.
Flavor improves upon standing -- try to cook it the day before and refrigerate.

Cesia Lederberger
Brooklyn, NY, U.S.A.
Submitted by her granddaughter Rivka Perlman

My grandmother was second to youngest in a family of 8. When her oldest brother, Abba was little, every day after coming home from school, he used to bring his great-uncle a freshly cooked lunch. The great uncle once asked his niece, Abba's mother, what she had to do to bribe her son to bring his old great-uncle food every day. She answered that she never had to bribe him, that Abba actually begged her for the privilege of delivering the food. The next day when Abba came with his daily food delivery, his great-uncle embraced him and blessed him that he would always have food on the table for his family, no matter what may come. Throughout the war all 8 siblings hid in Budapest, Hungary under false papers. They were frightened and shaken and petrified, but always had bread to eat. Even in the worst days when they had nothing else but bread, there was always enough bread for them all to eat.

I thought it was fitting to relay this story in a cookbook. Who knows what blessings we may receive through what we make for our day to day meals.

Cesia Lederberger Perlman

Morah Chanie Baron's Challah
parve

This recipe is made every Friday for Shabbos at Gan Israel Preschool with the children.

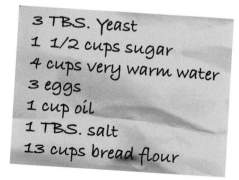

3 TBS. Yeast
1 1/2 cups sugar
4 cups very warm water
3 eggs
1 cup oil
1 TBS. salt
13 cups bread flour

Directions:
Preheat oven to 350 degrees

1.) Mix yeast, sugar, and water.
2.) Leave to proof.
3.) Add eggs, oil, salt, and bread flour.
4.) Kneed dough until smooth.
5.) Let rise 1 1/2 hours.
6.) Punch down, shape and let rise again for 1/2 hour.
7.) Brush on an egg and sprinkle with sesame seeds, poppy seeds, or leave plain.
8.) Bake at 350 for 30 minutes or until golden brown.

Eggplant Dip- Israeli style

parve

1 large eggplant (about 2 lbs.)
1 cup onion finely chopped
4 tablespoons olive oil
1/2 cup green pepper finely chopped
1 tsp. garlic finely minced
2 large ripe tomatoes, peeled seeded, chopped
1/2 tsp. sugar
1 tsp. salt
2 tablespoons olive oil
freshly ground pepper
1 1/2 tablespoon lemon juice

Directions:
Preheat oven to 425 degrees

1.) Prick eggplant with fork and place on a cookie sheet.
2.) Bake the eggplant for about 1 hour, turning it over several times until it's soft and its skin is charred and blistered.
3.) Meanwhile, cook the onions in 4 tablespoons of olive oil over moderate heat for 6-8 minutes until soft brown.
4.) Stir in the green pepper and garlic and cook, stirring occasionally, for 5 minutes longer.
5.) Put mixture in mixing bowl. Remove skin from eggplant and puree the inside.
6.) Add to mixing bowl along with tomatoes, sugar , salt and pepper.
7.) Heat 2 tablespoons olive oil in skillet over moderate heat.
8.) Pour in eggplant mixture. Bring to a boil, stirring constantly.
9.) Reduce heat, stir occasionally and continue cooking until moisture has evaporated.
10.) Stir in lemon juice. Season to taste.
11.) Transfer to serving dish and chill covered until ready to serve with mini rye or crackers.

Bitka (Blima Glaser) Goldberg

Akko, Israel

As told to Sarah Caras

Bitka Goldberg

Bitka Goldberg was born on October 26th, 1925 in the town of Chrzanow, Poland, where 15,000 Jews lived. Her family had lived in that town for four generations on her father's side. In the beginning of 1940, Chrzanow was turned into a ghetto. On February 18th, 1943, which was the day of the Fast of Esther, the Gestapo came to her home and told everyone to go outside for a "selection." Bitka, who was 15 and her sister, Fayga who was 17 were sent to a concentration camp in Czechoslovakia called Parschniz. Her mother and younger sister were sent to Auschwitz. Her father was supposed to go to a work camp, but paid off the Gestapo to allow him to go with his wife and youngest daughter. That was the last time Bitka saw her parents and youngest sister.

In the camp, there was a girl who had two prayer books for the high holy days, Rosh Hashanah and Yom Kippur. Because this girl had these books, they were able to keep track of the Jewish holidays. When Passover came, the girls didn't eat bread for seven days and instead only ate potatoes and beets. The kitchen of the camp gave the girls extra potatoes instead of bread during this time.

On the 9th of May in 1945, Parschniz was liberated by the Russians. Having no place to go, Bitka stayed at the camp for two more weeks. During this time she met her future husband, Yosek Goldberg. They lived in Germany until June 6, 1949 when they moved to Israel and settled in Akko where Bitka has been living for 57 years. She has two sons, four grandchildren and two great granddaughters, all of whom live in Israel.

Bitka & Yosek Goldberg c. 1946

167

Kapu'snak (Polish cabbage dish)

meat

1 can of sour cabbage in a can
1 onion chopped into pieces
2-3 medium sized potatoes
pinch of salt to taste
hot dogs if desired
2 tbsp oil

Directions:

1.) Cut onion into pieces.
2.) Peel the potatoes and cut each into 4 pieces.
3.) Put a pinch of salt on each one.
4.) Put the potatoes in a pot with water just covering them.
5.) Mash the potatoes a little-not so they are pureed.
6.) Put oil in frying pan, heat up oil and sauté the onions until soft and golden.
7.) Drain the water from the can and put the cabbage on top of the onions constantly stirring for about 15 minutes so it does not burn.
8.) Add the potatoes and stir it for 5 more minutes.
9.) You can cut up hot dogs and add it to the mixture if you desire and stir it for another 5-10 minutes until the hot dogs are soft.

Raisin nut babka

parve

Rectangular baking pan.
3 eggs
1 stick of margarine at room temp.
1 1/4 cup of sugar
3/4 cup orange juice or cream
little bit of lemon zest
450 grams of cake flour
    (if you don't have cake flour, use 2 1/2 cups of
    flour and 5 grams of baking powder)
1/2 tsp vanilla
1/2 handful of chopped up walnuts
1/2 handful of raisins

Directions:

Preheat oven to 350 degrees

1.) Mix sugar and eggs in a bowl.
2.) Add room temp. margarine to mixture.
3.) Alternate adding flour and juice slowly to mixture.
4.) Put in vanilla.
5.) Put chopped walnuts and raisins on a plate with a little flour and toss it so the raisins and nuts are covered.
6.) Fold in the raisins and nuts into the mixture.
7.) Put some oil on the pan, or use a baking sheet so the babka will not stick to the pan.
8.) Put the mixture in the pan.
9.) Let it bake for one hour until it browns a bit.
10.) Stick a toothpick in the center and it should come out clean.

Cherie Rosenstein

Dayton, OH, U.S.A.

It was April 1948. I was a five year old child named Maria Helena Chuchnowicz. As I flew on a plane over the Atlantic to my new home in the United States I left a shattered life of tragedy and sorrow. My parents, Joseph Chuchnowicz and Basia Bojarska, had perished at Bergen Belsen. Sadly I could not remember what they looked like. But I was leaving behind the orphanage that had been home to me and other children who had lost their families.

The orphanage , located in Ville Juiff in Paris, was one of many financed and organized by the Vaad Hatzalah, which means "Group to Save (Jewish People)". The orphanage was surrounded by high walls which concealed us from the outside. We knew the Nazis had hunted for Jews to bake in their ovens. We were warned never to venture outside because danger lurked beyond. Inside the orphanage there was warmth and comfort. The staff worked with compassion and dedication to ease our fears and traumas.

Since the orphanage was under the auspices of an orthodox Jewish organization, Judaism was very much part of our every day lives. We were provided with a Jewish education and also introduced to the Hebrew language in songs and prayers. We were given a bath once per week, on Fridays so that we could welcome in the Sabbath with cleanliness. After the Sabbath meals our dining hall echoed with the sounds and beauty of zemiros (Sabbath songs). Though the Germans had strived to kill Jewish life and culture, the embers of Judaism were rekindled in our orphanage.

Mr. & Mrs. John Moskowitz of Cincinnati were looking for a child to adopt, and when they were shown my picture from the orphanage I was the chosen one. Before I left Paris I was taken from the orphanage to the home of a French Catholic woman Eleanor Bohne-Hene. I was frightened but she and her two daughters eased my fears by offering friendship and candy. The next phase of "Operation America" was ready for execution. Mrs. Bohne-Hene applied for and obtained passports from the French government. Because America's quota system made it difficult to enter I was going as Monique Bohne, using her passport. My hair was bleached blonde to resemble hers.

When we finally arrived in Cincinnati Mrs. Bohne-Hene and I were met by an attractive couple who would become my parents, Libby and John Moscowitz. They were eager and thrilled to see me. But I had pangs of isolation when I realized that French was not spoken here. Everyone spoke a strange language, English, and I didn't understand a word.

Mrs. Bohne-Hene stayed with me for about a week to help me adjust to my new environment. I couldn't believe that I had a bedroom all to myself. At the orphanage I had shared a bedroom with fifteen other girls. Mrs. Bohne-Hene told me that I had a new mother and father who loved me dearly and would take good care of me. She advised me never to be afraid because my new parents would always be there for me. I cried for days when she finally left to return to France.

But soon I began to adjust to my new life in America. I met my new grandmother, who captured my heart when she sewed me a new dress. I was also blessed with dozens of aunts, uncles, and cousins. I went to Hebrew Day school and began to learn English.

But my past still haunted me and occasional nightmares disturbed my sleep. Would the Nazis ever leave me alone? One day when my parents took me downtown to an Armistices day parade I was terrified to see the soldiers and guns. I trembled with fear and started screaming. Were the Nazis after me and the other children? My parents understood and we left the parade.

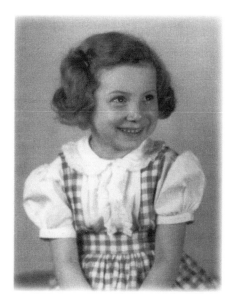

Before I became an American we had unfinished business to settle. Since I came to America illegally on Monique Bohne-Hene's passport the matter had to be resolved. My parents were working feverishly with lawyers, congressmen and immigration personnel to open the door for me. Finally after much time and bureaucracy an act of Congress was passed in Washington, DC enabling me to stay in America. It was a proud red white and blue day when, at the age of 10, I was the youngest to be sworn in as an American citizen.

I am deeply grateful to all who made it possible for me to come to America, especially my parents. My dad passed away in 1963 and my mom lives in a retirement home. But I have never forgotten my birth parents.

Today I am married over 40 years to my high school sweetheart, Stuart Rosenstein. We are the parents of two grown children, Johnny who works for CBS Sportsline.com in Ft. Lauderdale, and Shani, who works as U.S.Y. director for Tifereth Israel Synagogue in Columbus, OH. I am thankful every day for being blessed with wonderful family and friends.

In Washington, DC we spent an entire day at the Holocaust Museum searching for clues on my natural parents. We checked in one book after another for deportation dates from different towns, but we came up empty handed. I have so many questions that beg for answers.

How did I get separated from my natural parents? Did they entrust me to strangers to insure my survival? How did I wind up in the orphanage? Are there brothers and sisters, other relatives? What has happened to the other children from my orphanage? Where are Mrs. Bohne-Hene and her daughters today? Will these mysteries be solved?

After attending Washington University in St. Louis I graduated from Wright State in Dayton, Ohio. I have taught Sunday school, chaired programs, did publicity for community events, freelanced for area newspapers, written poetry, campaigned for causes and political candidates, led a Brownie troop, coached a soccer team, co-chaired a gift shop, was editor of my children's day school newspaper, and now I work for Chase Bank. None of these would be possible without coming to America. I was blessed with two sets of parents who loved (love) me and I shall remember them, because I must never forget.

***Current photo of
Cherie Rosenstein***

Corn Pudding

parve

This parve corn pudding recipe was one of Mother's favorite's and was enjoyed hundreds of times at family picnics, holiday barbecues, and dinners. I have shared this recipe with many relatives and friends; now they are making this recipe when I come for dinner.

1/4 cup sugar
1/2 cup flour
1 tsp salt
1/4 tsp pepper
8 eggs
1/2 stick unsalted margarine, melted
3 16 oz. cans cream-style yellow corn
1 11 oz. can of Mexicorn (corn with red & green peppers)-drained

Directions:
Preheat oven to 400 degrees

1.) Combine the first four ingredients in one bowl and mix well.
2.) Beat eggs until fluffy in a second bowl; add margarine and mix well.
3.) Add dry mixture to eggs and mix well.
4.) Add the cans of corn and mix well.
5.) Pour into greased 9x13 pan.
6.) Bake for 1 hour until golden brown.

Irving and Helena Zeidman
Argentina
Submitted by their son John Zeidman

Irving and his son

Irving and Helena lived in Poland. They were married with three children when the war broke out. Irving owned a wallet factory. One day he came back from work and the Nazis had taken his children. At this point he knew the situation had turned desperate, so he took his money and expensive jewelry and hid it in the woods. Helena was sent to work in a factory and Irving was sent to Auschwitz. There, he was put in a line with other Jews and shot. He fell back into the mass grave, along with everyone else, but he had been shot only in the leg. He played dead until nightfall and then climbed out, retrieved his hidden treasure from the woods, got his wife from the factory and fled to Argentina. They had a son and seven years later immigrated to America.

Beer Bread
parve

3 cups self rising flour
1 tbsp sugar
12 oz room temp. beer

Directions:
Preheat oven to 375 degrees

1.) Combine 3 cups of self rising flour with 1 tbsp sugar.
2.) Add 12 oz room temp. beer.
3.) Put it in a greased 8x4.5 pan.
4.) Bake at 375 degrees or 40 minutes, until brown.

* Slices best when bread is cold

Beer Soup
parve or dairy

5 cups beer
1 cup water
3 de-crusted slices of black bread
2 tbsp butter/margarine
1 tsp caraway seeds
1 tsp sugar
pinch of salt

Directions:
1.) In a pot, combine beer, water, black bread, margarine/butter and caraway seeds.
2.) Bring to boil, reduce heat and let simmer for 10 minutes.
3.) Force the mixture through a sieve and add 1 tsp sugar and salt to taste.

Samuel Burke
Mayfield Heights, OH, U.S.A.
As told to Joanne Caras

Sam as a child

Samuel was born Samuel Berkovits in the city of Chust, Czechoslovakia-Hungary. When he was fourteen he was sent to Auschwitz with his mother, father, two sisters, two aunts, his grandparents, his Rabbi, Chaskel Juni of Poland, who was hiding in his house because his family had already been deported, and was his private tutor, and also a neighbor. They were immediately separated into two lines, men and boys to the right, women and old people to the left.

As they stood in line they were told to look down and not to look back or whisper, to stand perfectly still or they would be shot. His mother, sisters, and aunts were being pushed forward as they marched by, in formation, so they would not have a chance to stop. But Samuel saw his mother walking by and he whispered to her "Anyu" (mother in Hungarian) and she said "Shmilu" (his name in Yiddish). Those were the last words they ever spoke to each other, and it was the last time Samuel ever saw his mother.

An older man showed Samuel the smoke from the gas chambers and told him that he would probably be kept alive because he was young so when he got out he must promise to tell the world what he saw there.

Before Samuel was arrested he had watched for hours and hours his neighbor studying and practicing to be a dentist. After he was sent to the camp he found out that they were looking for a dental assistant. Because he had learned so much he volunteered for the job, claiming that he had "studied" dentistry. Even at the young age of fourteen he was given the job.

So Samuel settled in to the dental office and helped the dentist take care of the teeth of the prisoners. But shortly after he got the job the dentist died and that left Samuel, at the age of 14 1/2, as the camp's only "dentist". One time he was visited by a German Air Force General who carried two swords and a professor, who said they wanted to visit "the little dentist." After talking to Samuel for an hour and a half the General allowed Samuel to keep his hair while the other Jews were forced to have a 1 ½ inch strip cut down the center of their heads to show that they were prisoners. He told Samuel "Keep your spirits up because the war will be over soon."

Because he was a "dentist" Samuel also had a little more freedom than other prisoners. He used that freedom to smuggle food out of the kitchen and give it to the old and sick, who were no longer being fed. This lasted a while but then Samuel was caught and beaten mercilessly with a shovel handle by an SS guard. The beating took place in front of the kids who peeled potatoes and the guard said "this is what will happen to you if you are caught taking a single potato!"

Just before the liberation a German Whermacht officer was ordered to evacuate the camp and to take all 5,000 of us to the Tyrol Mountains to be executed, but he promised that he would do everything he could to save the 5,000 prisoners. So he put them in a cattle car and ran them up and down the mountains until he ran out of coal. Then he waited for the Americans and saved all of those people from death.

174

After the war Samuel went back to Czechoslovakia and found his two sisters and aunt. He was privileged to meet General Eisenhower, who patted him on the head and shook his hand. In early November, 1945 Samuel was one of 150 children transported from the DP camp in Fuhrnwald, Bavaria, Germany to England. In 1971, he played for 200 young students the Moonlight Sonata where his young children, Kimberly and David attended elementary school. He received a standing ovation from those young wonderful students, teachers, friends, and his cousin Ruth Rosenberg, may she rest in peace.

Paprika Chicken "chicken paprikash"

Submitted by Marion Weinzweig

meat

2 chickens, cut in pieces
4 green peppers, sliced thin
6 large onions, sliced thin
1 tsp. each salt, pepper, garlic
1/4 cup chopped fresh parsley
3 tsp. paprika
28 oz. can chopped tomatoes
Oil

Sam and his sisters, Lili and Irene

Directions:
1.) Sauté onions in oil till lightly brown.
2.) Add green peppers till wilted.
3.) Season chicken pieces with salt, pepper, garlic and paprika, then add to onion mixture and brown chicken on both sides.
4.) Add tomatoes.
5.) Cover and cook slowly for 1 hr.
6.) Do not add water.
7.) At the end add parsley.

Sam in 2010
I used a similar foot-pedal dental-drill in Mühldorf Concentration Camp at the age of 14 in 1945.

Sam in 2007
On August 26, 2007, I performed the "Warshaw Piano Concerto" for 220 adults at temple Bnai Jeshurin, for Kol Israel second generation of Holocaust Survivors.

175

Edyta Klein-Smith
London, England

Edyta and her mother

On July 22, 1942 I was living in the Warsaw Ghetto when the "Final Solution" was declared. The deportations started immediately. At first 6,000 people per day, then 10,000. The first victims were patients in hospitals, orphanages, and old people. My paternal grandparents came to say goodbye. The deportations continued until mid-September and a total of 200,000 people were deported. My uncle Jozef was among those taken. When he was taken a Jewish policeman tried to pull him off of the cattle car but was unsuccessful.

We were always facing selection in rows of five. At one selection, standing in a row with my parents, I realized that we had no chance for three out of five to survive the selection. In a second I pushed my mother to the front and my step father to the back. Strangers automatically stepped into their spots to complete the row of five. We survived the selection. Did it hasten anybody's final moment? Who knows, but I do think about it.

One hot and sunny morning the Nazi director called everyone into the courtyard. He said that it was common knowledge that children were being hidden on the premises of my parents' workplace. He said the children "prevent parents from doing their best work and hamper the productivity needed for the Third Reich."

He said he had arranged for nurses to accompany the transport of the children to an open space for them to play and eat porridge. Thirty children came down the transport, including me. I was just about to join the group when a boy I knew stopped me and said "Come with me." He hid me in a safe place. That evening we realized that the children were not coming back." Parents were screaming and hitting their heads against the walls.

The worst day in my memory was September 6th. By that time at least half the population of the ghetto had disappeared. The rest of us were told to gather together in a couple of streets that had once been inhabited by the poor. One SS officer began beating people with a stick that had an iron ball at the end. My mother was hit in the head. That was catastrophic since sick or wounded people would never pass selection. In a panic I wrapped her head in a scarf and once again we survived selection. I estimate after that day that there were less than 100,000 left. About half the people were working, either in the factories or outside the ghetto. The rest were called "wilds" hiding wherever they could.

Amazingly, we were able to use bribes to get my mother and me out of the ghetto. The guards we bribed said they could not risk helping a man escape so only my mother and I got out. On November 4, 1943 all of the workers in our factory were taken to Poniatowa, where they were made to dig their own graves. They were all shot. One of the victims was my step father Stanislaw.

Mother and I watched from the outside as the Warsaw ghetto was burning. Part of us died with the others.

Cucumber Salad

parve

2 large cucumbers
1 tbsp sugar
1/4 cup white cider or vinegar
1 bunch fennel
Salt and pepper to taste

Directions:
1.) Take one husband to peel and slice the cucumbers very thin by hand. (No Jewish Princess should do this!)
2.) Cover bowl with saran wrap and put in refrigerator over night.
3.) The next morning the cucumbers will be very crisp.
4.) Add salt and pepper.
5.) Dissolve sugar in boiling water with white cider or vinegar.
6.) Cover with a bunch of finely chopped fennel.
7.) Leave in fridge until ready to serve (couple of hours).
8.) Drain.

Serve with fish, chicken, or meat.

Calf Brains

meat

Directions:
1.) Go to the Kosher Butcher.
2.) Cover brains in cold water with a couple of tablespoons of vinegar.
3.) Boil for 2-3 minutes. Drain.
4.) Carefully remove all veins (they will have turned dark).
5.) Mash with fork well. Mix with 1 sauted onion, 1 egg, 1/2 pinch fresh chopped parsley.
6.) Salt & pepper to taste.
7.) Mix well with 1/3 cup of bread crumbs or matzoh meal.
8.) Cut of the top of fresh rolls, scoop bread out of center, and fill them with the calf brain mixture.
9.) Put into oven at 350 degrees for 20-30 minutes.
10.) Serve with a wedge of lemon.

Add a martini and your party will be a success!

Sam Lauber
Dayton, OH, U.S.A.

Sam Lauber

By 1940 the Nazis occupied Belgium. Jewish families and their children were at risk of execution or deportation to concentration camps. Jews were stripped of all their basic rights and were forbidden to live or remain in their homes. They were also stripped of their Belgian citizenship. The Nazis required that all Jewish adults wear yellow stars with the word Juif (Jew) displayed on clothing for easy identification and Nazi determination.

Jewish children were prohibited from attending school, play outdoors, and associate with non-Jewish children. They were mocked by their teachers in school for being physically and psychologically different from "normal" Aryan children. Hence, Non-Jewish children would mock the Jewish children and pick fights with them as desired.

Terrified Jewish parents were faced with a dilemma. How can I/we save our children? Knowing that they were at risk their number one thought was to make whatever arrangements necessary, at whatever cost, to keep their children safe and alive.

Although there were no records kept, it is estimated that approximately 100,000 Jewish children were hidden during the holocaust in various European countries. That was my fate. I was born in Antwerp, Belgium in 1942 and can only recall that I lived with my parents at #10 Rue Gustav Fils in Brussels.

I only knew and spoke French as a child even though I was born in Antwerp where the local inhabitants spoke Flemish (similar to Dutch). Through arrangements with the Belgian Mother Superior and the church I was placed in a private home in Lalouviere, near Mons, Belgium. I was then escorted by my sister to the new family, The Detrys in Lalouviere, Belgium. This city was predominantly not Jewish and so it was relatively safe to stay. The Detrys never discussed me with the local inhabitants except for a physician whom they knew well.

My parents were extremely frantic, if not frightened considering what the future would bring for them and for me. In their minds were thoughts such as "Will we ever see our son again?" "Will he be safe?" "How long will he be gone?" "Will he have to convert to Christianity and attend church services?" They cried.

Although I was three when I left my parents and delivered by my sister to Lalouviere my thoughts were, "Why am I going to Lalouviere and the Detrys?" "Am I being punished?" "Did I do something wrong?" "Will I ever see my parents again?" "Who are these people that I will be staying with?" "I don't want to go!" I cried.

Sam Lauber

178

The Detrys had a son by the name of Jean Marie who was my age. We soon bonded and became brothers. I now had a step-brother who cared for me. We were inseparable although my mind was constantly preoccupied about returning home to Brussels, I cried a lot. I missed my parents terribly and I wanted to go home right away. Since I was so young I did not know or understand that I was Jewish or came from a Jewish family. I went along with the Detry family and was given a non-Jewish name, "Dede," their son. Lalouviere was strictly a gentile city and an industrial city. Had the local inhabitants been informed that I was Jewish I would have been at risk for deportation. Nine months later my sister picked me up and brought me back to my parents in Brussels.

How did my parents survive in Brussels? How did they eat? How did they escape from the Nazis? Were there any close calls? My parents never discussed the war, my separation from them, or what they did to survive the war.

All I knew was that after six years in Belgium, in 1948 my parents were discussing immigrating to the United States. They knew they could not remain in Belgium, having lost most of their personal goods and the feeling of being targeted as Jews. To them, the United States was a land of opportunity and religious freedom to grow and learn, and good schools, if not for them, for me.

In 1948 we sailed on the Queen Elizabeth I from Cherbourg, France to New York. On board were many refugees stemming from numerous parts of Europe all with the intent of starting a new life in America.

During the voyage my father took me to the ship's makeshift synagogue for Shabbat services. We ate in a designated lounge earmarked for refugees and viewed movies daily. My parents were both seasick and suffered the entire trip until we reached New York. Once we saw the Statue of Liberty we all had a bird's eye view of New York City and one could hear a huge cheer from all of the passengers. Seeing the Statue of Liberty, was like a symbol of a new life and prosperity.

On 12 April 1948 at approximately 11 p.m. we entered Manhattan harbor and disembarked at Ellis Island. Ellis Island was created to process new aliens and conduct medical exams to ensure that no serious diseases were brought into the States.

Like all the refugees of Western Europe my parents left most of their personal belongings as a result of the war, so starting a new life in a strange land was a challenge even though there were many Jewish inhabitants in New York City. My parents were already middle aged when we arrived in the United States and were prepared to make do with the few personal belongings that we had and make a fresh start.

All new arrivals to the United States were identified, examined and processed for settlement with an identifiable family sponsor. Those found with communicable diseases were detained for a week to see whether the ailment would dissipate or risk being shipped back to Europe.

The Hebrew Immigrant Aid Society (HIAS) was the Jewish organization at Ellis Island that processed incoming refugees at Ellis Island. People around me spoke a babble of different languages that was different from what I understood and difficult to comprehend. Although my parents were fluent in Polish, they also spoke Yiddish and French so they were able to communicate with the authorities in both languages who spoke these languages. After my parents finished the in-processing we were admitted into New York where we all settled in an apartment in mid-Manhattan on 100th Street between Amsterdam and Columbus Avenue. My parents felt that the United States had a lot to offer.

Since my parents had no money, my father had applied for financial assistance and employment through HIAS social service. He was called for an interview where the case manager assisted in securing some financial assistance and employment in areas where there were Jewish merchants

Since my mother could not secure employment, she opened up an artificial flowers shop down the block from our house on 100th Street. She later relocated and opened a shop near Gimbel's in Herald Square on 34th Street. Her skill was in designing artificial flowers for formal gowns. Because of her skill and hard work she was able to gain two prestigious clients, Saks 5th Avenue and Lord and Taylors 5th Avenue.

After we settled my father's next task was to enroll me into a Yeshiva, Manhattan Day Elementary School located on 102nd Street, one block west of Central Park. In the Yeshiva I studied Hebrew, Bible and the Ethics of Our Forefathers, Monday through Friday, and on Sabbath with my father.

I soon rebelled and transferred to a nearby public school, P.S. 52 Manhattan, and left the Yeshiva. My father and I still went religiously to Shabbat (Sabbath) services at Ohab Zedek on 95th between Amsterdam and Columbus Avenue.

In 1957 my mother passed away when I was 15 years old. In 1960 my father passed away after I graduated high school and I was 18 years old.

In 1969 I met my wife, Ellen at Hillel, a Jewish social club at the University of Buffalo where I attended undergraduate studies. On August 23, 1970 Ellen and I were married in Buffalo. In January 1973 I was accepted to the University of Michigan in Ann Arbor for graduate work in Social Work.

For years I wondered how I could get in touch with Jean Marie, my brother whom I stayed with during the war. In July 1975 I decided to write a personal letter to the Mayor of Lalouviere and see whether he could locate the Detry family. To my astonishment he passed it on to the Belgian Veterans Administration in Lalouviere who found the Detry family. I received a nice package from the Veteran's Administration and a beautiful letter from Aunt Nelly, Madame Detry's sister.

In 1989 while I worked for the US Army in The Netherlands as a civil servant I frequently thought about making contact and visiting the Detrys. One time during the High Holy days my family and I attended services at SHAPE (Strategic Headquarters Allied Personnel Europe) outside of Mons, Belgium. It might have been a coincidence or maybe fate that on our way to SHAPE on the expressway we always passed Lalouviere. One Friday I said to my wife that we need to stop in Lalouviere to see whether we could locate the Detrys. I phoned the Detrys and Aunt Nelly answered the phone. She said, 'Dede, cest vous?" Is that you Dede. I was stunned and thrilled to see Jean Marie. We spent three delightful days sharing stories and pictures of the past. I have kept in touch with him by mail to this very day.

Jean Marie informed me that the U.S. Army liberated Lalouviere on September 5, He informed me that I was never baptized because my parents had asked the Detry's not to have me baptized, although I attended church services with them.

Today my wife and I reside in Dayton, Ohio. I am currently working at Wright-Patterson Air Force Base Medical Center, department of Mental Health as a social worker.

Chalah a la Ellen (Ellen Lauber)

parve

4 cups of flour
3 eggs
1 cup of warm water
1 tablespoon of vegetable oil
2 tablespoons of sugar
Pinch of salt
1 3/4 yeast

Directions:

Bread machine

In order: Place water, oil, 2 eggs, flour, salt, yeast and sugar into machine and put on dough cycle. When dough cycle ends remove dough from machine. Knead the dough and braid it. Crack egg and brush it with the egg mixture. Place in a pre-heated 400 degree oven for 10 minutes.
Lower the oven temperature to 350 degrees for 20 minutes.

If making the challah by hand

- Put all the ingredients cited above in a large bowl and mix together.
- Turn on to a flour board and knead for 10 minutes.
- Return the dough in an oil bowl.
- Cover with a warm clean damp cloth and place into A warm oven for 40 minutes.
- Take the dough out and place in a flour board. Knead the dough slightly.
- Cut into three strips.
- Braid the three strips.
- Brush with the egg mixture and place in a pre-heated 400 degree oven for ten minutes.
- Lower oven temperature to 350 degree for 20 minutes.

Chalah will be done when you hear a hollow sound when tapping the chalah.

David Zauder

Pine, CO, U.S.A.
Submitted by his daughter Karen Z. Brass,
Holocaust Speaker and Educator
www.standupsters.com

David Zauder and his granddaughter, Shannah Rose Brass

My father, David Zauder, was born in Krakow, Poland in 1928 or 1931. He remembers being almost 10 years old when Hitler's Army invaded Poland, while he and his brother Soloman, and some friends watched them cross the bridge into his city, being welcomed with flowers by the Mayor of Krakow. There was great social unrest in his city, and great amounts of Anti-Semitism was felt by my father and all Jews daily. He couldn't cross the street without being attacked by the neighborhood bullies. He chose to not stay angry, because he knew it wasn't personal. How could it have been personal? He had a head full of white-blonde hair and blue grey eyes. This is what the Nazi called Aryan-looking; the perfect human race. Hitler's ultimate goal was to rid the world of all other people. The bullies knew that his family was Jewish- and that was all it took.

My father, who was 10 years old, and his family; his mother, Rose Lucks Zauder, and his father, Karl Zauder, both around 40 years old, grandmother, wheelchair bound and in her 70's and older brother, Soloman, who was 18 years old, were kicked out of their home in Krakow, Poland and taken to live in the Krakow Ghetto in the Spring of 1940. They killed his grandmother by pushing her down the stairs that day. His neighbors witnessed this and did nothing.

My father's father, Karl Zauder was an upstanding citizen in their community, a tailor and drummer in the local theater. He had fought in WWI, for the Austrian Army, then the Polish Army and then the Russian Army. After each battle, the captured soldiers were given new uniforms and told to fight for the opposition.

While living in the Krakow Ghetto, the Nazi's selected my Grandfather Karl to be in charge of the other Jews as the Fire Marshall, as well as in Plaszow Work Camp. He wore the hat with the yellow star of responsibility. My father, now 11 years old worked with his mother, Rose Zauder, making horse brushes. His brother, Solomon, now 19 years old, who was a violinist and learned to be an electrician, and worked putting up lights around the Work Camp, which saved his life. They stayed here from 1940 through 1943. My Grandfather was shot in the head by a Nazi who didn't look to discover first that he had his Fire Marshall hat on. His father's last words to him were, "You will live. You will work hard so that you survive, to go to America where you will be free and bear witness to this human atrocity which should never have been allowed to happen, and you will contribute something to the world." Grandfather Karl died two weeks later.

Karl Zauder, Fire Marshall

It took Uncle Soloman, now 20 years old and my father, now 12 years old, 2 nights digging a grave in a field to get Grandfather Karl into a grave. One day later, after the grave was finished and they had buried Grandfather, the Nazi's bulldozed the field, dug up the entire area and leveled it to build more of the buildings for the prisoners coming in to the work camp. While still in Plaszow, the Nazi's killed his mother in 1943, along with many other mothers with children. My Grandmother Rose saved his life by pushing him into another line. He was taken to Auschwitz by cattle car alone.

From April 1943 to November 1944 my father worked in Auschwitz. He hauled chopped wood for the crematorium and moved rocks; whatever they told him to do he did, 15-18 hours per day.

He drank water that had been seasoned with one potato as soup once a week, had a few pieces of bread, some of which were given to him by those who witnessed his high work ethic and relentless struggle to survive. Sometimes he'd get lucky enough to get a raw potato. To this day, his favorite soup is potato soup! As a survival technique he learned to speak 5 languages to communicate with everyone he was surrounded by, Polish, German, Yiddish, Russian and Czechoslovakian.

His life was saved again when his tattooed number on his inner arm was called, but since he was so young when they first put the tattoo on him, the last digit was an 8 but it had rubbed off from his hard labor and now resembled a 3. He did not move out of the line when they called his number and he lived.

In November, 1944, the Russian Army was closing in, so in bitter cold, the Nazi's moved out the prisoners they felt were still alive enough to make the journey and began the Death March. My father was 14 years old, wore wooden shoes, and only had the striped prison uniform on to protect him from the cold. In the snow they marched across Poland, Czechoslovakia, and headed into Germany. For 6 months, he had no clothes, no food and no rest. They walked at night to avoid being shot at and slept by day in the woods.

My father had not lost hope throughout his Holocaust experience. After one month of the march, he fell to his knees on a very snowy night and could not get up. He thought he was finished. He was frightened and alone. He looked up at the diminishing crowd passing him by and hoped a Nazi would not see him; for certain he would be shot and killed. He saw a man coming towards him wearing a blanket around his shoulders and my father reached out to him and asked in Polish, "Please help me, I cannot die here." The man bent down and lifted my father up and their eyes met. The man was his brother, Solomon. My Uncle Solomon saved my father's life, as he carried him the rest of the way into Germany.

Those who survived the death march were rescued by the sounds of General George P. Patton's 2nd Army, Tank Division. The Nazi's heard the tanks and made the prisoners drop in the snow in a line, execution style. They did not want to be caught with live prisoners. The Nazi soldiers fled as the roar of the tanks got louder. The prisoners got braver and finally one looked up and saw they had been abandoned. They cheered the tanks as they approached! My father and his brother joined the U.S. soldiers and rode the tanks, feeding the machine guns and helping to destroy other pill boxes of Nazi soldiers. Afterwards, they ran to a farm nearby and ate everything they could get their hands on, eggs, cheese, and milk. They fell terribly ill and had to be nursed by the farm owners, they hadn't eaten anything real in years. Then he and his brother rode a wagon into Frankfort, Germany and were nursed back to full health at the Displaced Persons camp.

My father then worked for the 7th Army who gave him room and board and there he learned to shine shoes, mop floors and cut hair while learning a little English. He was 15 years old. One day a couple of the U.S. soldiers dragged two young German boys off the street to give my father a way to get even with the Germans. They figured my father would want or need to take revenge. He looked at the two boys on the ground and saw the fear in their eyes. One boy was so distraught over having been brought there he wet himself and lost control completely-sobbing. My father pulled him to his feet and sent him out the door, saying, "Go home." After all he had been through he knew those boys had not caused his pain and horrible losses. My father has always said an eye for an eye only begets two blind people.

Rose, Soloman and David Zauder

My father arrived in The United States on May 20th, 1946 as a 15 year old boy, alone. He joined his cousins, Lil and Harry Markle. They had offered Uncle Solomon to live with them, too. My father lived with them, and helped his family in the milk delivery business. Even though he was safe in America he still slept with a deer knife under his pillow for protection.

Because my father was a very good musician, and he got suspended from school again for beating up the bullies, it was arranged for him by his Trumpet teacher, Leonard B. Smith, to be sent to the New York Military Academy on Full Scholarship for his Trumpet playing. My father Graduated #3 in his class of 80 student cadets and held a 92% grade point average at NYMA. He enlisted at the 1802nd Special Regimen Regular US Army stationed at West Point. He would have gone to Korea, willingly, but the Army chose to have him play in The West Point Band, serving in the USA. It had been 5 years since he came to America, so he could finally earn his Naturalization Papers now. He was a Sergeant 1st class when he got his United States Citizenship in 1952.

He was a freelance musician until 1957, often playing first trumpet for the Boston Pops conducted by Arthur Fiedler. In 1958 he joined the Cleveland Orchestra as first cornet and second trumpet. He continues to be a resource and mentor at The Cleveland Institute of Music where he served as a Master Teacher for years. He still plays the trumpet now even though he is 75 or 78 years old. He enjoys his golf, his friends and his grandchildren.

Momma Rose Lucks - Zauder's
Potato Soup
parve

3 large sweet onions
6 large potatoes
4 cloves of crushed garlic
oil
salt and pepper
1 cup of flour
rye seeds

Directions:

1.) Brown flour in dry skillet.
2.) Add to boiling potatoes in 1 quart of water.
3.) Fry onions and oil with garlic and seasonings.
4.) Add together and enjoy!

Erika Weibel Kuss
Frankford, DE, U.S.A.
Submitted by her daughter Marie McIntosh

Erika Kuss

My mother was born in Prussia in 1926. At the time Prussia was part of Germany. When the Nazi movement took hold in Germany my grandmother decided that it would be safer if they denied their Judaism. While this was confusing to my mother at the time, she had little choice. So the entire family pretended not to be Jewish. While they thought this denial would protect them, it did not.

When the Russians invaded that part of Germany the family was taken to a Russian concentration camp. My mother was 17 at the time. While a prisoner she was physically abused by the soldiers. After ten months she escaped from the camp and walked across the icy terrain with her feet wrapped in rags.

She met my father and married him in 1946. In 1960 she brought my brother and me to the United States and she worked day and night to support us, even working extra jobs so my brother and I could take music and riding lessons. She always instilled in us a love for reading, and we would go as often as possible to the public library to take out books.

Chicken Paprikasch
meat

1   8 ounce package egg noodles (parve)
Olive oil
1 pound boned skinned chicken breasts
   - chopped
8 ounces fresh mushrooms, quartered
1/2 teaspoon pepper
1/2 teaspoon salt
1/4 cup chicken broth
1 cup parve sour cream substitute
1 tablespoon paprika

Directions:
- Cook noodles according to package directions, drain and noodles.
- Transfer to covered serving dish.
- Coat a skillet with olive oil and place over medium- high heat, add chicken, and next 3 ingredients.
- Cook 5 minutes or until chicken is done.
- Remove from heat and stir in sour cream substitute and paprika.
- Spoon over noodles.
- Sprinkle with additional paprika.

185

William H. Donat
Purchase, NY, U.S.A.

Food was scarce in the Warsaw Ghetto in 1943. While my father and the other printers were marched to work under armed guard to the German printing plant outside the Ghetto, I would spend the day with my mother at the Ghetto's last pharmacy. I was only five years old and I could easily find distractions in the many nooks in the basement of the store.

Occasionally, my parents and the other people living in the building at 44 Muranowska Street were able to gather the ingredients to make a cholent. The ladies would wash and prepare the elements and send the pot down to the bakery that was located in the building where it baked overnight. When finally it was ready the next day we would all have a good meal.

Later that year it became clear to my parents that the Ghetto would soon be liquidated. Women with young children would be sent directly to the gas chambers of Treblinka. Because my father worked outside the Ghetto, he had an opportunity to contact some of his Christian friends to ask if any of them would take his five-year-old son. After trying many prospects, he finally found an older couple who were willing to take me.

There was little time. My mother prepared me by teaching me the prayers a Christian child would know from the moment he could speak. She told me to remember that I was never in the Ghetto and that my father was a Polish officer who was a P.O.W. and my mother was sick in the country. But there were so many things she didn't have time to mention.

Several weeks later, when I had been smuggled out of the Ghetto by my father pushing me in the handcart used for transporting paper to the printing plant, my new aunty Maria prepared an especially good dinner for me. She then asked me if I had liked it. "Oh yes, auntie, it was delicious, almost as good as cholent." On hearing that, she blanched. She scolded me never to say that word again because it was a word that could betray me to our neighbors, and could cause us trouble.

I never used that word again, but I was betrayed to the police anyway and had to spend the remaining two years of the war in an orphanage in the small town of Otwock, near Warsaw.

For more details of my family's wartime survival, see my father's memoirs –
Alexander Donat: THE HOLOCAUST KINGDOM, most recently published by the USHMM

William H. Donat

Cholent

meat

from the Engagement Cookbook
by Debbie Elstein

2 onions, sliced
1/2 cup kidney beans
1/2 cup white lima beans
1 cup pearl barley or wheat
1 piece flanken
3-5 potatoes, peeled and cut into large bite size pieces
1 onion chopped

Directions:

1.) Add to large pot in the order listed and completely cover the surface with heavy sprinkling of sweet paprika.
2.) Optional: add 1-2 tsp salt and 1 tsp pepper.
3.) Add water to completely cover.
4.) Bring to boil then reduce heat to simmer.
5.) Stir occasionally.

Ira Segalewitz

aka Israel Segalewitz

Dayton, OH, U.S.A.

I was born in Sarny, Poland in 1936. Shortly before World War II started, Germany and the USSR signed a non-aggression pact that would cede the Eastern part of Poland to the USSR as reward for not interfering with the Germany's Blitz krieg on Poland.

From September 1939, the start of WWII to June of 1941 my family continued to live under fairly benevolent Russian occupation. My father, originally from Pinsk , a barber was drafted in to the Russian Army and served locally.

When Nazis began their attack on Russia in June of 1941, my father was able to get my mother and me on a cattle train that was headed East, away from the bombs and the advancing German army. Shortly after the train left the station, German airplanes strafed our train killing and wounding many people. This scene was repeated a number of times for the rest of the day. That was the first leg of many that eventually resulted in our escape deep into the Ural Mountains, to a work camp called Raivka in the Bashkir USSR.

For over 4 years my mother toiled grueling hours under most horrific conditions manufacturing ammunition for the war effort. We lived in an unheated barrack without sanitary facilities and shared a 9' by 9' area with another family of 3. Food rations were barely enough to survive on. Hunger, cold and lice were our constant companions. As the only Jewish kid in the area I was called all types of anti-Semitic epithets, beaten up often and mistreated constantly.

After the war, my mother and I returned to a devastated Sarny. Our house was a pile of rubble and we could not find any of our relatives or their dwelling places. We soon learned that immediately after the Nazis occupied Sarny they established a Ghetto. In August of 1942 they murdered most of the 14,000 Jews in the Ghetto, including almost all of my mother's family. They slaughtered my grandmother and six of my mother's siblings as well as scores of cousins and other relatives. We also learned that my father was killed in the battle for Stalingrad. The only spark of hope that kept my mother from going insane during that bleak time was the knowledge that two of her oldest sisters immigrated to the US 10 years before the war.

She did not know where they were but she was determined to find them. We then joined a group of people that were headed for Palestine. After months of walking and occasional rides we arrived in a Displaced Persons (DP) Camp in Hallein by Salzburg, Austria. There we waited for transportation to Israel.

With the help of the HIAS we located my aunts in the US. They soon sent us a visa for the US. But due to US immigration quotas we waited five (5) more years in the DP camp for our turn to sail to America. In 1948 while in the Camp, my mother married Aron Turetsky. Aron survived the war as a partisan fighting in the forests but he too lost all his family.

The 3 of us arrived in NY, AMERICA on the S.S. Stewart in August 1951, I was 15 and half years old.

Today I have four sons and six grandchildren.

Me (Ira Segalewitz) with my mother Rochel and step father Aron Turetsky. This pix was taken in Hallein, Salzburg DP camp in March 1948

188

Taiglach

A fruit & nut collection for Rosh Hashanah

parve

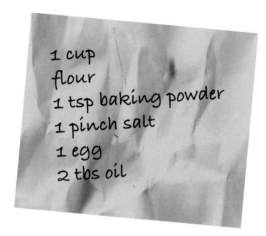

1 cup
flour
1 tsp baking powder
1 pinch salt
1 egg
2 tbs oil

Directions:

Preheat oven to 350 degrees

1.) Should be like a very flaky pie crust.
2.) Combine all ingredients, knead a few min until it holds together.
3.) Break off small amounts, shape into balls, drop on greased cookie sheet.
4.) Bake 350 about 20 min or until light brown.

While mondlelin is baking combine:

    1/2 lb honey (about 1 cup)
    1/4 cup brown sugar
    1/2 tsp ginger
    1/4 tsp nutmeg

1.) Cook about 15 min, add cooked mondlelin, then cook another 5 min.
2.) Add about 1 cup mixed nuts and about 1 cup candied fruit
    (cherries, pineapple, etc.).
3.) Make sure everything is coated very well.

Divide into 2-3 small bowls.

Otto Loewi
Ulrich, Anna, and Ruth Weiss
Portland, OR, U.S.A.
Submitted by Ruth Weiss Bolliger

Wedding photo of Ulrich and Anna Weiss

I was born in Usti nad Labem in Czechoslovakia. My mother was Anna Loewi Weiss and my father was Ulrich Weiss. They had two daughters, me and my sister, Margaret, born in N.Y. in 1945.

My grandfather, Otto Loewi, won the Nobel Prize in Medicine in 1936. Because of that, he and two of his sons were rounded up and imprisoned on the very night of the Austrian Anschluss, one week before I was born. He was forced to buy all three lives with the Nobel Prize money. Because of the Nobel Prize he had made connections which ultimately ensured his survival and indirectly allowed him to help us survive.

Ours was an odyssey of fleeing and hiding and fleeing and hiding across most of Western Europe, into England, and back to the continent. This continued from the time of my birth in March, 1938 until we could finally leave from Marseilles when I was a little over three years old. Although I had the amazing good fortune to survive with both of my parents, I have lived all my life knowing that I survived because of them, that even though I kept on breathing and did not die, and was always excruciatingly obedient, I didn't survive by any wits, intelligence, or skills of my own. My parents and grandparents were the survivors; I still occasionally question whether I was/am.

Today I live in Portland, Oregon. I have three daughters and two grandchildren.

Ruth Weiss Bolliger

Otto Loewi and Guida Goldschmiedt Loewi

Zwetschenkuchen

(this was my grandfather's all-time favorite dessert)

dairy

about 5 lbs. (or more) Italian prune type plums

4 eggs
3 eggs- weight of sugar
2 eggs- weight of flour
1 egg- weight of butter, melted

Directions:
Preheat oven to 350 degrees

1.) Wash, halve, and de-pit the plums.
2.) Separate the eggs.
3.) Whip the whites to a stiff snow, and refrigerate them.
4.) Cream the egg yolks and sugar. Blend in the flour.
5.) Gently fold in the snow.
6.) Spoon or pour the mixture into a well greased Pyrex baking dish.
8.) Pour in the butter and mix in carefully.
9.) Be sure that the dough entirely covers the bottom of the baking dish.
10.) Bake at 350 degrees for 5 minutes.

Remove from the oven.

Stand the plum halves in the dough on their edges, densely enough that they keep each other from falling over. It's fine if they are actually touching. I put them in 3 or 4 dense rows. Bake for another 45-60 minutes until the dough (which has risen around and between the plums) is nicely browned and/or a small knife or skewer pierced into the dough, not a plum, comes out clean.

191

Gizela Solomon Farkas
Silver Spring, MD, U.S.A.
Submitted by her daughter Sheva Farkas

Chaya (lying across) Laya & Gizela

My mother, Gizela Solomon Farkas, was in Auschwitz for a year along with her youngest sister. As a child growing up she told many stories of her life before and after the camps. She met and married my father, Jacob Farkas, in Czechoslovakia after the war, and immigrated with him and my brother in 1948. I was the only American born in my father's family. Both my mom and dad have passed away, but whenever I want to conjure up a memory, I make either her chicken soup, which I'm sure you have many recipes for, or Lokshen mit case (noodles with cheese). My husband and children also like it:

My mother was born and grew up in Drahova, Czechoslovakia, which is now part of the Ukraine. She was the middle child of seven. Two older children (Max and Suri) were born in the United States, and returned before the war to the US. Ironically, my mother's parents did meet in the U.S., married, and returned to Europe after two children. The additional five included Laya (who was in Russia during the war, tried to get to the US after the war, but ended up in Sao Paulo Brazil for the rest of her life), Toby (who hid in Budapest and stayed there after the war until her death last year); Fishel (who died in Auschwitz) and Chaya, who was with my mom, Gitta.

Auschwitz was spoken of often in our house. My mother and her sister survived by working outside the camp, using cement bags for warmth while constructing an airport. My mother lost her mother Sheva, and brother Fishel in the camps. The rest survived to adulthood. Now, only Chaya is alive in Montreal. There were nine children, eight of whom survive, along with eight grandchildren.

My father's family was not as "lucky" during the war. My father, Jack Farkas was in a camp in Siberia. His parents, two sisters and their families, and one brother and his family all died in the camps. Four brothers survived, all came to the US (two via Israel) and only the youngest, Yidel, survives today in New Jersey. The four brothers did have six children and eleven grand children.

Lokshen mit case
(noodles with cheese)

dairy

1 pint sour cream
2 Tbsp butter room temperature
1 lb cottage cheese (I use Breakstones)
salt and pepper
12 oz. bag of wide egg noodles, cooked.

Directions:

Preheat oven to 350 degrees

1.) Mix together the "sauce" ingredients.
2.) Add the noodles, still hot from being cooked.
3.) Put into a greased baking dish and heat, covered at 350 for twenty minutes.

**My mom and three (of four) aunts surviving.
It was taken in 1960, at the first reunion
of the sisters.**

Laya Wojcer
San Paulo, Brazil
Submitted by her niece Sheva Farkas

Laya was the second oldest of my mother's sisters. While the oldest two siblings, Max and Shirley, were able to get to America before the war, Laya was stuck in Russia for most of the conflict. During that time, she survived by scavenging and finding work when she could. She had a hard time in Russia, not knowing what happened to the family and assuming the worst. When my mother, Gizela, and her sister Chaya, escaped from the camps, they went in search of the two sisters they hoped were alive--- Toby in Budapest and Laya in Russia. First, they found Toby, who had assumed all her family was dead. The two sisters walked up to the door in Budapest, and Toby, by then pregnant with my cousin Laszlo, looked at them and fainted. They later found Laya in a refugee camp.

My mother met and married my father, Jacob Farkas, and Chaya married Sam Zelikovic. Both had children born in Czechoslovakia. Laya married Avram Wojcer. My parents and brother got to leave for America on visas from her oldest sister's family. Chaya and her family went with Laya and Avram to Palestine, now Israel. They hoped for visas to the United States, but at the time such visas were difficult, if not impossible to get. Through my Uncle Sam's family, Chaya and Sam made it to Montreal, where they live today. Laya and Avram had no such luck. They decided to take their chances and went to Sao Paulo Brazil in the hope that they could get visas to the US or Canada from there. Avram became a peddler, a quite successful one in Sao Paulo, bringing items and allowing credit among the Brazilians in Sao Paulo's poorest neighborhoods. They settled into a good life in Brazil, in a Jewish community that was formed after the war. They lived and died in Sao Paulo, never getting the visas they needed to come to the US. However, they did come to visit a number of times, and even when they could have come, they realized that their lives were now in Brazil. They had no children. Laya was a spectacular cook, making wonderful Jewish meals for all of us when she and Avram visited. Her specialty was cholent, a dish known in Brazil as feijoada.

Laya (with my brother Harry). My mom,
Gizela, and Chaya (with her daughter Hanna)
taken in 1948 before they left for Europe.

Cholent

meat

2 pound beef short ribs
1 piece of smoked turkey
1 pound of barley
1 pound of pinto beans
1 medium onion chopped
2 cloves garlic, pressed
1 teaspoon of paprika
salt and pepper to taste.

Directions:
Preheat oven to 300 degrees

1.) Put all the ingredients in a heavy dutch oven.
2.) Add water to cover by about 2 inches.
3.) Bake in a 300 degree oven for 3-4 hours until the beans
are soft and the beef falls off the bone. Add water if it
seems to be dry.

Lee Weinberg
Linden, N.J., U.S.A.

1946

I was born in Chrzanow, Poland on August 1, 1925. I was working in the ghetto until February 19, 1943 when the Germans liquidated the Jews from Chrzanow I was sent to the camp Klettendorf and Ludwigsdorff. We were liberated May 8, 1945 by the Russian army.

How did I survive the Holocaust? It is very hard to say. I think it was faith- Besheret.

I came to the United States in 1949.

My two sons, Norman and Steven Weinberg

Meat Loaf
meat

1 pound beef
1 pound ground chicken or turkey
1 small onion
1/2 cup bread crumbs
1-2 eggs
1 tsp. salt
1-2 tsp. fresh garlic
Pinch of pepper

Directions:
Preheat oven to 350 degrees
1.) Mix the ingredients with the meat well.
2.) Form into loaf and place in baking pan.
3.) Bake at 350 F for 60 minutes.

Harry Toporek
Chicago, IL, U.S.A.
Submitted by his daughter Esther Toporek Finder

Harry Toporek

I am Auschwitz #145183. I was born April 20, 1923. April 20 was also Hitler's birthday and that was important later. We were poor tanners. There were 8 children in a 2-room apartment. I was 16 when Germany invaded Poland. I fled with my oldest brother to Soviet territory. We got separated and, being a homesick teen, I returned to my parents. When I got back I realized I made a mistake that could cost me my life. I was in 12 concentration camps, including Auschwitz.

April 20, 1942, the lagerfuhrer asked if anyone had a birthday that day. I knew he wasn't going to bake me a cake so I kept my mouth shut. Other Jews were selected and hung as a birthday present to Hitler.

While working in a coalmine sub camp of Auschwitz, my brother Sam became ill. He was taken out of the infirmary and was about to be sent back to Birkenau to be killed. I had been doing extra work for the lagerfuhrer turning rabbit skins into useable leather.

When I saw my brother was about to be sent away, I asked the lagerfuhrer to let me keep my brother. He said no. I then asked if I could go with him. We all knew where Sam was going. The lagerfuhrer told me to go with my brother but at the last minute he pulled us both off the transport.

When the Auschwitz camps were liquidated we were marched out. There was a Hungarian teenager with us. After a few days he said he could not walk anymore. He begged me to hide him so I hid him under some straw in an outhouse by a farm where we had stopped. He was not discovered when we left and I hope he survived. During the Death March we stopped in Blechhammer and the guards fled. I went to the kitchen looking for food. Then I heard shooting. I hid in the large kettle that had been used to make coffee for the prisoners. Everyone else in the kitchen was killed.

My brother Sam became ill during the march and was put in an infirmary in Buchenwald. I spent whatever time I could with him and one day the doctor gave me a Red Cross armband and made me his aid. When he got transported out, I became the camp doctor. I later got transported out and that is how I got separated from my brother. Four of my brothers, including Sam, survived.

April 20, 1945. I was a prisoner outside Berlin and I saw the "birthday gift" the Soviet troops were delivering to Hitler.

My last night as a prisoner: I dreamt my mother told me to flee. There was one other prisoner with me who spoke my language and we decided to run. We got away and found Russians troops who gave us food. I got sick right away and could not eat. The other man ate too much and died. At daylight I showed the Russians where I was held prisoner. The others had been killed. I was the sole survivor.

Sweet & Sour Meatballs

meat

Meatballs:

1 - 1.5 lbs. of ground beef
1 egg
1 tablespoon of onion flakes
salt (to taste)
1/2 cup of water
2 tablespoons of bread crumbs

Directions:

Sauce

1 bottle of chili sauce
1 jar of grape jelly
3/4 bottle of water [use the empty chili sauce bottle]

Bring these to boil.

Make small meatballs and cook in the sauce ~90 minutes on low flame.

Faye Rothstein Toporek
Chicago, IL, U.S.A.
Submitted by her daughter Esther Toporek Finder

Faye Rothstein Toporek was born in Lask, Poland and spent years in the Lodz Ghetto until it was liquidated and she was sent to Birkenau. She survived with a brother and a sister but passed away in 1970 at the age of 47.

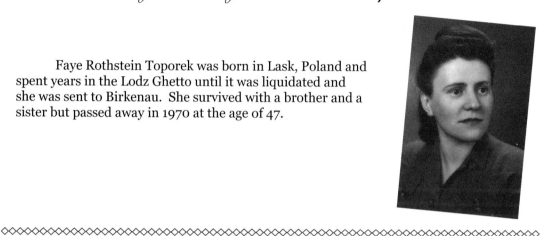

Cottage cheese salad
dairy

sour cream
- to your own taste but as least enough
  to bind with the cottage cheese
finely diced onions
salt and pepper
12 oz. cottage cheese

Mix all ingredients together well.

It is delicious with challah and butter.

Barbara Mekel Toporek

Rockville, MD, U.S.A.

Submitted by her step-daughter Esther Toporek Finder

Barbara Mekel Toporek, originally from Vilna, was sent to Siberia with her whole family during the Soviet occupation. As a young child she remembers having to be roped together with other children so she wouldn't get lost in the snow outside. Her immediate family survived in Siberia.

Matzo Stuffing

meat

1/2 cup oil
3/4 cup minced onion
10 unsalted matzot finely broken
1 tsp. salt
1/4 tsp. white pepper
1 tsp. paprika
2 eggs
1 can clear chicken broth
1/2 can of water

Directions:

1.) Sauté onions until golden.
2.) Bring soup & water to a boil in a large pot.
3.) Combine ingredients.

Stuff right before cooking the bird.

200

Barbara Schechter Cohen

Bloomfield, MI, U.S.A.

Barbara and her mother Jean Schechter

I was born in Bukaczowce, a small village S.W. of Krakow, Poland in Sept. 1941. My father was a lawyer, born in Krakow with a family of six sisters, my mother a bookkeeper from Stanislavov with a family of three sisters and one brother. As conditions became more and more oppressive, we went into hiding. A Polish farmer hid us for a short time, but it was getting too dangerous for him and his family, and we were told to leave.

My father was able to get forged papers stating that we were Polish Christians. Philip and Jean Schachter were now Philip and Jean Rogalska and their Barbara, or Basha, as I was called. My parents decided to separate, so that it would be easier to travel, and move more freely. My father was able to get work in a Polish labor camp, but my mother was frantic not knowing where to go or what to do, with a little baby. She was planning to go back to her hometown to be with her parents, but that probably would have meant death for us.

As luck would have it she stood by the church in the village square where she was told Germans were looking for farm laborers. She had blonde hair and blue eyes, and spoke fluent German and when the truck came by with bullhorns screeching that volunteers were needed, we were taken to Germany.

My mother was given heavy farm work to do, but she was unable to take care of me properly, as a baby needs constant attention. A German woman offered to take care of me. She was a single woman and wanted a child of her own. I was well taken care of dressed and fed well. There was even a dog for me to play with. I was taken to church regularly and knew all the psalms in perfect German. Little by little my mother's visiting privileges were taken away and I was getting used to this new mother..calling her "muti". My biological mother begged to see me one more time to take me for a little walk and it was then that she simply ran away with me...I was crying for my "muti", my German mother.

Now it was near the end of the war and we were on the road with many other refugees. Again, we survived a very close call. We were nearly killed in the bombing of Dresden, by our own American planes. We finally ended up in Stuttgart in a DP (displaced persons camp.) My father found us by some miracle with the help of the Red Cross. The American Joint Distrubution Committee, Hias, another agency and a distant relative in NY helped us to come to the U.S. We were on the very first ship of refugees after the war, the Marine Flesher in May of 1946. My father's five sisters, survived the Concentration Camps, but all of my mother's family was murdered.

Living in the U.S. was not easy. We lived in Brooklyn, in the tenements, five-story walk-up no elevator. My parents worked in the sweatshops doing piecework. We were very poor, but my parents were very grateful to be in this country, and their faith in G-d was not diminished. They associated with other "greeners" meaning other refugees like themselves and did not mingle with other people. We moved to Detroit with the help of friends when I was eleven.

The Holocaust has permeated my whole life. When I was growing up, I wanted to block it out, and just assimilate into my environment, and just live a "Normal" life. Now, that I am older and my parents are gone I feel as if I have a mission to speak of it, to honor my parent's memory, to honor the Righteous among the Nations. The Jews and non-Jews who risked their lives to save ours gives me hope that there is yet some goodness in the world. I want to pass on the legacy of remembrance to my children and grandchildren that they should never forget where they came from and their history of the Shoah.

That they should value their freedoms, the Bill of Rights, the constitution, and most importantly to vote. To be aware of bigotry and prejudice, to analyze the media, and propaganda, to speak out against intolerance.

Mandarin Orange Salad

parve

1/2 C Sliced Almonds
1 Tbs. Red Wine Vinegar
1 tbs. Orange Juice
1 Tbs. Honey
1 Tbs. Dijon Mustard
1/4 Tsp Salt, Pepper To Taste
1/4 C Vegetable Oil
1 Bag Mixed Salad
1 C Mandarin Oranges Drained
1 C Red Grapes Cut

Directions:
Pre-Heat Oven 375

- Bake Almonds 7-9 Min.
- Combine all liquid ingredients, and whisk, except oil.
- Add oil slowly while whisking.

* Double recipe for 8 and up

Piquant Meat Balls

meat

2 lbs ground beef
1 egg
2 tbsp bread crumbs
1 tsp salt
pepper
12 ounce bottle of chili sauce
6 ounces grape jelly
juice of 1 lemon

Directions:

1.) Combine meat, egg, bread crumbs, and seasonings.
2.) Shape into balls the size of a walnut.
3.) Heat chili sauce, jelly and lemon juice in a heavy skillet or dutch oven until blended.
4.) Add the meat balls, cover, and simmer for 30 minutes.
5.) Uncover and cook 15 minutes longer, stirring frequently to prevent sticking.

Serves 8 to 10

Thank you for the wonderful idea of a survivor cookbook....Barbara Schechter Cohen.

The recipe is a sweet and sour taste; like life, there is sweetness, and bitterness... let us pray for the sweet!

203

Bala Kisner, now Betty Chanan
Canton, OH, U.S.A.
Submitted by her daughters Ingrid Cohn and Rosalie Nathan

I was born Bala Kisner in the city of Bendzin, Poland. My parents, three sisters, brother, and I lived as any typical close-knit, happy family. My father owned a business, Kisner Monuments, where he cut and hand-carved headstones. My mother worked six days a week at her own store, selling fabrics and women's and children's coats, in addition to raising five children. I have warm memories of my childhood.

Everything changed, however, when the Germans marched into Bendzin on September 1, 1939. Three days after arriving, they took seventeen Jews from an apartment building, and they were shot in the market square. A week later, two hundred Jews were herded into the Grand Synagogue, and it was set on fire. For days, you could see the smoldering flames, which destroyed four city blocks. Many people were shot and killed that night. Soon a twelve-hour curfew was enforced, and we were ordered to wear a Star of David on our clothes at all times. Food became very scarce. Schools were shut down. Men on the streets were randomly kicked and beaten, and others were abducted from their homes and sent away to do hard labor. Most were never seen again. Jewish businesses were seized, and unemployment was the norm.

Early on the morning of December 15, 1941, when I was seventeen years old, police stormed into our home. We children hid behind a large wardrobe, but we quickly came out when we heard my mother being slapped across the face. With guns pointing at us, they demanded that two of my sisters and I leave with them. I quickly pulled a dress over my nightgown. Everything happened so fast that I never had a chance to look back or to say goodbye.

Outside were hundreds of teenage girls who had been rounded up. We were taken to the elementary school for what turned out to be the first transport of females to be taken away from our city. We stayed at the school all day and were made to march to the next town. As we left the school grounds, I caught a glimpse of my father in the crowd that had gathered in the street nearby. It still pains me to remember how helpless he seemed and how overcome with pain.

After two days, in the darkness of night we were taken to the train station and herded into cattle cars. It was freezing cold and completely dark. We had no food or water and given only ersatz coffee. Only once at night were we permitted to relieve ourselves in the fields by the train tracks with guns pointed at us the whole time. I was absolutely terrified and could not begin to comprehend what was happening.

We finally arrived at a small mountain village, Gabersdorf, in Sudetenland (now Czecho-slovakia), where I remained for the next three and a half years. I worked in a factory, operating a huge machine that converted flax into thread which was later used to make Nazi uniforms. Working this piece of machinery would have been challenging for an experienced adult, let alone for a scared young girl. One mistake or small problem could cause the many spindles on the machine to become jammed or the threads to tangle. The factory overseer was always pacing up and down watching. I was very fearful for there was absolutely no room for mistakes.

Camp routine was grueling. We woke at 4:00 a.m. and worked in the textile factory from 5:00 a.m. until 5:00 p.m. during the week and until 10:00 p.m. on Saturdays. There were no showers or hot water. Personal hygiene was essentially nonexistent. We were given one loaf of bread, which was expected to last for a whole week, along with some other meager rations of food. The hunger and exhaustion were overwhelming. The whole routine was repeated the next day and the next, over and over again.

I was so lonely during this time. I cried for two years. It was the first time I had ever been separated from all the people I loved. It is difficult to express the depth of this sorrow in words. The only thing that kept me alive was the burning desire to be reunited with my family again.

On March 21, 1944, the Gestapo arrived, which marked the change of our labor camp to a concentration camp. I became #22878.

Conditions then became increasingly worse. We had few clothes and no shoes or stock-ings, only wooden clogs, to protect us from the deep snow of the brutal winter. We lived in a constant state of starvation, exhaustion, and fright. In addition, we were totally exhausted and had no idea what was taking place outside the gates of the camp. I longed and prayed for a time I would see my family once again. A tuberculosis epidemic plagued the camp. I developed chronic kidney problems, which took many years after the war to resolve. Eventually the factory shut down due to the shortage of materials, and girls were sent to dig ditches. We lived in constant fear that we would have to march to another camp, a trek that many of us would not have been able to survive.

One morning we heard a loud, roaring sound, which to our shock and amazement, turned out to be Russian army tanks coming to liberate us. The camp gates were thrown open, and our liberators shouted that we were free. I remember everyone screaming with disbelief. Later that day, a young Russian officer, who was Jewish, asked that we be assembled so he could speak to us. He said, "Children, I am sorry to tell you I have bad news for you. There is no one waiting for you at home. There is no one to go back to." I remember the screams and cries and the chaos that followed. I can't even begin to describe how I felt. My reason for living, the dream of once again being with my family, that had gotten me through those years, was suddenly ripped away from me. To have endured the horrors of a concentration camp, only to find that my family had been wiped out, was beyond devastating.

In the Holocaust, I lost more than seventy family members: my mother, father, sisters, grandmother, aunts, uncles and cousins. Of forty-one grandchildren on both sides of the family, my brother and I were among the six who survived.

It still boggles my mind, and will until the last breath that I take, how this ever could have happened.

Soon after liberation I met the man who would become my husband. Young and lacking experience, we started our lives over again, In 1947, while we were still living in Germany, our first daughter was born. We immigrated to the United States in 1949 and made Cleveland our home. Our second daughter was born in 1953. Both girls have families and I'm happy and proud to say I have four grandchildren. I hope and pray for them to live in a better world.

Potato Soup from home

parve

Directions:

2 large potatoes
1 T. chopped parsley
2 T flour
2 T margarine
salt and pepper
1 medium chopped onion

1.) Cube potatoes and cover with water.
2.) Cook until soft. Do not discard water.
3.) Add salt and pepper.
4.) In separate pan, brown onion in margarine.
5.) Make a rue by adding flour and 1/2 cup water.
6.) Add this to the cooked potatoes.
7.) Add parsley and cook on medium heat for 5 minutes.

Herring Salad

dairy

1 cup of herring tidbits packed in wine
1 13-14 ounce can of pickled beets
1 large apple
1/2 cup of walnuts
1 pint of sour cream

Directions:

- Allow enough time to thoroughly drain the herring and beets.
- Separately chop each of the first five ingredients very fine.
- Combine thoroughly and then fold in sour cream.
- Refrigerate.

Enjoy!

Ralph J. Preiss
Poughkeepsie, NY, U.S.A.
Survived in the Philippines

When I was 4 or 5 I regularly helped my grandmother, Omi, prepare pancakes for breakfast for the family every Sunday morning. Her son, a surgeon who worked in a hospital in Berlin was fired in 1933 when Hitler came to power, and he emigrated to Shanghai, China. My other uncle was a lawyer in Berlin and he too got fired and left for Paris. My Shanghai uncle phoned his mother weekly and told her and my parents to leave Germany while the going was good. He said that we could all learn new languages and try to re-establish our lives elsewhere. But the warnings all fell on deaf ears.

My father, a physician working in Rosenberg O/S, was too busy helping deliver children, mend bones and sew up farm folks who had accidents with their farm equipment to notice the politics of it all... until in 1937 he received word that he was not allowed to medicate non-Jewish people anymore. Then he started looking around and answered an ad for 12 physicians needed in the Philippines. The Jewish Committee in Manila, Philippines under the leadership of the Frieder brothers of Cincinnati, OH had arranged to bring that number of physicians and up to 10,000 German Jews to the Philippines (read the late Frank Ephraim's book, Escape to Manila, for a fuller account).

My father was fortunate to be one of the physicians accepted, and after visiting my uncle's family in Paris on the way to the Philippines we sailed for Manila arriving in the spring of 1939. Omi Suessbach sailed on to Shanghai. In 1940 my family and I participated in a ceremony at which Manuel Quezon, President of the Philippine Commonwealth presented to the Jewish Community of the Philippines a piece of his own personal land for use as a model Kibbutz by German Jews in Marikina. I asked him for his autograph and a photographer took a picture (attached) which then was printed in Manila newspapers. But in December 1941 President Quezon fled as the Philippines was occupied by the Japanese. Fortunately, the immigrant community was left to carry on since we could show them our German passports (expired of course).

I went to elementary school in Manila. One of my classmates was Jose Laurel Jr. In October 1943, on the occasion of the granting of independence to the Philippines by the Japanese and the inauguration of Jose Laurel as first President, our class participated in the ceremony and I met Premier Tojo of Japan who presided. In 1945, during the liberation of the Philippines, my family was rescued by Filipino guerrillas (freedom fighters) and taken into the mountains just before the Japanese started killing all white people. We found our house bombed out when we returned after the fighting was over. My Paris uncle and family had been deported to Auschwitz and never heard of again. My grandmother died in Shanghai of old age soon after the war.

I came to the USA to study engineering in 1949. My Shanghai uncle followed on the heels of the Communist take-over in China, and my parents joined my family in 1969 after retiring from a pharmaceutical company in Manila that my father ran and whose chemical product helped stamp out the rats that were devouring the sugar crop in the Philippines.

Ralph with Philippine President Manuel Quezon

Omi Suessbach's Pfannkuchen

(German Pancakes)
dairy

3 eggs
2 cups of flour
2 cups of 2 percent milk
2 pinches of salt
1/4 lb salted butter

Directions:

Makes 8 thin pancakes or crepes. Serve with syrup of your liking or sweet jam (blueberry, strawberry or raspberry)

1.) Crack eggs into deep bowl.
2.) Add flour, salt and milk.
3.) Use whisk to stir into a smooth mixture, 3 to 5 minutes.
4.) Use 8-inch frying pan over medium heat and melt a teaspoon butter, then ladle 1/4 cup smooth batter into the browning butter spreading the mix over entire pan bottom.
5.) Wait till batter looks dry on top, then flip over (with spatula) and brown bottom side to same color.
6.) Slide crepe onto a dinner plate and repeat process for next pancake.

Ralph Preiss (in the chairs) with Omi

Dr. Egon Suessbach
Submitted by his nephew Ralph J. Preiss
Poughkeepsie, NY, U.S.A.

My mother's brother, Dr. Egon Suessbach, was a surgeon operating in Berlin hospitals before he was forced from his job when Hitler came to power in 1933. At that time, no visas were required for the international settlement in Shanghai, China so he and his bride emigrated to that far off country.

In Germany, we did not hear from the couple for a very long time and I saw my grandmother become very worried, especially after her husband, Egon's father, died and no one had an address to send him the news. My grandmother finally decided to send him a letter addressed to Dr. Egon Suessbach, China, even though everyone thought that the action was foolish as China was a very large country. However, some three months later, she got a phone call from her son. Egon miraculously had received the letter and the sad news and he promised to keep in touch thereafter. He kept his promise, and at first, once a month, and later weekly, she received a phone call from China and he gave her all the news about his working at an international hospital in Shanghai and suggesting that my parents and she also move to Shanghai before my father would lose his job under the Nazis as a family physician in Upper Silesia. This went on for years till 1937 when Egon's prediction came true and my parents left Germany for the Philippines at the end of 1938, while my grandmother joined him in Shanghai.

During the Japanese occupation, my uncle continued his work in the hospital uninterrupted since, after all, he had come from Germany, and that country was allied with Japan. After the war, my grandmother died and he continued his work till the Communist take-over of China in 1949. Then, he managed to obtain a visa for the USA to work as an anesthesiologist in the TB hospital on Staten Island, NY. After retiring from a similar position at the Jamaica Hospital in New York, he moved his family to California to live near where my parents had retired.

When my mother had my uncle for dinner, she served his favorite dish, Koenigsberger Kloepse.

**Dr. Egon Suessbach and wife,
Margot, in China**

Koenigsberger Kloepse

(Meatballs)

meat

1 1/2 lbs ground beef
1/2 cup water
salt and pepper
1/2 cup bread crumbs
1/2 finely chopped onion

Gravy

1 egg beaten
2 ounces of lemon juice
2 to 3 tbsp sugar
1 tbsp capers

Directions:

1.) Mix together in a bowl and add sufficient water to form the gravy base.
2.) Put one Tablespoon margarine and one Tablespoon flour in large frying pan or Dutch oven and let fry until light yellow.
3.) Pour in gravy mix, stir and boil until thick.
4.) Add meatballs and simmer for an hour.
   (Add white wine during simmering if too lemony and more capers to taste).

Serves 6.

Rena Finder & Rozia Ferber
Framingham, MA, U.S.A.

Lost Opportunities

I remember scenes and times from my early childhood when I couldn't be more than 3 years old. I remember a scene from the play in the nursery school when I had to recite a poem about a spot on the floor fighting with the broom. I still remember the first verse (in Polish, of course).

I remember a sunny day in the country, playing with my cousins. Our parents were hiking in the mountains when a sudden storm erupted. It was so dark, thundering and lighting and we were so frightened. Our baby sitter sat down with us and we prayed for our parent's safe return.

I remember the many times my father took me to the soccer games on Sunday morning. The ride in the ambulance when I was 5 and got scarlet fever. In those days you had to be quarantined in the infectious special hospital where the nuns took care of us in a huge ward. For the first time in my life I was separated from my parents. It was so scary.

My parents, my Bubbies and Zaide, my aunts came to visit every afternoon, outside and we waved behind the windows. I remember it so well.

And yet I can't remember my father's face, not the real face with the twinkle in his eyes or feel the warmth of his hand when we walked together. I see him only as he appears in the few photos I was able to find after I came back to Krakow after the war to the ghetto apartment of my grandparents.

My father was killed in 1942. I never knew him as a person, only as my Daddy. I knew that he doted on me, his only child. He was so proud of me. My mother and I survived together. We were on Schindler's List.

My mother, Rozia Ferber, lived for 20 more years after the war. We were so close, and yet we never talked about the war, our terrible losses. Her husband and parents, sisters and brothers were murdered. Why didn't we share our grief? I know we tried to be strong for each other, we tried to be brave.

But oh, how I wish now that we had talked and cried together, that I could have known my parents not only as my Mother and Father but also as people with their dreams and feelings.

Now that I am old enough to ask questions, there is no one to answer. So I stand in front of the pictures and remember how much love was in our lives. And maybe this is the most important thing to remember. My mother loved to bake and these were our favorites.

Rena Finder

211

Brownies

parve

2 cups sugar
1 scant cup flour
4 eggs
1/2 pound of sweet margarine
4 squares baking chocolate
1 TSP rum flavor

Directions:
Preheat oven to 350 degrees

1.) Melt chocolate and margarine over slow boiling water.
2.) Cool.
3.) Mix with the eggs, sugar and sifted flour.
   * Don't over beat.
4.) Pour into an oiled 9x12 baking pan.
5.) Sprinkle the chocolate chips over the top.
6.) Bake in a 350 preheated oven for about 16 to 20 minutes.
7.) Test with toothpick.
   * Do not over bake.

Hinda Tenenbaum-Margulies
Brooklyn, NY, U.S.A.
Submitted by her daughter Rena Chertoff

My mother, Hinda Tenenbaum-Margulies was born in Tomaszow-Mazowiecki on June 14, 1907. She was one of five children of Hersh and Raizel Tenenbaum. The children were Zalman-Icio, Rivka, Josef, and Chava. Zalman-Icio and Rivka immigrated to Argentina in the 1920's.

Hinda was the third child and she was very talented. She became a seamstress and had her own workshop. She employed three people. She was very beautiful and got married to Abraham-Chaim Margulies. She has two children, Rivka (Rena) and Reuben (Romek).

During World War II she was in the ghetto, Tomaszow. She cooked twice a week cabbage soup that she distributed to poor and hungry Jews that came to our house. Later on she was transferred to labor camp Blizyn with her husband and her two children, Rena and Romek.

In 1944 she was transferred to Auschwitz-Birkenau where her beloved son Romek was gassed and cremated at age 9. Her husband Abraham-Chaim Margulies was shot while on a death march one day before liberation in May 1945, by a German SS-man near Freilassing, Germany.

I, Rena Chernoff, am submitting this recipe of sweet and sour cabbage that she frequently cooked in her memory.

Hinda and Rena

Sweet & Sour Cabbage

dairy

1 medium-sized red cabbage-shredded
2 tablespoons sugar
1 tart apple, pared and sliced thin
1/2 teaspoon ground allspice
2 cups boiling water
1 teaspoon salt
5 tablespoons vinegar

Thickening

1 tbsp melted butter or oil
1 tbsp flour
1/2 cup cabbage liquid

Directions:

1.) Cook all ingredients together except thickening for 15 minutes.
2.) Make a paste by adding butter or oil to flour.
3.) Stir until smooth.
4.) Add the sauce and cook 10 minutes longer.

Serves 6 to 8

Emilia Siegel

New York, NY, U.S.A.

I was born in Krakow, Poland. When the war broke out in 1939 I was 10 years old, living in Plasrov, and working in the carpet factory.

I was sent to Weilierka where I worked in the salt grube. Later I was sent to the Flossenberg Concentration Camp where I worked in a factory making Meser-Scmidts for the Germans. Eventually I was liberated by the American soldiers.

Falafel
parve

1 cup dried chickpeas
Half a large chopped onion
1 teaspoon baking powder
4-6 tablespoons flour
2 tablespoons finely chopped fresh parsley
Soybean or vegetable oil for frying
Chopped tomato and cucumber for garnish
Diced onion for garnish
1 teaspoon salt
Tahina sauce
4 cloves garlic
1 teaspoon cumin
Pita

Directions:
Yields about 20 balls

1.) Put the chickpeas in a large bowl and add enough cold water to cover them by at least 5 cm. Let soak overnight, then drain. Or use canned chickpeas.
2.) Place the drained, uncooked chickpeas and the onions in the food processor. Add the parsley, salt, hot pepper, garlic, and cumin. Process until blended but not pureed.
3.) Sprinkle in the baking powder and 4 tablespoons of the flour, and pulse. You want to add enough bulgur or flour so that the dough forms a small ball and no longer sticks to your hands. Refrigerate for several hours.
4.) Form the chickpea mixture into small balls with a falafel scoop.
5.) Heat 10 cm of oil to 180 degrees in a deep pot and fry 1 ball to test.
  * If it falls apart, add a little flour. Then fry about 6 balls at once for a few minutes on each side, or until golden brown. Drain on paper towels. Stuff half a pita with falafel balls, chopped tomatoes and cucumbers, onion. Drizzle with tahina thinne with water.

Helen Schoenberg
New York, NY, U.S.A.

I was born in Chrzanow, Poland. I was young and very good looking. I learned how to sew and I used a sewing machine in the ghetto making uniforms for German soldiers.. After two years I was sent to a Concentration Camp Neusolz until 1944.

I then went on the Toden March for six weeks. After the march I wound up in the Flosenburg Concentration camp for two weeks. Then I was sent in a cattle car to Bergen-Belsen. A big epidemic broke out there and I was very sick and lost my memory. We were liberated in 1945 but for a long time I knew nothing about myself. I went to school after the war was over to learn what I had lost.

Minute Steaks
meat

Helen Schoenberg

Directions:
1.) Sauté onion and fresh chopped garlic in a small amount of oil.
2.) Add a little water, short steak beef (sliced), paprika, a chicken bullion cube, pepper, and a small can of tomato sauce.
3.) Cook on a small flame for about 1 ½ hours.

Easy Gefilte Fish
parve

A and B frozen gefilte loaf
1 chopped large onion
2 sliced carrots)
Salt, pepper, sugar
2 oz. chopped almonds

Directions:

Fill a large enough sauce pan to fit the gefilte loaf with water. Add 1 chopped up onion and sliced carrots. Add salt, sugar, and pepper to taste and bring to a boil. Take off first wrapper of gefilte loaf. Add to water. Lower the temperature and cook for ½ hour over a small flame. Take off second wrapper, and let cook for another 45 minutes. Add chopped almonds and cook for 15 more minutes.

Dora Krulik (Oma)
Baltimore, MD, U.S.A.
Submitted by her daughter Bertha Schwarz

My mother was born in Cologne, Germany. She married my father Usher and moved to Antwerp, Belgium where they had three children. In 1940 when the Germans invaded Belgium we escaped to southern France. My father was arrested by the French Gendarme and deported to Auschwitz. So were my mother's parents, who escaped with us to France.

After the war we arrived in Palestine where my mother remarried and started a new life for herself. She worked in a ceramic factory and developed lung disease. She lost her second husband and never remarried. She lived to be 87 and had a lot of "naches" from her nine grandchildren. She had a very hard life but wanted very much that we, her three daughters, would never have to live the life that she had to go through.

Let us never forget.

My mother used to make her gefilte fish for Friday night and later in life when the Holidays came along her job was to make the gefilte fish. My children who came from the USA could not wait to taste them. Nobody made them as well as she did. For Passover it was Oma's gefilte fish that made the seder. The whole neighborhood knew that Oma was preparing for her family this most favorite dish. She passed away several years ago and none of us daughters can come close to the taste of her gefilte fish. As the High Holidays approach I would like to dedicate this recipe in her honor, from the family Schwarz, Pessach, and Mandelbrot and all her grandchildren who loved her very much.

Dora Krulik at her 80th Birthday

My mother's Gefilte Fish (Oma's)

parve

1 pound ground carp
1 pound white fish ground plus bones and head
3 big onions
3 hard boiled eggs
2 uncooked eggs
1/2 cup sugar
2 tbsp matzo meal

Directions:

1.) Mix grated eggs and grated onions with fish.
2.) Add salt and pepper.
3.) Add ½ cup sugar to taste.
4.) Add 2 Tbsp. matzo meal to the 2 uncooked eggs.

In a flat pot make the sauce:
3 big onions chopped
3 cups of water
2 slices carrots

1.) Cook onions and carrots. Add salt and pepper and 3 Tbsp. sugar to taste. Let cook until it comes to a boil. Taste the sauce.
2.) Make fish balls and add sugar to sauce if needed (check one ball to see if it holds). If loose add more matzo meal.
3.) Cook together for one hour at low heat. The fish should be cooked with the sauce. Drain the liquid and take out the fish ball from the sauce into a colander. Separate the head bones form the fish balls. The sauce should be refrigerated and served with the fish. You can add the carrot ring for decoration. This should be made one day ahead.

Apple Cake
by Oma
parve

This recipe Oma always had in the freezer to take out when guests came to visit.
We all loved that recipe. My sister in Israel always has that cake ready for any occasion.
It always tastes good even after a few days. It freezes well and defrosts quickly.

3 cups flour
1/2 cup sugar
1 1/2 sticks margarine
2 egg yolks
1 tsp. baking powder
1 tsp. vanilla

Directions:
Preheat oven to 350 degrees

- Mix the dough in mixer until smooth.
- Slice 5 apples- 2 apricots or plums
    - 3 Tbsp. sugar
    - ½ tsp. cinnamon
    - 1 Tbsp. vanilla and bread crumbs
- Slice apples, add cinnamon, and sugar.
- Arrange half the dough in bottom of 3x9 pan.
- Put apple and bread crumb mixture over the dough.
- Put second half of dough and pour the apple mixture on top layer.
- Put bread crumbs, vanilla, and sugar mixture on top layer.
- Bake 45 minutes in 350 degree oven-ration.

Inge Schopler
Milwaukee, WI, U.S.A.

Inge at 6 years old

We left Vienna, Austria in Sept.1939 after the "Anschluss" but before Kristallnacht. We went to Brussels, Belgium where we were refugees for one year. There, we were the guests of a banker and his wife, Raymond and Ida Levi, who were friends my parents met on one of their travels in Europe. They were philanthropists and wonderful people who really saved our lives. We immigrated to the US at the end of 1939. My father had to go back to dental school while my mother gave body massages and in the evenings worked at Loehman's in sales. After two years in dental school my father opened an office in Manhattan. I went to Julia Richman HS and Hunter College.

Inge and Harry Schopler

Original Painting by granddaughter Lisa Schopler

Flourless chocolate cake
dairy

5 oz. sugar (little less than 1/2 cup)
5 oz. unsalted butter,
5 oz semisweet chocolate chips
(melted w. little water)
2 cups (7 oz.) finely ground almonds
6 egg yolks
6 egg whites

Original painting by granddaughter Ellen Schopler

Directions:
Preheat oven to 350 degrees
1.) Mix sugar, egg yolks, melted choc., add almonds.
2.) Add beaten egg whites in greased 7 inch floured spring form.
3.) Bake 45 minutes at 350.
4.) After cooled cover with apricot jam & chocolate frosting--melted choc chips with a little powdered sugar & a pad of butter.

Eva Dorothea Tikotin-Licht
Jerusalem, Israel
Submitted by her daughter Ilana Drukker-Tikotin

My mother was born in Berlin and had one older brother. My grandmother, her mother, Helene Stein, had been born in Switzerland. After WWI both her parents died in the influenza epidemic. An aunt, Tante Liese, raised her. During the time of the Great Inflation in Germany her aunt had to make some extra money to feed her two sons and the two children of her brother. She used to bake cakes and have them delivered to private homes by the four kids.

My mother kept her recipes, but they were written in Gothic script, which I couldn't decipher and threw away before I realized what a treasure they must have been. However I still possess her beautiful heavy wooden rolling pin and use it a lot.

Thus, when Hitler rose to power and my mother had to quit her studies at age 21 (she had wanted to become a simultaneous translator). She approached her three well-established uncles in Bern for assistance. They replied that it would be hard for them to get her a work permit and having no other choice, she fled to Holland. There she met my father Felix Tikotin (another refugee from Germany) and initially worked for him as a secretary.

During the years of the war after having put me and my younger sister into hiding, she was very active in the resistance and apparently a 'hero', but never spoke about it. Afterwards, and I do not want to dwell at this time on the 'hell' after the Shoa, she became ill and spent most of the rest of her life in and out of hospitals.

However, whenever she did come home and felt better, she prepared for my father the favorite dishes he had known from his early childhood in Silezia.
In her honor and memory I would like to send in the recipe of a dish that I have never encountered anywhere else. It was usually served during Hanukkah.

Eva and her daughters

Schlesische Mohnpielen
(Silesian Poppy Seed Dish)
dairy

250 gr. ground poppy seeds
125 gr. sugar
125 gr. raisins
1/2 l. milk
6 slices of old white bread
1/4 l. milk

Directions:

1.) Boil the ground poppy seeds with the sugar and the raisins in the milk.
2.) Let the poppy seeds expand for about ten minutes.
3.) Fill a glass bowl in layers with the bread and the poppy seed mixture, ending with the poppy seeds on top.
4.) Boil the remaining milk with a little sugar and pour it after about an hour over the dish until it no longer absorbs any liquid.
5.) Let it rest at least overnight in the refrigerator.
6.) The desert should be served with an ice-cream scoop in bowls.

Dorothea Benjamini
Cherry Hill, N.J., U.S.A.
Submitted by Christine Koxnat

Mrs. Benjamini was born on the border of Austria and Romania. She remembers as a child her Ukrainian maid baking and cooking for her family. Unfortunately, she didn't have the opportunity to acquire those recipes because the war broke out when she was sixteen. Her family was taken to a labor camp in Romania for four years. Luckily they were freed and sent to a camp in Cypress. From years of starvation, her family contracted Typhus and her mother did not have the strength to survive. She, along with her father and sister, recovered and were freed when the war ended. She later moved to Israel and it was in Israel that she found what she considers her favorite potato kugel recipe. She has included this in the cookbook for everyone to enjoy- her taste of freedom!

Childhood picture from Austria

Mrs. Benjamini's Potato Kugel
parve

6 Idaho Potatoes
4 eggs
1/2 cup oil
1/2 cup matzoh meal
1 tsp baking powder
1 greased 13x9 pan

After the war in Israel

Directions:

Preheat the oven to 350 degrees

1.) Grate potatoes.
2.) Drain in colander but keep the drained water in bottom of the bowl for later.
3.) Add oil, then matzoh meal and toss until potatoes are coated evenly. You might need a tad more oil.
4.) If mixture is too dry add the saved starchy water. Add salt and pepper to taste.
5.) Add baking powder until blended.
6.) Pour into pan and bake at 350 until top browns.

223

Fira Kaplan

Southfield, MI, U.S.A.

My life in the Minsk ghetto during World War II.

I was born in Minsk, Belorussia on July 7, 1936. Three weeks later my father, Kaplan Tsalia, was arrested by the Communists without any explanation. They took him at night time to prison like they did with thousands other people. My mama, Bella Muroch-Kaplan was never able to find out where they sent him and why. She became a single mother with two children, 7 year old son Gershon Kaplan (Grisha in Russian) and a three week old baby, that is me. She was very young, only 25 years old. Some relatives and neighbors avoided her as the wife of an "enemy". Only her older brother Uda, Yuri Muroch, helped her with getting food. He knocked at the window at night and brought milk, potatoes and other kinds of food. It was an extremely hard time for my Mom.

But a more horrible time came when the fascists attacked Belorussia and other areas and occupied Minsk in June 1941. At that time my mother worked at a sewing plant as a bookkeeper. My brother was 12 years old, he went to school. I was 5 years old at the beginning of the enemy's occupation. It was a warm beautiful summer in 1941 (usually summer in Belorussia is wet and not very warm). My Mom sent me to the summer camp in a green suburb, which belonged to her working organization. Nobody could predict that World War II would begin in a couple of days.

I remember, it was a bright shiny day when suddenly children were plunged in the train carriages at a very fast pace. It was panic as the train was ready to depart and teachers tried to gather all children. We arrived by train to the Minsk train station. My uncle Aizik saw me through the window, picked me up quickly and brought me to my crying Mom. But many children were missed. I remember the other mothers asking me with tears in their eyes: Firele, did you see my Berele or my Sarele or…" It was crowded and noisy. Later I heard from adults that the train had been bombed and some carriages were destroyed.

Then I noticed many strange men dressed in green uniforms and heavy boots. I asked Mom who are they and why so many? Our life was changed completely.

All Jewish people were moved from their houses to one area surrounded with barbed wire which got the name "ghetto". Several different families settled in one small house. I remember many details of my unhappy childhood. Nobody was allowed to get out from the territory ghetto. The Gestapo would shoot people with no warning. We, small children, became smart and mature. We were on the alert playing hide-and-seek and other simple games. Sometimes we played on the forbidden empty street outside of barbed wire and watched the street so that if the Gestapo appeared we would warn others: "Hide, Gestapo". One time my clothing got caught in the wire and I could not move. An older boy gave me a hand and we ran away from the dangerous street into the ghetto. We were always hungry.

Fira Kaplan Lupyan

My brother Gershon, 12 years old, understood that he must support Mom and his sister somehow. There was only one way to get a little food: get out from the ghetto at night and go to the village to trade or exchange any items for eggs or milk and bread. And he did it. During that time I started to notice that some adults disappeared. It was a big secret, where they went away.

Germans and many Russian traitors organized "oblavas": all of sudden they would surround houses, walk in and look for somebody to kill. People started to hide in basements, which usually were cold and served for keeping vegetables in winter time. Basements were wet, dark, no windows, no lights. When somebody would warn: "Oblava" people jumped down and sat quietly until the enemies went away from the house. It was very difficult to keep babies and small children in the basement and keep them quiet.

One day I and my girlfriend Olga, 4 years old, were late to jump down to hide. We sat down on the bed near the wall. An old man with a beard was lying in the bed opposite us. He was very old and sick. Two policemen walked in, glanced at us and looked at the old man. They aimed a rifle at old man, silently, very long time, and then killed him. Those scenes stay in my eyes even now.

I can not forget the boy's voice outside of our house who tried to run away from police. He was one of my friends, neighbor Nohemka, he was running away and crying:
" Please, don't kill me. I'm still a small boy, please, please". But he was killed. He was only 11 years old, but he was too late to hide. We grew up during the time in ghetto and we were witnesses and participants in this somber life.

Our family occupied a small part of house: my Mom's parents, uncle Aisik, 19 years old, my brother Gershon, 12 years old and Mom with me. Aisik was the first person who disappeared. Nobody recalled his name and I didn't ask. I understood that it was a secret. Much later I heard that he became a member of an underground organization. Members of this organization helped many man and women run away from ghetto to forests and fight with enemies or save children. Aisik blasted five enemies' trains with weapons being a partisan. Brave Aisik was killed in battle. My Mom received an official letter after the war from an office that her brother Aisik Muroch was a brave partisan and he had perished and was buried in common grave with many other fighters.

Then we lost my Grandparents. One day the police came in the house and ordered us to send out one person from each family to the central plaza voluntarily. Grandfather and Grandmother decided to go together. That was their last day in the life: nobody returned to their houses, everybody in the plaza was killed.

Then we lost my uncle Uda's wife Anna with her son Misha, 6 years old. They were killed on the street inside of ghetto, because they were 15 minutes late for curfew, 5 or 6 p.m. My Mom and many other women became slaves: Germans with weapons conducted women in columns to the train station to perform dirty jobs. In the beginning the Germans did not pay attention to the children and the women would take their children with them. While the women worked, we quietly hid and played invisibly. Later, the Germans made a strong rule that children were not allowed to go to the working place with their mothers. But my mother refused to leave me alone in the house. I was still a small child. So, two women put me between them, covered me with their long skirts and we walked tightly together and that's how my mother took me to work with her.

Once I noticed a man on the ground, he called me and asked me very quietly to bring him a piece of bread. He promised me a toy. I ran to my Mom for a piece of bread and I returned quickly back to the man on the ground. He thanked me and gave me a wood toy. I was happy. Suddenly a tall German appeared in front of me, angrily took me to my Mom in the kitchen, lifted me by my hair and put me on a high metal table. He took out a revolver and touched my forehead with the cold end. I was silent and just looked at him at gun point.

I remember how my Mom and her girlfriends fell down on their knees and begged him not to kill this small child. So, he dropped me on the floor and said if he saw me again he would kill me without a word.

Once, my mother decided that she would try to save me by giving me to a non-Jewish orphanage home. She did not tell me anything, she just took me to some little white house with a porch and told me to knock on the door and tell whoever would open the door that I wanted to stay with them. Then she turned and walked away. I was standing on the porch and looking at my mother walking away down the street. Then I turned and ran very, very quickly after her and grabbed her hand and told her that I would never leave her and I would stay with her. After the war was over, my mother was told that the orphanage was bombed a few days later and everyone inside got killed.

My Mom was not able to watch her son Gregory who was 12 years old. He became an independent mature person. He went out every morning and returned back home late in the evening, sometimes with a little food for us. He didn't tell us were he went and what he was doing in day time. Later my Mom realized that he became a link between partisans in the forest and the underground organization in the ghetto. He climbed over barbed wire and ran away to the partisans. One of his duties was to find and collect pieces of metal everywhere and bring them to the people who would secretly melt them and make bullets. He had many other duties. One day a traitor saw him behind the barbed wire and denounced him to the Gestapo. Gregory, 12 years old, was immediately arrested. A couple of days later somebody told my Mom:" Bella, go to see your son, he is in the German truck with Russian captives." My Mom ran to see him and with tears in her eyes brought him a piece of bread, a bar of soap, and a towel. Grisha said: Don't cry Mama, I'll return." We never saw him again. I still believe that maybe he survived. My Mom wrote letters to the Red Cross and other organizations hoping to find her son. He was a brave courier, adults called him Grisha Sorvanyetz , what means in Russian courageous.

Joanne, you asked me how I survived. My Mom lost all loved ones beside small daughter, me. The ghetto was closed at the end. The Germans and the policemen felt that Russian Red Army was coming soon so they must finish with Jewish ghetto as soon as possible. One gloomy day they gathered all ghetto population to the train station plaza and started to move people to the gas chamber trucks in line. My Mom understood that it was the end, no way she was going to stay in line. She took my hand and went into the kitchen. Nobody paid attention on us, it was crowded, noisy, sad. The Germans were busy.

There was a second door in the kitchen, which led to the railroad. We went down the railroad about 200 meters away. Suddenly we met a man. He came closer and asked quietly where we were going. My Mom said: "I don't know, I am going where my eyes look". He said: "You have to take off the yellow star from the front and from the back. Let me help you". He covered the faded spots with some "shmata".

Then he pointed ahead to the haystack to hide and stay till darkness and told us to move further into the forest after dark. He said: "Don't try to meet and ask anybody, just go in the right direction." My Mom and I didn't eat for two days until we reached the first people in the forest. Thus began the next chapter of our life, also terrible and dangerous, because nobody believed that it was possible to survive from ghetto.

Passover Bagels (gebrukts)

parve

1/2 cup vegetable oil
1 1/2 cup water
2 cups Matzo Meal
1 tsp sugar
1/2 or 1 tsp salt
4 eggs
1 tbsp fried onion

Directions:

1.) Mix 1.5 cup water and 0.5 cup vegetable oil and pour in a small sauce pan. Heat until boiling.
2.) While the water with oil is heating up, mix 2 cups of matzo meal, salt and sugar in a small bowl.
3.) Take off the boiling pot from the fire and slowly pour into the boiling liquid matzo meal mixture, mixing all the time. Add fried onion to the batter and cool.
4.) Add 4 raw eggs and mix in to the cooled batter. Refrigerate for at least 10-15 min.
5.) Pre-heat the oven to 375-400 degrees.
6.) Make balls the size of about 2" or 2,5" from the batter and place on a greased cookie sheet. Flatten the balls with the wet spoon and make holes in the middle with a wet finger.
7.) Place the cookie sheet into the hot oven, bake until slightly browned, approximately 15-20 min.

Makes about 10-12 Passover bagels

227

Stuffed Chicken Neck (hutzel)

meat

1 skin of chicken neck
   (or take the skin off the chicken)
chicken fat,
      cut into small chunks with small pieces of meat
      attached. (About 2 tbls)
1 onion, chopped
1 cup flour or farina (or more)
1/3 cup of water

Directions:

Preheat oven to 350 degrees

1.) Remove the fat from the chicken neck or chicken skin, rinse well. Wipe inside with paper towel and then sew up one end of the chicken neck. If you have just chicken skin, sew it up so that you have a small bag about the size of a chicken neck, open at one end
2.) Prepare the filling. Fry small chunks of chicken (or goose) fat on a low heat until fat melts. Increase heat, add chopped onion, and continue frying until the onion gets soft and slight brown. Set aside.
3.) Fill chicken neck with the batter, sew up the open end.
4.) Boil water in a small pot and put the chicken neck into the boiling water. Lower the temperature and cook for approximately 40 min.
5.) Preheat the oven to 350 degrees, put the chicken neck into a small casserole dish and bake until browned.

Ceil Brauner
Linden, N.J, U.S.A.

I was born in Berlin, Germany in 1921, the youngest child in a family of two boys and two girls. My father was a businessman. In 1938 my older siblings left Germany and went to Palestine. In October, 1939 my father was transported to Poland because he was originally from there. A short while later my mother and I joined him there.

On May 3, 1941, in the middle of the night, Nazis with big flash lights banged on our door. I thought they were after my father, but instead they saw that he was too old so they took me instead. I was taken to a work camp. I was only twenty years old.

I never saw my parents again.

I worked in four camps. One job I had was to weigh the powder for ammunition. This changed the color of my hair and eyebrows to an ugly yellow color. I had to breathe that too. Eventually I was sent to several Concentration camps. Because I was lucky enough to survive all of the camps I was finally liberated from Ludwingdorf, Germany in 1945.

Right after the war I met and married my husband Samuel, who was also a Survivor from Poland. My brother from Palestine was in the Jewish Brigade in Belgium and he came to take us to Belgium where he was stationed. Then we set out illegally to go to Palestine in 1946. But my husband and I were caught and put into a military camp near Haifa for six weeks.

Finally in 1957 I came to the United States with a young daughter. Today I am blessed with a wonderful daughter, son-in-law, and two grandchildren.

Mandel Bread
parve

1 cup sugar
1 cup oil
4 eggs
6 oz chocolate chips
3 cups flour
1 tsp vanilla
8 oz chopped nuts

Directions:
Preheat oven to 325 degrees

1.) Mix sugar and eggs together.
2.) Add oil.
3.) Then add all of the remaining ingredients.
4.) Divide dough in half. Spread into long loaves on greased sheets.
5.) Bake at 325 degrees for 30-35 minutes.
6.) Remove from oven.
7.) Slice and bake for seven more minutes.

Fred Rose
Brooklyn, NY, U.S.A.
Submitted by his daughter Esther Posner, Southfield, MI

My father, Fred Rose, trained as a butcher in Germany and part of that training required an apprenticeship in a kosher restaurant where he learned a lot of the cooking basics. He always teased my mother that he taught her how to cook and she vehemently denied this.

Fred was born in 1910 in a small town in western Germany. In 1933, when Hitler came to power, he moved to Amsterdam, Holland where he soon opened his own butcher shop. When he felt he could support her, he sent for my mother, Ellen Westheim, his childhood sweetheart. I was born a year later. Fred and Ellen then successfully brought their parents and several sisters to Amsterdam to get away from the German threat to Jewish lives. However, after Holland was invaded, most of these relatives were deported and murdered in Sobibor.

My parents and I were taken to the Schouwburg (Dutch theater, now a museum, used by the Germans for deportation of Jews) but we were sent back home twice because my father was able to show special professional exemptions. The third time, we were on the truck that was to take us to the train station. In the thick fog, my father jumped off the truck, pulling my mother and me behind him and we escaped. With the help of the Dutch underground, a hiding place was quickly found for us in Enschede, an industrial center near the German border, and we spent a year hidden in the home of a young family whose 2 children did not know that there were 6 people living in their home with them. We all lived and slept in one room. I could not walk or talk aloud or play with other children or go to a dentist or bounce a ball. Once, German soldiers searched house to house and we hid behind a bookcase that opened into a narrow passage while the Germans searched the room we had just left. Subsequently, we were in various homes, at times separated, at times together, in Enschede and Delden and were liberated by the Canadians in April 1945.

What I remember most about my father during our years in hiding was his enthusiastic optimism that we would survive, his trust and faith in G-d and how he made me feel that because I was just a child, nothing bad would happen to me.

The recipe below is one that my mother, Ellen Westheim Rose, made when I was growing up in Brooklyn, after we left Amsterdam and settled there in 1949. I make it for my family and guests and my kids and husband have always eaten spinach because of it.

Fred and Ellen Rose

Creamed Spinach

parve

2 packages frozen chopped spinach
1 medium onion chopped fine
3 T margarine
2 T flour
salt and pepper

Directions:

1.) Cook spinach according to package directions.
2.) Do not drain.
3.) Set aside.
4.) In saucepan, brown onion in margarine.
5.) Stir in flour and continue to cook and stir until flour browns.
6.) Stir in the liquid from the spinach.
7.) Stir until smooth.
8.) Add spinach and season to taste.
   If too thick, you can add a little more water.

Sophia Machtinger
Brooklyn, NY, U.S.A.
Submitted by her daughter Ruth Faller

Sophia was born Zosia Fidler in Lodz, Germany in 1920. In 1940, as a young Jewish woman, she and her husband Pinio (Paul) were forced to move into the Lodzer Ghetto, where they endured unimaginable hardships.. They lived in constant fear, never knowing what the next day would bring.. In 1943 the Germans surrounded the ghetto and began selecting people to be taken away in trucks. Her sister and niece were taken away to Auschwitz, where they perished.

Sophia and Paul with their grandsons Bryan and Scott Faller

Finally, in August, 1944, Zosia and Pinio were taken to Auschwitz, along with her mother and several members of Pinio's family. A month later they were loaded onto cattle cars and taken to Stutthof Concentration Camp. Later they were taken to Dresden to work for the Germans. There they witnessed the Allied bombing of Dresden. On April 12, 1945, as the German army began to crumble, they were ordered to walk. For eleven days they walked across Germany into Czechoslovakia, surrounded by SS men. Finally, on May 8, 1945 they were released as the war came to an end. In 1946 Zoisa gave birth to a daughter, Ruth. And on March 22, 1949 they were finally able to immigrate to the United States.

In 1989 Sophia Machtinger published her memoirs. In the prologue she wrote the following:

This is my autobiography beginning with September, 1939 when World War II broke out. In 1955, in the United States, in Brooklyn, NY, where I live today, I decided to write about my husband Paul and myself during the war years, the Lodz Ghetto in Poland where we lived for five years before we were sent away to the concentration camps in Auschwitz, Struttholf, Pirna, and Theresiestadt, the longest-lasting ghetto feeding the ovens of Auschwitz with Jewish bodies gassed in the chambers. I felt I had to tell my story to my dear children, to my friends which I made in the U.S. and to everyone about the Jewish people who perished, about the atrocities inflicted upon us simply because we were Jews.

Sophia, Paul, and their children arriving in the United States at New York Harbor. Sophia is pointing to the Statue of Liberty.

Jews were surrounded with barbed wire, electrical wire without means to protect themselves and to fight against guns pointed at them. I am not a writer but I decided in my plain words to tell the world how innocent men, women, and children were slaughtered: how mothers who held their children next to their bodies, because they didn't want them to die alone, sacrificed their lives and went with their children to die together in the gas chambers.

We were lucky, just married, and then the war broke out and we didn't dare to think of a child when our lives were at stake, and then our survival was a matter of fate. Not that we both were stronger, it was just a matter of fate.

Each Holocaust Survivor has a different story to tell from this tragic war. This is my life story and my legacy to my children, the Jewish People and the world, with the hope and belief that mankind might learn a lesson from the past, that this history must never be repeated, and people must try to improve the world and provide a better future for generations to come.

Sophia Machtinger

Editor's Note: These excerpts were taken form "Memoir from My Life's Experiences" by Sophia Machtinger, copyright Brooklyn, NY 1989. The entire manuscript is available through the United States Holocaust Museum.

Chinese Cookies
parve

Paul Machtinger

1 egg
1 cup sugar
2 3/4 cups flour
2 sticks margarine

1/2 tsp salt
1/2 tsp baking soda
3 tsp almond flv.
6 crushed walnuts or peeled
half almonds

Directions:
Preheat oven to 350 degrees

Put flour, sugar, salt, baking soda, crushed nuts and 2 sticks of margarine from the refrigerator into a bowl. Knead and crush margarine with your fingers, mix into crumbs. Drop in an egg and almond flavor, mix, absorb all flavor and form a dough.

Use a dry cookie sheet, take between your fingers a chunk of dough, form into a ball, size less than a walnut. Make it flat in your palm and put on the cookie sheet. Glaze the cookies with a beaten egg. Trim the cookies with a piece of nut. Bake in preheated oven 350 degrees for 15 minutes. Watch they shouldn't burn.

Good luck!

Salmon Soufflee

One red can of salmon with
liquid
6 eggs
2 cups cornflakes
1 cup milk
1 midium onion—diced and sauteed
1 stick butter, drop of salt +
pepper to taste

_____

Separately blend eggs + salmon
the rest mix everything together
bake at 350º for 45 - 1 hour
Use pirex round dish
and grease before using

Hanna Green
Silver Spring, MD, U.S.A.
Submitted by: Hanna Green, Ari Nathanson, Regina Berthold, Kenny Berthold, Helene Goodman, Camille Butler, and Jessica Stover

Hanna Green miraculously escaped death while her entire family perished in the hateful fever of the Holocaust. Her survival and passion for life have since flowered into beautiful new generations of sons and daughters, grandchildren, and great-grandchildren. We are all survivors through Hanna—our matriarch.

She was born Hanna Greenbaum in 1918, and raised in the shtetls of Kalisz, Poland, a small town with a centuries-long Jewish history. The seventh of ten brothers and sisters, Hanna was a free spirit. She smiles even now when she recalls how, as a teenager, she would run off with her friends to a nearby lake to tan on the shore. And the smile is accompanied by a giggle when she describes how she used to playfully scare her friends by standing up and rocking their small rowboat in the middle of the lake even though she herself never learned how to swim.

Hanna and Morris posing for a photograph shortly after their engagement in 1939

When she was 21 years old, Hanna met Morris (Avraham Moshe) Fajwlewicz, a 27-year-old textile worker from Lodz, Poland's second largest city. After a brief two-week engagement, they married. The year was 1939.

The wedding came at a difficult time for the Greenbaum family, as Rivka Bina, one of Hanna's older sisters, had passed away due to a stomach ailment a short time before. The ceremony was kept small out of respect for the family's loss, and was held in the Greenbaum's household. No music was played.

The newlywed couple moved in with one of Hanna's sisters while they looked for a home of their own; a place to start a family. But anything resembling a normal married life halted only four weeks after their wedding, as the Nazi movement in Germany—boiling with hatred—launched its assault on Poland.

Morris, knowing that a Nazi occupation of Poland would spell horror for the country's Jewish population, used the dowry he'd received from the wedding to purchase train tickets that would take Hanna and himself close to the Russian (then USSR) border. Gary Fajwlewicz, Morris's brother, fled with them.

235

Hanna had no way of knowing that, after boarding that train, she would never again see another member of her immediate family. All eight of her remaining bothers and sisters—Shalom, Menachem, Esther Frydal, Sarah Gittel, Yitta, Kayla, Dovid Yaakov, and Yisrol Srulik—were murdered in Nazi concentration camps. Her parents, too, Chaya Hinda and Hershel Tzvi, both still alive and well when she left for Russia, were taken and killed.

When they reached the Polish border, Hanna, Morris, Gary and the rest of the passengers were taken off the train by German soldiers and forced into two lines; Jews in one, everybody else in the other. Before any of the Jews were allowed to leave Poland, they were searched and interrogated at gunpoint by German officers. Other soldiers had German Shepherds on short leashes and goaded them to ferociously bark and lunge at the Jewish emigrants to inspire fear and compliance.

In the line, Hanna was in front of her husband and brother-in-law. The Nazi guards asked her if she had any money, to which she lied and said no. (She had actually sewn her money and jewelry into the seams and linings of her clothes. She later used the valuables as currency to live on.) Fortunately, the Germans believed her and she quickly began walking through the security zone to the Russian border.

Morris was next in the line, but he did not fare as well as Hanna. In his haste to leave Poland, and among the gun-wielding guards and their vicious attack-dogs, he had forgotten to take off his watch made of fake gold. The Germans spotted the timepiece and, thinking it was real and that Morris was concealing more valuables, robbed and beat him.

Hanna turned back and pleaded with the soldiers to let Morris and Gary through, and miraculously was successful. The three of them crossed the border into Russia together.

Early on, nobody knew how serious the war would be. After a short time in Russia, the authorities asked Hanna if she would like to stay there or go back to Poland to find her family. She chose the latter; believing Polish propaganda reports stating that Poland's army was a mighty force that was sure to beat back the Nazi invaders. In reality, however, Poland was under German rule less than a month after the September 1, 1939 Blitzkrieg attack was launched. Before the Russians had time to take Hanna back, the border to Poland was sealed.

Morris' brother Gary opted to join the Russian army and was later shot in the knee in a battle with the Germans. No longer able to fight, he waited out the war in Russia and used his status as a Polish citizen to immigrate to the United States.

Meanwhile, Hanna and Morris were out of options. They knew nobody and had nothing—circumstances that were not tolerated by a government as guarded and suspicious of outsiders as the Soviet Union's. As such, they were packed into a train and sent to a penal colony in Siberia. It was a painful, cramped journey that lasted for weeks and got colder and colder as they crossed the thousands of miles that make up Russia's vast landscape.

Their destination was a labor camp somewhere in a Siberian forest, where the yearly average temperatures range from zero to -20 degrees Celsius. For protection, they were given nothing but rags to wrap around their feet and drape over their bodies. Hanna and Morris had become slaves; forced to spend their days cutting down trees under the watch of Red Army guards. Payment for their servitude was one bowl of soup and one piece of stale bread per day.

It was in this harsh environment that Hanna and Morris had their first son, Chaim Shmuel, who tragically passed away in February 1941 due to complications from pneumonia. He was one year old. Hanna and Morris were eventually allowed to leave Siberia and fled to a more forgiving climate. For a time they sought refuge in the city of Jalal-Abad, a mountainous region in the small Central-Asian country of Kyrgyzstan. Here, in a land noted for its lush walnut forests and snow-covered peaks, they had their second child, Rivka Bina (Regina), in 1943.

When the war ended in 1945, Hanna was finally allowed to re-enter Poland, so the small family packed their things on a train and went home. But post-war Poland contrasted sharply with Hanna's pre-war memories. "When we got back, there were no Jews left. It was all discrimination," she recalls.

Realizing that Poland was no longer the Jewish hub it had been, the three made their way into an American zone where they were given the option to start new lives in either the U.S. or Israel. Hanna had an aunt and three uncles who had moved to Washington, D.C. before the war broke out, and decided that was where they would go.

On October 11, 1949—Columbus Day—Hanna and her growing family arrived at Ellis Island on a ship called the General Moore. In the interval she had another son, Yechezkel (Charles Haskell), in Poland in 1946, and currently was pregnant with a second daughter, Helene (Faiga Chaya).

Hanna, Morris and the children found a little apartment near Hanna's relatives and soon found a cozy house near the corner of 8th Street and Kennedy Street in Northwest D.C., where a third daughter Camille (Tzivya) was born in 1951.

Despite language barriers, Morris found work as a tailor and quickly opened up his own business called Sun Bright Cleaners. Hanna helped her husband as a seamstress in addition to watching over her four children and taking care of the home.

After Morris passed away in 1976, at the age of sixty-four, Hanna married Joseph Green, a great man who had been a family-friend for many years. Joseph, too, was a native of Poland and a survivor of the Holocaust. A sheet metal worker by trade, he had enormous, powerful hands and a heart and soul to match. He was a jovial man who rode a bike, bowled with Hanna on a league, and showed the warmest gratitude and affection for the children and grandchildren he inherited through Hanna. He sadly passed away in 1998.

In 2001, Hanna reconnected with her first cousin Henry Greenbaum, who had also escaped the German concentration camps by fleeing to Russia and, after the war, to France—eventually making his way to Los Angeles, California. After years of telephone correspondence and a couple of visits, Henry moved from L.A. to Silver Spring, Maryland, where Hanna currently lives, and was warmly embraced by more than thirty family members he never knew. Henry, too, was the only survivor from his family. His mother, father and two sisters were killed by the Germans during the war.

Our family owes everything to the bravery, love and devotion of the few people mentioned in this story—these survivors of horror. They each lost so much, yet have given so much back. They will never be forgotten.

My mother's entire Greenbaum family. The only
survivors from that picture are my mother (#18)
and her first cousin Henry Greenbaum (#23).
Hanna and Henry married four years ago.
Everyone else was murdered in the Holocaust.

Sugar Cookies

parve or dairy

4 eggs
1 cup sugar
1 stick margarine or butter
4 cups flour
1 tsp vanilla
2 tsp baking powder
salt

Directions:

Preheat oven to 350 degrees

1.) Mix the flour, baking powder, and salt together in a large mixing bowl.
2.) Place the butter and sugar together, and beat with an electric mixer.
3.) Add in the egg and vanilla.
4.) Gradually add the flour mixture.
5.) Use a little water or milk if the mixture is too thick.
6.) Beat together ingredients until the mixture pulls away from the side of the bowl.
7.) Divide the cookie dough in half, wrap in waxed paper, and refrigerate for two hours.
8.) Using a floured rolling pin, roll the dough out thin (about 1/4 inch) on lightly floured surface.
9.) Use cookie cutters to cut out your desired shapes.
10.) Sprinkle with sugar crystals if desired.
11.) Bake on greased pan at 350 degrees for 8 to 10 minutes or until golden around the edges.
12.) Let cool for 2 minutes on cookie sheet.

Enjoy!

Apple Cake

parve

4 cups flour
1 tsp salt
1/2 cup oil or margarine
4 eggs
2 cups sugar
2 tbsp baking powder
1 tsp vanilla
5 large wine sap apples, peeled and thinly sliced
2 tsp cinnamon
1 cup walnuts or other nuts (optional)

Directions:

Preheat oven to 350 degrees

1.) Mix the oil, eggs, and vanilla together.
2.) In a separate bowl, mix together the dry ingredients.
3.) In a third bowl, mix thinly sliced apples and sugar together thoroughly.
4.) Set aside.
5.) Add the egg mixture to the dry ingredients, mixing until combined (add nuts if desired).
6.) Pour 2/3 of the cake batter into a greased 9" by 13" baking pan.
7.) Gently spread the apple mixture in an even layer over the bottom layer of batter.
8.) Use the remaining 1/3 of cake batter to cover the apple mixture.
9.) Bake for 50-55 minutes or until a toothpick placed in the center of the cake comes out clean.

Bronia Furst
Linden, N.J, U.S.A.

I was born in Stanislav, Poland. My father was a businessman and I had a brother. I was 9 years old when the war started. We were taken away to four camps. My father was shot and killed at one of the camps and I was separated from my mother and my brother. We were all starved at the camps.

I was eventually liberated by the Russian Army in Ukraine and I was placed in an orphanage. A Jewish officer from the Russian army came to the orphanage looking for his daughter. I fit the description of his child so they brought me to him to see if I was his daughter. I knew that my father had been shot but I said to the man in Yiddish "Please get me out of here."

The man left but came back the next day and somehow took me out of the orphanage. He took me to the train station and put me on a train, where I stayed for two weeks until I arrived back at my home town. Because I was a young girl traveling alone people on the train gave me food to eat.

When I arrived at my home town I asked someone where the Jewish Market was. They told me it no longer existed. A woman asked me who my family was. When I gave her my name she said she thought that my aunt survived. She took me home, washed me, fed me, and put me to sleep. The next day she went out to look for my aunt and brought her to me.

But it wasn't my aunt...it was my mother! And my brother was alive too.

**Bronia (Netzler) Furst
and Abraham Furst
at their wedding party**

Parve Apple Cake

parve

1/3 cup margarine
1 cup flour
1 tsp. baking powder
1 scant cup brown
sugar
2 eggs
1 tsp. vanilla
8 cooking apples
Salt

Directions:
Preheat oven to 375 degrees

1.) Use a square glass pan.
2.) Cut apples in 1/8 pieces and line them into the bottom of a greased floured pan.
3.) Add brown sugar, eggs, margarine and vanilla.
4.) Sift flour, baking powder, and salt.
5.) Mix all together. Pour mixture over apples and bake for 40 minutes at 375 degrees.
6.) Walnuts and raisins can be sprinkled over the apples before batter is added.

Rugalach (my mother's recipe)

parve

2 sticks margarine
1 egg
1 egg yolk
1 pkg. dry yeast
1/2 cup warm water
1 tsp sugar

Sidney Furst's daughters' Bat Mitzvah in 2001: Bronia Furst is on the left, Bronia's son is in the back, Bronia's grandson David is in front and her granddaughter Ariel Lisa Furst is on the right.

Directions:

Preheat oven to 350 degrees

1.) Mix together margarine, eggs, and egg yolk.
2.) Let all other ingredients sit for 1/2 hr to proof.
3.) Add yeast mixture to top mixture.
4.) Add 3 cups flour to form dough.
5.) Divide into 3 equal parts.
6.) Add flour to rolling pin and roll out each part into pie shape.
7.) Filling:
   - 3/4 cups sugar
   - 3/4 cups walnuts
   - 1 tsp. cinnamon
8.) Combine above and spread on top of dough.
9.) Use a knife to cut into little triangles, roll them up from wide to narrow side to make rugelachs.
10.) Bake at 350 degrees 30-35 minutes on a cookie sheet with parchment paper.

Joshua Laks
Tel Aviv, Israel

September 1945, taken in Lodz, Poland 4 months after the liberation

Joshua Laks was born in 1927 in the town of Zaklikow, Poland, the son of Avner and Rachel (nee Weinreich). He was the middle son, between the first born Moshe, and the youngest, Herzel. Upon the outbreak of the Second World War and the Nazi occupation of Poland, the family remained together, living and working in the ghetto until its liquidation. On November 3, 1942 his parents, brother Herzel, and members of their extended family were sent on a transport to the Belzec extermination camp. Joshua and his brother Moshe were sent to the Budzyn labor camp.

At the outbreak of the war Joshua was a boy who had not yet celebrated his Bar Mitzvah. In the coming years he would grow in a daily struggle over each crust of bread and scrap of potato peels just to survive. From that day in November, 1942 he began a grueling odyssey that went on for years, from one concentration camp to the next, through Poland, France, and Germany- ten in all. On May 2, 1945 he was liberated by the US 82nd Airborne Division in a camp named Woebbelin in the Northeast of Germany.

A few weeks later he left Germany and headed back to Poland only to discover that not one member of his family was alive. He resumed his studies for some months then returned to Germany as a counselor for youth groups in Displaced Persons camps.

In 1946 he left Germany once more crossing Austria and Italy to arrive in 1946 in Palestine. He went to a Kibbutz and lived there for five years. In 1948 during Israel's War of Independence he took part in battles on the Egyptian front.

Recent Photo of Joshua Laks

In 1951 Joshua went to Tel-Aviv, and in 1957 married Jona Fuks, a former inmate of the Auschwitz and Ravensbruck camps. The couple has three sons and six grandchildren. Joshua and Jona Laks are very active in organizations and institutions memorializing the Holocaust.

The above was taken from Joshua Laks' book "I WAS THERE, ZAKLIKOW, A Small Town to Remember" Copyright 2005, Achdut Printing: Tel-Aviv, which he generously sent to us.

Krupnik Soup
meat

I believe the name is coming from the Polish or Russian, Slavic language. This was a very popular soup with a basis, like we used in our famous Cholent. You can also call it, the 3 B' soup.

Beans-Bones-Barley (pearl)

We have eaten this soup in the cold Autumn/Winter season. In Alaska you can eat this wonderful soup all around the year. Warning !! it is a rich calorie soup. No diet.

With the materials used I excluded the meat since I think that the bones will give enough effect. Generally at home in Poland my mother prepared the soup in a pot for 10 people.

We were in the family only 6 (six). But to be on the safe side maybe guests will come. At home in Poland we also entered in this soup a piece of Kishke about 3/4 mtr. but I am not doing it today. This is an option. Be careful not to have the Kishke burst. God forbid.

Ingredients:

1 glass of white, small, beans
5-6 bones suggested of cattle knee bones
2 potatoes 400 gr.(chopped by grater)
1 celery 150 gr. (chopped by grater).
3 tablespoon powder soup, mushroom or beef
1/2 teaspoon white pepper
2 table spoon of white flour

3/4 glass of Pearl barley
3.5 ltr. hot water
2 carrots 300 gr. (chopped by grater)
50 gr. dry mushrooms (suggest champigon)
1 tablespoon salt
1 flat tea spoon of garlic chopped or powder
3 tablespoon of oil or shmaltz

Directions:

1) Put the beans ahead in hot water for at least 6 hours.
2) Take a pot of 5 ltr. with a thick bottom with 3.5 ltr. hot water.
3) Enter first the bones, the beans and the powder soup and let boil on a middle fire for about 30 minutes.
4) Upon that enter the materials, mushrooms, barley and vegetables.
5) Reduce the fire, to low.
6) After a while take the flour and the oil/schmaltz into a pan and make a unified mixture and put into the pot. Mix the soup.
7) After another hour of cooking please taste the soup and add the salt, pepper and garlic. Check if you like it.
8) If the soup is thick you can add a bit of water, if thin a bit flour.
9) Let the soup on fire all together about 21/2 hours. The best test if the soup is ready is when the beans are soft.
10) Make the last taste and add what you think is needed.
11) On the top you may put a bit of dill, preferred fresh.

Israeli Sweet & Sour tomato and onion salad
parve

5 to 6 red tomatoes (if available also yellow around 600 to 750 gr)
2 red or blue onions about 250 gr
2/3 glass about 180 cc water
1/3 glass of vinegar 5 percent 70-75 cc
100 gr about 2 full tbsp white sugar or sweet a low - proportional

Directions:

1.) Cut tomatoes into slices of 3-4 mm thick. Same with the onions, but only 2 mm thick.
2.) Take water, vinegar and sweetness and mix them for a while, to get an unified taste.
3.) Put the tomatoes with the onions into a glass or a ceramic bowl, and mix.
4.) Put the water mixture into the bowl to cover the vegetables.
5.) You may lightly press the tomatoes to get juice out (creating a real mixture of tastes).
6.) You can play with the sweetness or sourness, as you like, to your taste.
7.) Put the bowl into the refrigerator for an hour or so to have the salad chilled.
8.) The salad can be eaten as a part of a appetizer, or beside a meat or fish meal.
9.) Your attention is drawn, no salt or pepper is to be added.

Beteavon, Bon Appetit!

243

Gittel Hunt
Des Plaines IL, U.S.A.

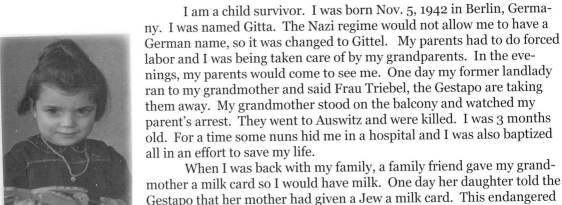

I am a child survivor. I was born Nov. 5, 1942 in Berlin, Germany. I was named Gitta. The Nazi regime would not allow me to have a German name, so it was changed to Gittel. My parents had to do forced labor and I was being taken care of by my grandparents. In the evenings, my parents would come to see me. One day my former landlady ran to my grandmother and said Frau Triebel, the Gestapo are taking them away. My grandmother stood on the balcony and watched my parent's arrest. They went to Auswitz and were killed. I was 3 months old. For a time some nuns hid me in a hospital and I was also baptized all in an effort to save my life.

Gittel in 1945

When I was back with my family, a family friend gave my grandmother a milk card so I would have milk. One day her daughter told the Gestapo that her mother had given a Jew a milk card. This endangered her life. My grandmother's husband was Catholic and that protected her until he died. When he died and my grandmother was to go to a concentration camp, this same lady who worked for the underground told my grandmother that she thought that my best chance for survival was to go to the camp with her.

I was in Theresienstadt (also known as Terezin) from about the age 1 ½ to 3 years old. I was in a nursery and my grandmother told me that on hot days she would beg the nuns to at least give us some tea. She had to scrub the sidewalks and stairs with cold water. I remember that for most of her life her hands would turn blue in winter because of this. She also told me that one day she was told to undress herself and me and we were sent to the shower room. She waited for the gas to come out and at the last minute they changed their minds and let us come out. Out of 15,000 children that were in Terezin, I am 1 of 100 that survived.

Theresienstadt was the show place for the Red Cross. This is the camp that the Red Cross was taken to and were told how good Jews had it. It was our own community. Concert, soccer games, mail, school classes for children. All show, not reality. It only happened while they were there. The Jews were watched carefully so they couldn't let the Red Cross know the truth. We came out on the last transport at the end of the war.

After liberation, my grandmother and I went back to the same apartment waiting for my parents to come back, which didn't happen. I met my husband shortly after I graduated from high school when I was a volunteer at the USO. He grew up without religion and had been looking for one for 10 years. He thought he would be comfortable with Judaism but didn't know how to explore that possibility. He went to Rosh Hashanah services with me and as we came out he asked how he could become Jewish. He finally found the religion he was looking for. A few months later, we were married.

Gittel's granddaughters

All went well, the first 6 months, and we had our first fight. I didn't know married couples fought. I never saw that at my friend's home even when I spent the weekend there. So, I thought this marriage is not meant to be.

Gittel with her husband

Rabbi Goldhammer recently blessed us for our 44th anniversary. I have to tell you that I'm told that I am a lot like my mother. She had decided that at a particular age she was going to have a baby. It didn't matter what the world situation was, she was going to have that baby. If she was deported to a camp, her mother would take care of the baby and when she came back, she would take over. It never occurred to her that she wouldn't come back. All I ever thought about was having children. Then the Dr. told me I couldn't conceive for a couple of reasons. We got a puppy and 3 days later I conceived. No one was going to tell me I couldn't have kids.

We now have 3 sons and 5 granddaughters. I didn't miss having parents, how can you miss something that you know nothing about. I did learn about that after having my own children. I didn't know siblings fought. I was an only child.

Of course there are family events and holidays that we had no one to share with. My sons ran into problems with prejudism at school. Imagine what would you say as a Jew let alone as a survivor when your son comes home from school after the series on TV about the Holocaust and he is told a joke I don't remember, but it ended with all you need is an ashtray for 6 million Jews. I thought my sons were normal and had no hesitation telling me what I did wrong as a mother.

But, when it came to the subject of the Holocaust, they were protective. My oldest son had a problem in high school. Some kids were passing anti-Semitic notes to him and they got worse as time went on. He finally showed it to his dad, and the kids got an in school suspension. I don't know to this day the contents of the notes. Another son was upset every time there was Grandparents Day at Sunday School because he didn't have any. Then there was the incident when someone made a Swastika and the word Jew on our front lawn with used oil. This can not be removed. We had to destroy the lawn to get rid of it. There are people who have said to me that there is no more prejudism in the world. You'll never convince me of that. I wasn't into this Holocaust thing through these times. I used to say, my grandmother survived and my parents didn't. I never put myself in that picture until I went to the World Gathering of Holocaust Survivors in Israel in 1981.

My oldest son was in a work/study program in Israel at the time and left the program early to join me at the gathering. We went to a kibbutz comprised of survivors from Terezin. There I met other children that survived the camp. We instantly bonded. A man who helped transport children out of Terezin, didn't know there were young ones like us in the camp. I was taken to a room with racks full of documents. He found my name and filled out a paper for me which says how many were on the transport, and how many survived. That's when it hit me, wow, this happened to me. From there my life changed a lot. I am a part of a Child Survivor group, and it means so much to me. That is the one place I don't have to explain myself. We know each others feelings and reactions to things. I have had a couple of things happen that they couldn't help me with. I left a job because I was threatened and harassed about being a survivor. I found I couldn't deal with it and felt I shouldn't have to.

Then I joined a very special congregation. The love and acceptance means a great deal to me. Last Simchas Torah service I was telling someone my story and was told what a miracle I was. That statement affected me a lot that day. Then I touched a Torah for the first time. It was the Holocaust Torah and it survived the same country I survived in Terezin. It has burn marks. The Nazi's tried to destroy it. Then Rabbi Chen called me over and showed me the tattoo the Nazi's had put on it because it was meant to be destroyed. It was such a powerful experience for me that I didn't sleep that night.

Many years ago, I tried finding out things about my father's side of the family only to be told that all the records were destroyed by fire during the war. Imagine my surprise when a few weeks ago I received a letter from a second cousin once removed who found me while looking at the Shoah Victims' Data Base on the Yad Vashem website. He traced my family back to the 17th century. He asked me if I would like the information. Through the wonders of e-mail, I received the family tree and he also sent me some very old family pictures.

I now find that I am telling my story more than I used to. I am feeling an urgency to tell it, time is running out. Our children must keep the story of the Holocaust alive.

Economy Matzo Balls

meat

1 c matzo meal
1 c boiling water
2 tbsp. melted fat or oil
1 egg, well beaten
1 tsp. salt
Dash of white pepper
2 tbsp. chopped parsley

Directions:
1.) Combine matzo meal and boiling water thoroughly.
2.) Add fat, egg, salt, pepper and parsley.
3.) Mix well and place in refrigerator for about 1/2 hr.
4.) With hands wet in cold water, make balls about 1 inch in diameter.
5.) Drop into gently boiling water.
6.) Cover and cook for 25 minutes.
7.) Serve in hot soup.

Makes 16.

Creamy Noodle Kugel

dairy

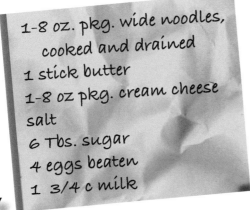

1-8 oz. pkg. wide noodles, cooked and drained
1 stick butter
1-8 oz pkg. cream cheese
salt
6 Tbs. sugar
4 eggs beaten
1 3/4 c milk

Directions:
Preheat oven to 350 degrees

• Cream butter and cream cheese; add salt, sugar and eggs.
• Gradually add milk and blend.
• Stir in noodles.
  (Mixture will be very liquidly.)
• Pour into a greased 13x9 inch baking dish.
• Bake at 350 for 1 1/2 hrs.

Makes 12 servings.

Carrot Mold

parve

3/4 c. shortening (I cut that in 1/2)
3/4 c. cake meal
rind and juice of a lemon
2 eggs
1 c. grated carrots
3/4 c. sugar
1/2 tsp. salt
3 Tbsp. water or orange juice

Directions:

Preheat oven to 350 degrees

1.) Blend shortening and sugar, add eggs beat well.
2.) Add carrots and other ingredients.
3.) Put into a well greased mold or 9 inch pan and bake 1 hr. at 350 degrees.

Gittel's three sons

Gittel's grandchildren

1860 Czech Torah that survived the Holocaust by being stored in the basement of a synagogue in Prague.

Morris and Norma Lipow
Washington, DC, U.S.A.
Submitted by their son Hershel Lipow

My parents Morris and Norma Lipow met and married after the war in Munich. As displaced persons surviving Dachau and Auschwitz, they made their way to Paris where my Uncle Leon, who had come to America between the wars, discovered my mother's name on a Red Cross survivors list.

Uncle Leon went to Paris to bring them back to America and more specifically, to a small town in Mississippi where he had settled with his wife's family. Imagine their sense of loss and longing for anything familiar and comforting. Ethnic food became that bridge, as European favorites rivaled Southern cuisine for a place at our table and our hearts.

Years later, I told my mother that I was dating a nice girl from Birmingham – a third generation Southern Jew. Upon meeting Susan, Mom immediately invited her to dinner. "I'll make stuffed cabbage" – code for "when's the wedding?" Fortunately, Susan fell in love with me and my mom's cabbage.

My mother passed away some years later without leaving us the recipe for her stuffed cabbage. Hopefully, I opened the cookbook published by Susan's family to look for a replacement recipe. As meant to be, the very first recipe I found was one for rolled cabbage submitted by Susan's mom Rosalyn in memory of her family's Shabbat dinners.

At our wedding, the Rabbi commented that it was ordained that our families should join together. My family was small, devastated by the war, and Susan's was huge, nurtured by America's freedom and prosperity. This recipe honors them all.

***Morris & Norma Lipow and their daughter-in-law
Susan Siegal***

Rolled Cabbage

meat

1 large cabbage
2 lb hamburger meat
1 1/2 cups corn flakes
1 TB salt
1/2 TS pepper
1 cup chopped onion
1 1/2 cups water

Sauce

1 TS salt
1/2 stick margarine, melted
2 cups water
1/2 TS pepper (to taste)
1 cup onions (fried)
2 cups tomato paste or 4 cups tomato sauce
1 cup celery, cut up
2 cups ginger snaps (broken)
Juice of 6-8 lemons

Directions:
Preheat oven to 325 degrees

Put cabbage in boiling water until leaves are limp (Freeze leaves for 30 minutes to help cabbage go limp). Cut thick parts out of cabbage leaves. Mix up hamburger and make balls. Roll meat into cabbage. Put in sauce. Bake at 325 degrees for 1-1/2 hours.
Makes 12 leaves.

249

Felicia Bryn
North Miami Beach, FL, U.S.A.

When Felicia Bryn was five years old, she and her younger brother were hidden by an aunt as Nazi soldiers searched the family's Warsaw ghetto apartment. After surviving that ordeal she was sent to live with a Catholic family. She practiced Christian rituals and moved frequently to avoid the Nazis. The following excerpt comes from her autobiography "Never Forget to Lie." The book is available by going to the following website: ***www.trafford.com.***

My Aunt Frania told me that my Mother was very beautiful before she was sick, and I would often shut my eyes and try to imagine her differently than as she lay in the bed next to me. Now her hair is tangled on her head and there is always sweat on her face, which Aunt Frania wipes away with damp rags. Mother's hands are now terrible to touch, hot and damp as the rags. I used to love my mother's hands. She liked to scratch my head and ruffle up my hair and then carefully pull it apart, twisting it in her fingers to make little curls.

I was just 5 years old when my Mother died from typhoid. It is 1942 in the Warsaw Ghetto. Aunt Frania will not let me go near the windows to look out. I have not even been able to go outside to play for weeks. I am tired of being inside. I have only one crayon to color with and Yurek, my baby brother has broken it into pieces. Suddenly, our door flies open. In the hallway people are screaming and running.

I hear the words "lapanka" ("roundup!") and "wysiedlenie" ("deportation!"). Aunt Frania grabs Yurek off the bed and drags me by the hand to the coal box next to the stove. She shoves Yurek inside and shouts at me to crawl in. Before I am even crouched on the sharp pieces of coal, she shoves the lid over us. "No! No!" I scream, Don't leave us in here!" but Yurek is screaming louder inside than me. It is black and I can hardly breathe. I try to push up the lid, but Aunt Frania has lifted the water pail onto it. The lid will not move. Pieces of coal are pushing into me. The blackness is terrible, but Yurek's screaming is more terrible. I want to get out of this box. I want to get away from this screaming. I want to breathe. I want to live!

Yurek's cries are sucking all the air out of the box. I can hardly catch my breath. "They will hear him, the Germans will hear him," I am thinking and shriek at him, "Bad boy, bad boy! Look how you cry-- that's why Aunt Frania did not take us. Who can hide with a child that cries? Now there are German voices in the hall and pounding on the stairs. I hear the dogs snarling and barking, people screaming, Yurek screaming, doors of the other apartments being kicked open.

"Raus, Raus Fafluchte Jude!" (Out, out you Jews!), the Germans are shouting. There is crashing and more crying and Yurek screams louder than ever. "We'll die if you don't stop!" I shout at him, suddenly shivering. It is so hot inside this box, but I am shivering. Big drops of sweat are falling into my eyes--drops like the sweat that was on Mommy's face. I am wet all over now, hot from the box and cold from fright. And Yurek's screams are like hard sharp spikes breaking apart my ears. I want to live! I want to live!

The crashing and pounding are on top of us. Before I hear the door to our apartment burst open, I shove my fist into Yurek's mouth: he stops crying and I hold him close and whisper, "I love you, I love you, you are a good boy." Boots come pounding into the room. I hear crashing all over. The curtain in front of the stove is being ripped. They are right in front of us! Yurek and I stop breathing. The boots go away. The screaming in the halls stops.

Felicia Bryn's Pickled Salmon

parve

12 pieces of salmon
2 c. water
3/4 c. vinegar
2 1/2 tsp. salt
1/2 c. sugar

Directions:

Cover, turn to boil, and cook for 20 minutes.

Add 8 bay leaves, 8 black pepper corns, and boil for 10 more minutes.

Remove salmon from the pot (remove skin from each piece if you wish), and arrange in a deep dish. Cover with 3 onions (sliced very thinly), juice of 1 lemon, and the cooking juice from the pot.

Refrigerate and serve cold.

Enjoy!

Rose Glazman
Submitted by her daughter Maria Lachs
Blue Bay, NSW, Australia

Rose Glazman

My mother, Rose Glazman, born in Mezritch Poland, was the third youngest child, and the youngest daughter of 9 siblings. Her father was a Chassid and she also had an extensive, extended family of uncles, aunts and cousins. In early 1948, my mother, aged 34 and single mother of two, was a Polish refugee in Paris.

I was at that time in school, attending a prize giving ceremony during which, for the first time, I received a prize. I had been fortunate enough to receive a silver prize representing second place in my class. As a rule, my mother was too busy to attend these functions as she had to work to earn money so that we could have food on the table.

It was only two years earlier that my teacher thought I was retarded. She failed to take into account that I had been in a sanatorium for the treatment of pulmonary tuberculosis for over a year.

Consequently I was academically more than a year behind most of the children in my class - hence her diagnosis.

So now, with my book of the Tales of Hans Christian Anderson wrapped up neatly in silver paper under my arm, I was ecstatic. I was eager to relate to my mother that I had won this second prize at school. I skipped joyfully, most of the way home. I was still happy when I reached my courtyard. I heard the raucous voice of a woman howling, crying loudly and painfully, almost continuously. As I started up the staircase towards my apartment on the second floor, I thought I could actually hear my mother's voice in some of the sobs. When I reached my door I realized that the howling did indeed come from inside my apartment.

I opened the door and found my mother slouched over her sewing machine, sobbing uncontrollably, her body shaking with each sob which also caused a paper she was holding in her hand, to wave up and down, in wide arcs in the air. I examined my mother and she did not seem to be physically injured. I tried to catch her attention, but she was too distraught to notice me. She had a vacant look. I spoke to her, trying to attract her attention again. "Mummy! Look! I've been given a prize, the silver prize. Only one person was better than me. Are you not glad for me?"

Mother continued to howl, but now, slowly realizing that I was home, she tried to explain herself to me "Mimi, they are all dead. My whole family is dead. Even my house in Poland no longer exists in my street. I no longer have anyone but you. You are now my only family. You will have to replace my father, my mother, my sisters and my brothers, my aunts, my uncles, my cousins and all my friends. I have no one else but you."

I stood quietly, stunned by the enormity and the seriousness of the request. I knew that I could not replace all these people. That was too tall an order. But replacing her friends, this I believed I could do. I have genuinely tried to always be my mother's best friend until her death in 2003. I helped her sew in her work, I helped to translate when she saw a doctor or a public servant, I helped her cook and clean and look after my little brother. I helped her in every possible way I could.

In her memory, I include the following two Passover Cake recipes . . .

Flourless Chocolate Cake

parve

120 gms Sugar
150 gms dark chocolate
    melted in bain-marie
6 eggs separated
1 1/2 cups almond meal

Directions:

1.) Beat 6 egg whites with half the sugar to thick snow.
2.) Beat together 6 egg yokes with other half of sugar.
3.) Add melted chocolate to egg yolk mixture and beat.
4.) Add 1.5 cups of almond meal to mixture and then,
5.) Gently fold in the beaten egg whites.
6.) Pour into baking-paper lined and greased tin.
7.) Bake for 1 hour at 180 C.

Citrus Dessert

parve

3 or 4 navel oranges
6 eggs
1 cup sugar
1 1/2 cups ground almonds
2 tsp baking soda

Directions:

1.) Boil, then simmer, the oranges (no pips) or 6 limes (cut in half with pips removed) for 2 hours in enough water to cover them.
2) Then mash fruit in blender.
3.) In another bowl beat the 6 eggs with 1 cup sugar and 2 tsp baking soda.
4.) Add ground almonds to egg mixture.
5.) Lastly add mashed citrus fruit.
6.) Bake in greased and grease proof-paper lined tray for 1 hour at 180 C.

253

Shimon Glazman

Submitted by his niece Maria Lachs
Blue Bay, NSW, Australia

Shimon Glazman

In early 1948, my mother had received information from reliable sources, that she was the sole survivor of her entire family. About six months later, she was overjoyed when two of her brothers, contacted her from Russia and she organized for them to travel to Paris so that they could be reunited.

Imagine her astonishment when she found out that another relative with her maiden name, a second cousin, whom she hardly knew because he had lived in another town, was also searching for his family. She arranged for him also, to come to Paris from Poland. He had lost his wife and two little children in the Auschwitz crematoria, as well as the rest of his immediate family in Majdanek. He was quiet and shy, a sad little man, constantly wondering why he had been spared and why he could not have died with his loved ones.

Mother decided to act as a matchmaker, so she asked her acquaintances to introduce him to possible marriage partners. When he seemed to become friendly with another Holocaust survivor, Luba, who also had lost her husband and extended family members during the Nazi occupation of Poland, my mother urged them to forge a new family.

Luba had survived with her small daughter and my mother tried to point out to both of them how much they needed one another. He was alone and sadly still pining for his family, and had no one to help him to live comfortably while he worked so hard making hairbrushes. He earned money but had no one to spend it with. She needed help to bring up her daughter, and would be able to provide him that housekeeping help, comfort and companionship if they formed a family.

Soon they agreed and the wedding date was set. Many people came to share in the wedding festivities on the day. In those days, soon after the war, because so few people had any relatives to invite, total strangers would be welcomed into the synagogue for any family celebrations. In this way, people could have witnesses to special events as well as make-believe family members, who shared in, and doubled the joy of the celebrants, and sometimes even contributed with provisions or towards the expenses. When the synagogue was fairly crowded and the bride had arrived, the groom, my Uncle Shimon, who had been sighted in the synagogue earlier, was now nowhere to be seen.

Since my mother was also missing, I went all around the synagogue building, looking for her. In the back of the synagogue there was a steep staircase, leading up to an apartment. On each step of the staircase stood various strangers, among whom my mother appeared to be waiting on one of the highest steps. I began to insinuate myself upwards, towards where my mother stood. At the top of the staircase, a door was ajar, revealing my uncle Shimon, sitting on a chair with his hands on his temples, crying his eyes out while he was reiterating to a companion that he could not go on with this wedding.

He was still in love with his wife and he felt it would be unfaithful to her if he remarried. He could not bring himself to go down to this wedding, even though he did not intend to hurt Luba by leaving her at the altar. His eyes were red and swollen, he was sweaty and disheveled and his white shirt stained with tears and crumpled.

Eventually, the person who was speaking to him, left him, shaking her hands in the air in an act of exasperation, as if praying to God for help. Another person, at the top of the stairs then entered the room and again tried to convince him to come downstairs. Shimon did some more sobbing and explaining, and this person was equally unsuccessful. My mother was next in line on the staircase. And as the previous person walked out of the room, my mother walked in like a bulldozer, telling him to stop thinking of himself and to start thinking of the pain and embarrassment he was causing Luba. She was a fine woman and did not deserve this insult.

He would get married today and divorce later if it did not work out. But now the wedding was going to take place. While she spoke, she pulled down his shirtsleeves and buttoned up his shirt. She picked up a tie lying on the back of his chair and tied it up for him, speaking all the while. She picked up two cards that he seemed to have been focusing on, from off the table and told him "They are dead. Kiss them goodbye and tell them you will always love them and that no one can ever take their place. But you must put them away."

He sobbed again and kissed both photos tenderly. Mother wiped them dry with her hankie and she placed them into the left inside chest pocket of his suit jacket which was also hanging on the back of the chair behind him. She stood him up and put the jacket on him and dragging him by the arm, she moved him towards the staircase. By then, he could not have had anymore tears left. He was totally exhausted and as if in a daze; in a childlike manner, he followed my mother without paying attention to where his feet were going. He nearly fell down that first step. She supported him all the way down, and at the bottom of the stairs she ran her fingers through his hair to tidy it up. She gave him a kiss on both cheeks and whispered "good luck" and walked him right around to the front of the synagogue building to enter the portals of the synagogue. She took him all the way to stand beside his bride, who was now smiling happily at him. They were married that day in 1949, beneath the Chuppah. The members of the synagogue yelled the loudest shrieks of delight and Mazel Tovs that a small community could produce when he crushed the glass beneath his feet at the end of the marriage celebration.

When I returned to France in 1964 and went to visit him, he showed me two photos: one of a beautiful woman, the other of two darling infants. I had never seen these before, and so I asked him "Who were they?" He answered "My first wife and children." I said something like "What a sad loss!" And tried to return his photos to him. But he refused them. He explained that his adopted daughter did not understand her parents and laughed whenever either of them cried, due to a sad reminiscence of their past. So he felt he could not entrust his two valuable photos to his daughter. He wanted me to have them, explaining "when I am gone, who will be left to love them if not you."

I have kept and honoured his photos, but when I handed them in to the Jewish Museum for posterity I realized I did not remember their first names. In honour of my Uncle Shimon who remained married to the end, I would like to offer the following recipes – Impossible Pie, Easy Chocolate Mousse and No Knead Apple Pie.

Easy Chocolate Mousse
dairy

Ingredients:
- 2 eggs (separated)
- Pinch of cream of tartar
- 1 jar of pure cream
- 2/3 of a 200 g pack of dark chocolate

Directions:
- Beat egg whites with a pinch of cream of tartar into snow.
- Heat but don't boil the cream in a saucepan.
- Remove cream from heat and stir in chocolate to melt. Stir until chocolate has dissolved.
- Add egg yolks while still warm and stir.
- Allow to cool completely, then whip to thicken. Gently fold in egg snow and pour into cups.
- Refrigerate.

255

Impossible Pie *(The recipe can be sweet or savory)*

dairy

60 g butter
1 cup sugar
1/2 cup sifted self raising flour
pinch of salt
1/2 cup desiccated coconut
4 eggs
1 1/2 cups of milk
grated rind of 1 lemon
juice of 1 to 2 lemons

Directions:
1.) Grease flan dish.
2.) Place butter and sugar into food processor and blend.
3.) Add flour, salt and coconut. Blend on pulse setting.
4.) Mix together eggs and milk with fork then add to the mixture above.
5.) Add rind and lemon juice. Pulse again.
6.) Pour into flan dish and bake for 1 hr. in moderate oven at 180 degrees Celsius.
7.) Cake will sit on top of a lemon custard.

For savory version, replace sugar, coconut & lemon with vegetables as listed:
With 60 gms butter, 1 cup SR flour, 4 eggs, 1.5 cups milk, 1 garlic clove crushed, 1 tbs finely chopped parsley or coriander, a couple of spoonfuls of finely chopped spinach, grated carrot, peas, onions, shallots, red capsicum or chili, 3 to 4 tbsp grated cheese or cottage cheese, +/- salmon, tuna or smoked salmon.

No Knead Apple Pie

dairy or parve

Directions:
1.) Combine last four ingredients in a bowl and mix.
2.) Use an ungreased 9 inch square cake tin.
3.) Cream butter, sugar and add egg yolks and vanilla.
4.) Add SR flour with a wooden spoon to a consistency that does not stick to fingers.
5.) Take small amounts of dough the size of a walnut and pat flat between palms of hands to the thickness of a banana skin and place on ungreased tin.

- 2 eggs (separated)
- 4 ozs unsalted butter or oil
- 4 ozs sugar
- 1 tsp vanilla
- 1 1/2 cups self rising flour
- 6 apples (peeled, cored and grated)
- 1/2 cup sultanas soaked in juice of 1 lemon for at least 1 hour
- 1 tsp powdered cinnamon
- 1/2 tsp powdered cloves

6.) Keep making little flat patties and place them overlapping one another across the bottom and sides of ungreased tin (leaving less than a quarter of the dough mixture for the covering of this cake).
7.) Brush egg white on the bottom layer of crust before filling with apple mixture.
8.) Make little patties to line the top of the apple cake, again overlapping one another but leaving a small central air hole for steam to escape.
9.) If there is any egg white left, brush top of the cake with it (optional) and sprinkle with sugar.
10.) Bake for 1 hour at 180 C or until cake dough is golden brown.

256

Agnes Mandl
Buenos Aires, Argentina
Submitted by her daughters Mirta, Agi, and Marga

Mandl Family

Agnes Mandl was born on May 4th 1924, in a small town called Sárosd, located in the province of Féjer, approximately 80 km south of Budapest. Its name, which means muddy, boggy, probably derives from the swampy surrounding lands that make farming very difficult.

In the year of her birth, a little more than 2,200 inhabitants lived in that town, most of them were Roman Catholics. Among them there were 30 Jews that played an important role in the local economy since they owned the only mill, the only grain storage house and the only stock yard.

Imre Mandl- that was the name of her father- ran a general store, located in what was called "Mandl Corner". Besides, he was a grain trader, milk collector and oil sales agent. Her mother, Gitta Kellner, divided her time among helping her husband with the business, the household chores and the upbringing of their children.

Sandor, whose nickname was "Shany", was two years younger than Agnes and was pranky and playful. The paternal grandmother completed the primary family group.
Sárosd´s Jewish collectivity did not have a synagogue. When the high celebrations approached, they traveled to Seregelyes, a nearby town, or they hired a seminarist that went specially from Budapest to celebrate and fulfill the "minion".

Agnes´s childhood was like any other at her time. It became a period of her life that she would remember with yearning; surrounded by the love of her parents, the tenderness of her brother and the company of the other Jewish families of the town; Deutsch, Goldner, Heisler, Weisz, Lehner and Medak. When she finished her primary school, her parents sent her to study in Budapest. She entered the "Skot Iskola", a Scottish- Anglican school where many Jewish students went. At first she was a boarder and then she rented a room in the house of a Jewish family. She expected the weekend with anxiety because it was then when she returned home at her hometown in order to meet the beloved ones.

Although in the year 1920 there was already in Hungary a law that limited the entry of Jews to the University. In 1938 there started the enactment of laws that progressively restricted their rights. In 1933, the National Socialism, with Hitler as a leader, had officially gained the power in Germany and under Nazi pressure, there appeared many clearly discriminatory measures in Hungary such as the expulsion of professionals from business associations, the prohibition to enter the civil service, to publish newspapers and magazines, mixed marriages, the punishment of sex relations between people of different religions , the withdrawal of citizenship, the expropriation of real property , etcetera. At that time, for convenience reasons, all the members of the Mandl family had changed their original last name to Mero.

257

The afternoon of March 19th 1944, after having lunch at the maternal grandparents house and while she was watching a movie, the show was suddenly interrupted by the German forces that had occupied Hungary. That day, Agnes´s life would do an about-turn.

Agnes and her brother had not returned home that weekend. As soon as they received the news of the occupation, they phoned their parents who ordered them to take the first train and return to Sárosd the following day. Unfortunately that was the last time they would hear their parents' voices. Shany, despite being only 18 years old, refused to return home. He thought that if they stayed in Budapest, a much bigger city, they would not be noticed. However, Agnes obeyed the order because, among such uncertainty, she needed the warmth of her parents.

The following day, very early in the morning, she packed some belongings in a small suitcase and, together with her brother who escorted her to the train station, took a tramway that was supposed to take them to the terminal station. They never reached their destination. During their trip, German soldiers, SS, with their frightening dogs strongly ordered all the Jews to get off the tramway. Agnes and Shany immediately stood up. –"But, Miss, you are not Jewish", a Hungarian policeman that was taking part in this proceeding said. "And my brother?" asked Agnes. "Oh, no, your brother, no". Agnes did not hesitate and between the opportunity of freedom and the possibility to stay together with her brother that had been so kind as to escort her to the station and whom she loved deeply, she chose for the latter option although that would lead her to the most cruel experience that a human being can undergo.

That same day, she was transferred to "Mosony Tolonchaz", the most famous prison in Budapest for sheltering the worst criminals of the city. Together with other women that were in the same situation, she was placed in an aisle between the cells of the prisoners, in a maximum security section. Another female prisoner approached her and asked: "Are you Agnes Mero? Because in the cell at the back there is someone who knows you and asks for a cigarette". Agnes could not move. Fear and desperation paralyzed her. Until today, she wonders who could have been the prisoner who said he knew her.

After midnight, she was transferred to "Kistarcza", a concentration camp in Hungary where there were political prisoners, professionals with "dangerous" ideas and war prisoners. She would stay three weeks there. In a situation of extreme deprivation and very poor sanitary conditions, she lived in a warehouse, sleeping on the floor, surrounded by other women that shared the same suffering. After some days, it was the festivity of Pesaj and the association that grouped Jewish entities sent some food "Kosher le Pesaj" that they had to eat with their hands because they did not have cutlery.

As the days passed by, Agnes felt she was recovering her inner strength. However, when she thought about her parents waiting for her at the train station in Sárosd and that she would never get to her destination, she had a feeling of deep anguish, impossible to describe.

After almost a week after her arrival to "Kistcarcza", to her surprise, a Hungarian policeman called her and led her to the camp infirmary. She was assigned a bed and a political prisoner, who had important contacts outside the camp and who tried to obtain better conditions for the prisoners, informed her that her parents were doing their best and were paying very high amounts of money to take her out of there.

The infirmary was the threshold to freedom. Those who obtained the contacts and paid an amount of money, pretending to be ill, abandoned the camp to be hospitalized at the Israeli Hospital. Agnes remained ten days laying in bed and without moving. At night, all the "patients" would abandon the camp. Moments before leaving, there appeared a political prisoner in charge of the proceedings.- "Miss Agnes, if you want to go, you have to pay",.- "But how is it possible? If my parents have already paid enough".- "No Miss, you don't understand. You have to pay", answered the prisoner with the evil and pride of he who considers himself the owner of the destiny, the body and the life of others.

258

That same night, everybody abandoned the camp, except Agnes that returned to the warehouse, which at that time was full of Jewish women infested with lice and conjunctivitis, humiliated, frustrated and with a justified feeling of pain that ate her up.

One day, just after midnight, while they were trying to fall asleep, Agnes and her partners were violently interrupted with the order of getting up and making lines and they were obliged to go into cramped cargo wagons and deported. More than a hundred persons traveled in those wagons, piled up, in places that were locked from outside. They had to travel standing up and there was no container to be used as latrine for their physical needs. Among the deported ones there were elderly people, children, ill persons, women that breast-fed their babies, men and women that became crazy from the ordeal they had to tolerate, religious people that prayed and prayed. The trip lasted two days. Those that died during the trip were thrown from the train. A humiliating, degrading and traumatic experience. A humiliation to the human dignity with unprecedented evil.

Agnes did not have any idea as to where they had just arrived. Hell on Earth. The deported ones were submitted to the process of selection or classification through which people were labeled as "non usable" and deserved the gas chamber or "usable" and entered a new dimension, unknown until that moment of the human history: Auschwitz. A scene that cannot be described. Gas chambers, summary executions, common graves, crematoriums, subhuman works, living corpses, burnt and putrid flesh, denigrating practices from SS. Just as Primo Levi points out the way of being hungry and cold in Auschwitz requires new definitions to describe the sensations that have nothing to do with what we usually construe as hunger and cold. As Victor Frankl described: it was better to become a prisoner of the most terrible nightmare than having to wake up and return to the reality of Auschwitz.

Agnes has just arrived to the annihilation and extermination camp. She is taken away all her dignity and is obliged to take off her clothes. She will only keep a photograph of her family that is returned to her by a polish woman that is in charge of keeping the objects seized from the deported ones. She is given a manly shirt that is very big for her, a shoe for her left foot and a boot for her right one. She is shaved from head to toe. And from the moment Agnes sets foot in Auschwitz, she loses her name and becomes 80264; this number is tattooed in the left forearm; a mark that will never go away and will accompany her for the rest of her life; as living evidence of her survival of the most tragic and cruel situation that a person could ever live.

80264 was taken to a barrack. She slept with seven other "numbers" in a "Koya" or kind of bed where if one turned, the other seven had to do the same. At four in the morning the strong reflections of the searchlights woke her up. She had to go to the "Appel", a denigrating ceremony that took place every morning when the Nazis called the roll and each number had to call out "present". Sometimes they made them stay standing, without moving, for hours. As 80264 was strongly built, she always placed herself in the first line with the objective of covering any companion that could be sick and therefore sent to the gas chamber.

The only food they had every day was a loaf of bread and a brown liquid similar to a soup. There were no spoons so they had to lick it, just as dogs do. To make their physical needs they used collective latrines. It was not easy to get used to obliged hours and the presence of the following person in the line. Bathing was one of the most traumatic experiences. Sometimes when they were still using the soap on their bodies, the water was closed. They never knew if the shower would be of water or of Ziclon B gas.

80264 arrived in Auschwitz on the first transport from Hungary. The polish women received them with evident aversion: "Here come the Hungarian whores", a phrase embedded in a deep resentment, although logical for those who had been in the camp for more than two years. At the entrance of the camp, there was a sign that read: "Arbeit macht frei" (Work will make you free), another sample of the evil irony of the killers.

Inside the camp, there was no space for trees or for birds. Only death and diseases like typhoid fever, tuberculosis, botulism and dysentery. Despite the deathly cold that froze the limbs, because no underwear was used, she never caught a cold. As if losing the condition of person and human dignity had modified her physiological structure enabling her to overcome situations that under normal conditions she would have never tolerated. She thought many times that it had been a miracle from God that generated a logic contradiction since most of the time she wondered that if there was a God, how He could allow something like this.

Despite the fact that when she arrived, someone had told here that nobody had left Auschwitz alive, 80264 never lost hope. She had the internal belief that she was going to survive. Notwithstanding the terrible conditions of life, she never had the idea of suicide. However, some acts of desperation, such as throwing oneself against the electrified fence that surrounded the camp- acts that happened daily- were not judged, and much less, considered as coward.

In the concentration camp, there was no place for emotions and feelings, but 80264 kept her identity thanks to one thing. Every time she looked at the photograph of her family, she felt pain in her soul, a spiritual tear, impossible to describe and that would never repeat in her life: neither in the intensity, nor in the form all through her life, even, many years later when she suffered the loss of other dearly relatives.

This is how 80264 passed her days in the death camp. Until one day when Josef Menguele, the doctor that made the medical experiments and the "selections " in Auschwitz, set her apart, gave her other clothes and moved her to another barrack. For twenty days, she was submitted to a million studies and medical examinations and finally put her in a wagon with hay on the floor and a barrel as bathroom. Agnes was part, with other 155 persons, of the first transportation of prisoners that left Auschwitz alive. She was taken to the "Pashnitz" camp, located at what today is the Check Republic, at that time a protectorate of Germany. When she left Auschwitz, her sensitivity appeared and tears dropped from here eyes along her soft cheeks. She fainted due to the emotion.

The director of the camp received them and said: "In this camp, no one has died of artificial death yet; but do not say where you come from". Every day they had to walk 4 km in the snow under the supervision of German soldiers that escorted them with their guns and dogs in a constant threat to get to the factory where they had to work. For that time, Stalingrado battle and the disembark of allied forces in Normandy had already taken place and Germany was slosing the war and needed slave workers to produce the goods necessary for the war.

Agnes worked in a spinning mill, making clothes for the soldiers that were in the front. One day, while she was working, she felt a terrible pain in one molar. An SS soldier took her to the dentist. At the door, there was a sign that read: " Jews will not be examined". Due to the insistence of the SS, the dentist, unwillingly, accepted to see her. He did not even make her sit down. Without anesthesia and while the SS held her head, the dentist took out the molar. Some time later, the pain would appear again. A healthy molar had been taken out. She would bear the toothache with the pain killers that another Jewish prisoner, a dentist who visited the factories to assist other prisoners, gave her. When she was released and returned to Hungary, her dentist would find that the molar affected was joined by its root to the other teeth. Had the dentist taken it out without an operation, he would have pulled out all the teeth.

During the weekends, she had to work in the garden of the factory director. It was so cold that her hair froze. The prisoners that accompanied her in the garden were sometimes so hungry that they stole the food of the director dogs.

One day, they took some radishes that grew in the garden. When the little son of the director realized, he obliged each one to put their foot on the footprint that was beside the plant. As everyone wore wooden shoes, the boy could not determine who the responsible one was and set the dogs free.

One midday, while they were at the camp, there was a general call by the loudspeakers and the director of the camp, standing on a table, informed that the Jews were free and threw them the keys of the camp. On the other side of the wire fence, Russian soldiers passed on their tanks yelling "Drasztutyi Tovarisz" (Welcome, partners). German women that had worked with them at the factory were also waiting for them with baskets full of food.

Agnes spent the following days at the director's house that was in front of the spinning mill where she had worked. The first night it was impossible for her to fall asleep on a soft bed so she had to sleep on the floor. The owner of the house begged her not to remember them as dogs. His wife offered them all her jewels and told them that it was their turn to suffer what Jews had suffered.

Some days later and after long and tiring proceedings she returned to Budapest. She went to the house of a friend of hers. When she arrived, her friend's mother started to cry. Agnes asked her for her parents but the woman did not know or could not answer her. When Agnes met her friend, they hugged each other and began to cry. When Agnes asked again for her parents, her friend closed her eyes and breathed deeply. There was no answer. However, Agnes had a feeling: "They committed suicide.... It was a very good decision". She had a contradictory feeling. On the one side she was very sad for the tragic end her parents had on the other she was certain that her parents would not have been able to undergo any situation similar to hers and that they could never have survived it.

What could she do? A young Hungarian, 21, cruelly humiliated; absolutely alone; without parents to give her warmth, ignoring the situation of her brother. Everything was loneliness in Hungary; it was devastated by the war and she did not want to stay any longer; her heart was" oppressed and the wounds were still open.

Temporarily, she began to work at a place where they accepted refugees until she got sick with hepatitis. A year before, she would have died from it. However, this was the passport to a new life because, while being at the hospital, she met Arek, a very handsome Polish, eight years older, also a survivor of Shoá, who had lost his wife and his eight year old son in Auschwitz, who worked for "Hashomer Hatzair" and who was recovering from pneumonia.
It was love at first sight. A love that would last all their lives. In less than three weeks, they decided to get married. When Agnes told the news to an Aunt, she answered her that she was crazy and that she had to go to a psychiatrist. On the other hand, her cousin told her to do whatever her heart told her to and that she would always be welcome.

An improvised "Cupáh" in an intimate ceremony only attended by the bride and the groom and the person who acted as rabbi, sealed the love pursuant to the Laws of Moses.
They decided to go to Palestine, which was under British control. After passing by Rumania and Yugoslavia, they met Arek´s brothers in Italy. When they were about to leave, Agnes received news from the Red Cross informing her that her brother was alive. She decided to postpone her trip in order to meet him. But for the situations of life, they could meet only 17 years later.
Finally, Agnes and Arek´s destination was not Palestine. Arek´s brother, who had already left, could not reach Palestine because the English did not let them and were sent to a prisoners camp in Cyprus. Agnes and Arek stayed three years in Italy, in the cities of Udine, Selvino and Milan earning a living by selling shirts. As they could not stay any longer without any documenter, they got papers to migrate to Paraguay. The adventure finished in 1948 when they entered Argentina. They rebuilt their lives and had two daughters: Margarita and Mirta.

Buenos Aires, December 1999

One of those warm days, typical of the summer in Buenos Aires, something happened and made me meditate upon an important aspect in my life that was rather asleep.

That morning I was walking near the Courts and I overheard a lawyer making a comment explicitly denying the Holocaust and the annihilation of six million Jews by the Nazis. The words I had just heard annoyed me though I did not have the courage to interrupt the conversation and to address the person who had just hurt my feelings. I wondered what I really knew about Shoah. As third generation of survivors it was not enough to attend yearly a commemorative act of the Holocaust. My grandmother, Agnes, had always told her experiences in Auschwitz. First to my mother and my Aunt, and then, to her grandchildren. However, I had not realized that my commitment in the effort to perpetuate the memory had been scarce and that I was closer to indifference than to an active commitment and I began to feel that I had to change my attitude. I could not stay with my arms crossed any more. The words of this man sounded in my head again and again and hurt my heart. Just as this person who denied Shoah, there were many others with the same idea that I could meet in my life. I was not going to let another situation like this pass by I reacted.

On the other hand, soon there would be no living survivors of the Holocaust. If the descendants of survivors did not do anything to perpetuate the memory, who would? "Learn from the past, learn from history so that things do not happen again". This is how a story that could not be interesting for another person lit in me the fire to meet my roots and to investigate what had happened. I decided to make a trip to visit the places where my grandparents had grown up and had lived. I want to tell you an anecdote of the trip. The day I visited Sárosd, I woke up very early to take the first train from Budapest bound for my grandmother's town. It was not easy to make myself understood since most Hungarians do not speak English. But despite this fact and after two hours of a tiring trip- endless, because the train stopped in every little town- I arrived. The town was just as it was fifty years ago. When I was walking along the route that goes from the station to the center, and a little before arriving to the main street, I noticed, on the side, a stone structure that called my attention. The first thing I thought was that it was some kind of monument in honor of a well known person in town. But as I approached I began to see a list of names carved in the stone. When I was near and did not need to make any effort to see, I could read: "URCOLTAK ES ULDOZOTTEK". I did not understand the meaning of these words. (I would then find out later that the translation is "Persecuted and Deported"). When I looked down and while reading the names of the list, my heart stopped for a second, my eyes got wet and my breathing was stronger. Among the names of the list appeared "MERO MANDL IMRE AND MERO MANDL IMRENE", my great grandparents.

New Year 2007 at Marga's home with the complete family and friends. Agi is in the right corner of the photo.

Filled with emotion, I ran to the post office and bought a phone card, and from the only public phone in Sárosd, I called my grandmother. She could not believe her ears; she did not know this monument existed. Unluckily I could not take any picture because the previous day, my camera had broken and there were no disposable cameras in town. I promised my grandmother that she was going to travel to see it. That night, when I returned to Budapest I laid my head on the pillow for a minute and I thought everything had been a dream. Apart from the thoughts, I was more and more convinced that from then on my voice would be the one of all those people whose lives had been destroyed and that claim Never Again; that of the victims of Shoá.

The year 2000 was a difficult year for Agnes. Her health was not good and her life was in danger.

262

Thank God, she could overcome this problem and on July 2001, she traveled to Hungary with one of her daughters and her granddaughter. There she found, Marisia, her sister in law, who had traveled specially from Israel to join the group. The night previous to the visit to Sárosd, Agnes could not sleep. She was very nervous and excited. She was so moved that, fifty years later, she had the same sensation she had in Auschwitz while looking at the photograph of her parents. Maybe because it was like meeting the soul of her parents.

The next morning, she woke up early, had a coffee with milk, with "Dóbos" cake and left for Sárosd. When she arrived, she walked from the station to the town as she used to do every Saturday when she came from Budapest. When she saw the monument, built in 1993, she stopped, lit two candles, looked at the sky and closed her eyes. In a very soft voice she began to utter: "

ITGADAL VIETKADASH SHEME RABÁ....

Agi, and her two daughters.
Marga and Mirta during a visit
in Budapest.

This is a photo of Agi´s family in Hungary.
She managed to hide the photo during all the
time in the camp. To protect it because it was
beginning to break she sewed it on a piece of
cardboard that she found on the floor, taking
a thread from her prisoner's uniform.

Hungarian Walnut Cake
Buenos Aires style
dairy

Flour 1/2 Kg
Butter: 250 Grs
Sugar: 60 Grs.
Yeast: 15 Grs.
Cream or Milk: 3 tbsp
Yolks: 2
A bit of salt
Marmalade
- (peach or raspberry)

Stuffing: Mix 250 Grs. walnuts plus 200 Grs. sugar.

Directions:
Knead the flour, the butter, the yeast (previously mixed with a little bit of sugar till it becomes a liquid) and the milk.

Let stay the dough 30 minutes at room temperature and divide into three pieces.

1 - Stretch one of the pieces and lay it over a pan for the oven, previously covered with butter and flour.
2 - Spread on a layer of marmelade.
3 - Cover with a layer of the nuts mixture.
4 - Place the other piece of stretched dough over and repeat.

The last layer must be the third piece of dough which has to be pierced with a fork Bake slowly until becomes pale brown.

COVER:
On the fire, mix 140 Grs. sugar plus 20 Grs. cocoa (powder) plus three black coffee (strong) tablespoons, until it gets dense.
Put off the fire, add 50 Grs. butter and mix it.
Pour the mixture on the cake.
When at room temperature, cut the cake in squares.

Agnes Merö Kupferminc won a prize at the Holocaust Museum in Buenos Aires. This work is a box containing two objects, the only two objects that Agi and her husband Arek brought with them from Europe. One is a belt that Arek took from a Nazi official at the moment he was liberated, and when he took the belt, he gave the Nazi the string he wore during all the time in the concentration camp.

Evelyn Pike Rubin
Jericho, NY, U.S.A.
Survived in Shanghai, China

Evelyn and 3 of her 4 children in front of her former Ghetto home in Shanghai (one daughter not pictured)

Eighteen thousand European refugees survived in Japanese occupied Shanghai, China during World War II. I am one of them.

Born in Breslau, Germany, when no country would let us in after the Nuremberg laws were promulgated, we went to the place of last resort – Shanghai. My father had just been released from Buchenwald where he had been incarcerated since November 11, 1938, right at the end of the Kristallnacht pogrom. He had to sign in with the Gestapo every week that he and his family would leave Germany within two months.

On February 13, my parents and I boarded the "Hakozaki Maru," a Japanese ship, leaving from Naples, and arrived in Shanghai, March 14, 1939. My grandmother would follow us a year later.

We were welcomed by the American staff members of the Joint Distribution Committee, who came with American funds to help the refugees settle in what was thought to be a temporary refuge.

Aside from the culture shock, what greeted us were the horrific unhygienic conditions, which produced epidemics of wide proportion. We had to get inoculated against cholera, typhoid, para-typhoid three times a year and smallpox once a year. All drinking water had to be boiled at least five minutes past its boiling point and the same had to be done for all fruits and vegetables.

My mother sold the personal possessions we had brought with us, to purchase an apartment in the residential French Concession and to establish a typewriter business which she and my father ran. I continued my interrupted schooling at the Shanghai Jewish School, a British school.

The sub-tropical climate, with cold, wet winters, monsoon rains that constantly flooded the streets, the summers with temperatures, measured by today's humidity index reaching sometimes 140 degrees Fahrenheit in the shade, took its toll on the western Europeans, already subjected to all the diseases around them. While in Buchenwald, my father's war wound, sustained as a German soldier during World War I at the battle of Verdun, had acted up and was left untreated. The climactic conditions in Shanghai only worsened the problem. He succumbed

Shanghai Jewish School, 1943

under these conditions, at the age of 43, leaving my mother, my grandmother and me.

On December 8, 1941 (we were on the other side of the international date line), we woke up to a tremendous explosion in the harbor of Shanghai and witnessed the parade of the occupying forces - the Imperial Japanese Army and Navy. Soon thereafter enemy aliens of Japan and Germany were interned in camps where they were going to remain for the duration of the war. At the moment, the refugees were left alone. A tremendous food shortage developed, only slightly alleviated with sugar, flour and rice rations.

The American staff members of the Joint were repatriated to the United States and no financial help was forthcoming to help the stranded refugee community. On February 18, 1943, the Japanese issued a Proclamation to the refugee community stating that we had three months to "relocate to a designated area." In effect we were going to live in a ghetto in the Hongkew (slum) area. My grandmother died right before our move. My mother and I relocated, with three other families, into a three room house (hovel), one toilet, cold running water, and no heat. We did our cooking on a little Chinese stove on the rooftop, forming egg shaped coals from coal dust mixed with cold water. The food shortage became even more acute and refugees were not just dying of disease but of starvation and despondency.

American planes constantly strafed us. Unfortunately, Germany's surrender on May 7, 1945, did not end the war for us in the Pacific Theatre. On July 17, 1945, American fighter planes bombed the ghetto. Some thirty refugees were killed and hundreds more were wounded. Our liberation came six weeks later, with the arrival of American Liberation Forces from Chungking, under the command of Maj. Gen. Claire Chenault.

Over the years, those of us who had survived Shanghai, got together at various reunions here in the U.S., and in Israel. This past April, was the most exciting reunion ever. It took place in Shanghai – the city that had given us refuge.

Three of my children accompanied me to this reunion. They were very excited to see the city where their mother and grandmother survived the war. It was hugs, kisses and tears as we met up with old friends again, mainly from the U.S., Canada and Australia. The first official program took place at the Center of Jewish Studies, which features a permanent display of the history of the former Jewish communities in Shanghai.

We were welcomed by local dignitaries, as well as our official host, Prof. Pan Guang, who was instrumental in the establishment of this Sino-Judaic Center at the university. They all joined us at a special dinner that evening, in celebration of Sino-Jewish friendship and to honor Shanghai for its role in Jewish history. Before the war there had been two large Jewish communities – Russian- fleeing the 1917 Revolution, and Baghdadi who had arrived in the mid 19th century.

Among the 120 reunion participants, were approximately 30 second- and some third generation young people. As they lined up for a photo session, tears were in everyones' eyes, as, again, realization dawned on us if it hadn't been for our Shanghai haven, none of these young people would be standing there. It was a most poignant moment.

The following morning we visited the Ohel Rachel synagogue (which has been visited by President Clinton). This building is on the grounds of the former Shanghai Jewish School, where I had received my education from 1939-1947 and where I learned English, French and subsequently Japanese, which was added to the curriculum in 1943. As part of our religious studies, we would visit that synagogue quite often. Those of us, who had attended this school, were crying as we entered the synagogue which has now been refurbished as a museum, commemorating the Holocaust and the wartime refugee community. Paparazzi dogged us everywhere. We were briefly permitted to enter the former Shanghai Jewish School. Again, a very emotional scene for those of us who had attended that school.

Our next stop was one of the highlights and most exciting part of our trip – Hongkou (Hongkew, the former ghetto). Again, we were most warmly welcomed by local government officials. For the edification of the press, who were present in great numbers, the speeches were first in Chinese and then translated into English for us. The officials were most anxious for us to visit Huoshan Park, where a large plaque in English, Chinese and Hebrew, commemorating the refugees, is located at the entrance. We signed a petition, to be submitted to UNESCO to designate this area of Tilinquao, the former ghetto, as a historic landmark, a World Heritage site.

I had wanted to show my children the room my mother and I had lived in during the ghetto years. Alas, workmen were in the process of demolishing the area. We stood in front of house #8, where we had lived during the ghetto years. The door was locked – no one lived there any more and there were signs on the door - one didn't have to know the language to know that these signs stated "No Entry – Dangerous – Keep Out." The workmen were kind enough to stop their hammering while we took photos and as soon as we departed, they continued their job of demolition.

On Friday evening a bunch of us attended services at the Shanghai Chabad, located in a beautiful house, within a gated compound, in an upscale residential area. We were warmly welcomed by Rabbi Sholom Greenberg and his beautiful wife Dina. After services, we were treated to a wonderful Shabbat dinner. Rabbi Greenberg then gave a little speech, welcoming our group. How exciting – Shabbat services at Chabad in Shanghai. Who would have thought of it!

Thus ended a great, wonderful, emotional and meaningful get-together. After some tearful good-byes, and "we hope to see you sometime soon," we all dispersed for post-reunion tours to various destinations. We went on to Beijing.

Author GHETTO SHANGHAI, lecturer, featured in award winning documentary "Shanghai Ghetto," narrated by Martin Landau **Note**: *During the Cultural Revolution, all western cemeteries were demolished, which also included the Jewish ones. My father's and grandmother's graves are non-existent.*

Evelyn's family at her son's wedding, 2005

Mother's German passport, which includes the government proscribed middle name "Sara"

Parve
Lokshen Kugel
parve

Pass issued to Evelyn by the Japanese occupation authorities, allowing her to leave the ghetto area

1 lb broad noodles
2 eggs
1 1/2 cups sugar
1/4 lb parve margarine
1 tsp cinnamon
1 tsp pure vanilla extract

Directions:
Preheat oven to 400 degrees

1.) Boil noodles about 6 minutes and at the same time melt stick margarine in lasagna size pan (can be aluminum foil pan) in oven.
2.) That way pan will be greased and margarine melted by the time noodles are ready.
3.) Beat eggs with the sugar, add cinnamon and vanilla.
4.) Mix the rinsed noodles into the mixture and then add the melted margarine.
5.) Mix well and then pour into pan.
6.) Cover with tinfoil and bake at 400 degrees for 40 minutes.
7.) It can be served right away, however, it is easier to slice into squares cold the next day.

267

Blanche Potchinsky

Lauderhill, FL, U.S.A.

Submitted by her daughter Gerda (Bierzonski) Bikales

Blanche Potchinsky was born in Skierniewice, Poland, as Blime Levkowicz. She moved to Germany where, upon marriage to my father, Viktor Bierzonski, she became Bronia Bierzonski. In hiding during the Holocaust years, her false papers identified her as Blanche Bergé, a name she liked well enough to keep after she immigrated to America. She later married Abe Potchinsky, and was known as Blanche Potchinsky until her passing in 1994.

My mother's kitchen was her kingdom, and cooking was her passion. It was a privilege to be allowed into her kitchen while she was busily preparing her special dishes, but rarely did the invitation extend to me. Though I was her much-loved only child, I was a clumsy bookworm with little aptitude for the domestic arts, of no help and in the way.

Her culinary wiles were an important survival tool in the years of relentless persecution when she and I were perpetually on the run. Living illegally in Antwerp (Belgium) without any means of support, she started a chocolate business on a Bunsen burner in someone's basement. After that enterprise fizzled, she launched a "restaurant" in our small furnished room that kept us afloat for a time.

Later, living in hiding on the edge of starvation in Lyon (France), she magically transformed the animal-feed rutabagas that were the mainstay of our diet into something close to edible. Still later in our constant wanderings, she talked herself into a job in a restaurant kitchen, where despite wartime food shortages her cooking attracted a clientele of soldiers of the occupation army. Until we had to flee again, the restaurant leftovers kept both of us alive, as well as several other undernourished Jews of our acquaintance.

Blanche and her daughter Gerda, Grenoble, France 1946

In the years of post-war abundance, my mom went back to serious cooking, eastern European style. Her first job in America was as a cook in a Yeshiva. When she became a grandmother, she was distraught over my little daughter's finicky eating habits which failed to do justice to her culinary creations. My son made up for it – he had a hearty appetite and enjoyed the food lovingly served at my mother's table.

When the opportunity arose to contribute my mom's story and a recipe in the Survivors' Cookbook, my children agreed that her "Compote" deserved to be featured. There was just one problem: my mother was not inclined to share her cooking secrets. When asked about ingredients or technique, she was reluctant to go into details. And quantities? Fuggetaboutit! "A little of this, a hint of that, a handful of these..." And so it went.

Note: Gerda Bikales is the Author of a Holocaust Memoir, "Through the Valley of the Shadow of Death: A Holocaust Childhood."

My mother's compote

parve

This is my reconstruction of my mother's simple but delicious compote recipe, based on furtive observing, fond memory and never-ending experimentation.

1 package of mixed dried fruit (7 oz)
1 package of dried apricots (6-7 oz)
1 package of dried pitted plums (7 oz)
4 apples preferably tart
a few thin slices of lemon, halved
about 2 tbsp brown sugar

Directions:

Cut up large pieces of mixed dried fruit into smaller ones; also cut up the dried apricots into smaller pieces. Leave dried plums whole.
Wash the lemon, dry and cut off thin slices; cut in half.
Peel the apples, cut into chunks.
Place all the fruit (including lemon slices) in a 4-quart pot and cover fully with water. Cook on medium heat to boiling, then reduce heat to maintain gentle boil for 30 minutes. Add water as it evaporates to keep fruit covered.
Taste the compote when cool enough to do so. If not sweet enough, add two tablespoons of brown sugar. If more is needed, add it in small increments, being careful not too over-sweeten this dish. Should that happen, don't hesitate to add some fresh lemon juice, a few drops at a time.

This compote is very forgiving. Proportions of dried plums to other dried fruit, apples, water, sugar and lemon can be changed, producing subtly different versions of the compote. It would be hard to spoil it. *Serve cold. Will serve 10 -14, more in a pinch.**

* *When unexpected company arrived, my mother was not beyond serving smaller portions of her compote on a bed of applesauce, homemade or commercial, explaining that this rich-tasting desert shows off best against the refreshing smoothness of plain applesauce.*

The Wagschals

Silver Spring, MD, U.S.A.
Submitted by Nicole Wagschal Rubloff
Daughter of Jack (Jacques) Wagschal

My grandparents were second cousins – Solomon was from Kosno, Poland and Yetta was from Germany. Solomon made his living first as a furrier and later as a diamond cutter, a profession common in the port city of Antwerp, Belgium where he had settled prior to WWII. My grandmother's job was to raise her three children, Sabina, the oldest (1935), Sam (1937) and my father Jack (1939). A fourth child, Israel died at 6 months of age. Their scant pre-war memories describe her as a dainty woman who loved dancing, music and poetry. They maintained a kosher, orthodox home, strict with rules and sometimes isolated from outsiders. Sometimes turbulent, sometimes humorous, family was first and foremost in the Wagschal household.

The Gestapo came for my grandfather first, rounding up the men in their apartment building. Shortly thereafter, my grandmother became very ill with Crone's disease and a bleeding ulcer. She underwent 6 operations and was taken directly from her hospital bed loaded on the last transport from Belgium to Auschwitz. When she arrived, her face flushed with illness, she stood before Dr. Mengele who mistook her red face as a sign of health, and not the illness she was experiencing. Yetta was subsequently sent to the "arbeit" (work) group.

Meanwhile the Wagschal children were not left alone. There was an active Jewish underground in Belgium of both Jewish and non-Jewish women. I came to learn later that this group had a name – l'Association des Juifs en Belgique (AJB). I came across a French book "Ils N'ont Pas Eu Ces Gosses" by Sylvain Branchfeld that is the one piece of documentation that I have to piece together the memories of my dad, aunt and uncle, which will be much easier when I have the book translated into English. The manifest of this home lists my father and his siblings as arriving at the Wezembeek house on Feb. 11, 1943. Their names are part of a list of 450 children who were there at the time. They were divided into various houses, in an atmosphere much like an orphanage. The major difference was that the Nazi's knew they were there and would periodically come and take children to help fill their transport quotas. Sabina remembers 60 children being taken away on their very day of arrival.

After 3 months, Sam was taken to a Catholic school, but still required to wear his Jewish star. From there he went to the home of a Catholic priest who would hide the children under his bed at night. Sam's worst memory is a soldier pointing a gun at them through the window.

While Sam was being protected by the Catholics, Sabina remained at Wezembeek with the head mistress, Madame Rosie Rothschild, of whom she has only fond memories. Perhaps realizing the power of the sun and nature to instill hope in her children, she granted every child a small plot of land to use as a garden. Sabina still speaks of how the sunlight helped keep her spirits alive. Sabina does, however, have many unhappy memories including abuse by a non-Jewish 12-year old boy. She described the home for Steven Spielberg's Shoah tapes as "hell on earth", lots of sirens and bombs, simply not knowing if you were going to live or die. They came after Madame Rothschild several times and they finally had to flee to the countryside. After they were gone, the Gestapo came and for lack of Jewish children took the 12-year old boy that had tormented Sabina, creating horrible conflicting emotions for the 8-year old girl when she discovered his fate.

As for my father, he was so young at the time – just 4 years old, with fear and hiding being the only life he had ever known. He moved around more than the others, probably because of his young age. He vividly recalls spending time in the woods, living off of berries. Despite his diabetes, he still has certain foods that he will not touch – peanut butter and popcorn among them – government surplus foods that were his only sustenance.

While their children were hiding in Catholic homes and in the countryside, Solomon and Yetta were surviving by just as thin a thread. When Solomon was taken, he was first sent to a French labor camp. He worked for a while and then managed to escape. He then found himself walking the French countryside and came across a farm. Realizing that his accent would give him away, he decided not to speak at all. Posing as a deaf-mute, he went to work on this farm, which belonged to the mayor of this small French village. He was never discovered. Yetta found solace in the sisterhood of women at Auschwitz. Weighing just 68 pounds at liberation, she somehow found the strength and the mindset to survive. She must have known deep inside that her children shared her strength.

The family was reunited at a D.P. (displaced persons) camp. My father, the youngest, was the one to recognize my grandfather, a miracle in itself because every Wagschal had changed not only by the impossible lives they were leading, but also by age itself. My father, who was now 7 years old, was found in just a pair of underwear and wooden shoes.

When I look at my two young boys – the youngest of my parent's 7 grandchildren, I think about the determined, strong and willful family that they come from. I also can't help but think that if one small detail in that story had gone a different way, then they would not be here today. Matthew (6), Evan (3) and their cousins did not get a chance to meet my grandparents as they died in 1979 when I was just 10 years old, but they are truly blessed to have their "Umpah" still in their lives as well as our Aunt Sabina and Uncle Sammy.

Yetta Wagschal, passport photo upon leaving Europe, 1957

Cholent
meat

Jack and his daughter Nicole

Ingredients:
Chuck roast, onions, carrots, potatoes, celery, flour, oil, water

Directions:
- Brown chuck roast in pan with flour and oil.
- Fill pot with water.
- Add in browned chuck roast.
- Add in chopped vegetables – onions, carrots, potatoes, celery or whatever vegetables could be found.
- Bring to bakery and have it cook/simmer for 24 hours.

Note: *My Dad couldn't give me exact measurements – they basically tossed in a bit of this and a bit of that. The dish was traditionally made prior to the Sabbath and was taken to the local bakery, where they would put it in an oven to cook, until my father would pick it up once the Sabbath had ended.*

Sweet Potato Soufflé
parve

This is a more modern recipe – two of his (and my) favorite foods to eat during holiday meals are sweet potatoes and cranberry sauce. The cranberry sauce comes from a can, but here is the sweet potato recipe:

Ingredients:
- 3 cups sweet potatoes
  (or 5 – 6 medium raw sweet potatoes)
- 1 cup sugar
- ½ cup melted margarine
- 2 eggs
- 1 tsp vanilla

- Peel potatoes then microwave (approx. 8 min. per potato) to soften.
- Mash into large bowl.
- Mix in sugar, margarine, eggs and vanilla.

Solomon Wagschal
Catskill Mountains, 1967

Topping:
1 cup brown sugar
½ cup melted margarine
1 cup chopped pecans
1/3 cup self-rising flour

Mix with wooden spoon and cover top of casserole.
Bake at 350 for 30-40 minutes or until bubbly.

Blintz Soufflé
parve

(Our family's favorite Yom Kippur Break Fast dish.)

Sam, Sabina and Jacques
Wagschal (l to r), after
the war (probably 1947)

Directions:
Preheat oven to 350 degrees
Mix all ingredients together in greased rectangular baking dish. Beat with fork. Roll blintzes into mixture so covered. Bake at 350 for 40 minutes – check often.

Ingredients:
- 3 eggs, 4 oz. sour cream
- 3 T sugar
- 4 oz. orange juice
- 4 T oil
- 2 pack frozen blintzes

Margarete Diener Levy

Silver Spring, MD, U.S.A.

Margarete and her brother, Jerry (Yonkele) in DP camp, 1948

My name is Margarete Diener (Dyner) Levy. My parents were Holocaust survivors, and I am a member of Generation After. My mother was Sara Sagalawa (Dyner) Diener, and my father was Towia (Ted)(Dyner) Diener. I was born in Russia in 1945, and my brother Jerry (Yankel) was born in DP Camp in Traunstein, Germany in 1948. We came to the United States on Sept 25, 1951. I was 6 yrs old and clearly remember the over-crowded US troopship carrier, the General Blatchford, enter-ing NY harbor after a very stormy crossing with most of the refugees being extremely seasick. As we stood on deck, the rain stopped, and a long shaft of sunlight descended theatrically to highlight the Statue of Liberty. She was beautiful...the land of Freedom was beautiful, and we were all crying with the joy of finding this sanctuary. My parents are no longer with us, and this is a good way to remember their lives and love...and the families they came from. In memories, life can continue, and we survive.

Mama was born in Kiev, the Ukraine. She also lived in Moscow, and Mama drank (tea) "tay", when it was to be had. Daddy was born and raised in Vishograd, Poland, and, when it was available, drank "tie"(tea). A luxury for Mama was to drink her tay with cherry pre-serves, and for Daddy..he drank his tie with sugar cubes, lots of sugar cubes. Both of them found themselves alone, the only survivors of their families, running from two different directions, from the same foes, the Nazis, and ending up in a small town in the Ural mountains, in Russia, called Votkinsk. Votkinsk was at the base of a mountain whose other side was Siberia. The climate was the same as Siberia, the streets were mud when not frozen, and everyone was cold, hungry, and exhausted from running. The town's only claim to fame was that, at some point in time, the composer Tchaikovsky actually lived there.

Margarete and her brother Jerry, as adults

(left to right) Towia, Margarete, Jerry, & Sara Diener, 1949 Traunstein, Germany

Daddy was a shoemaker, and Mama's shoes had worn out. Some-one pointed her to Dad, the shoemaker. Daddy took one look at the curvy, petite, blue-eyed fiery redhead, and fell instantly in love. He agreed to make her a pair of shoes, but kept on delaying their comple-tion. They got to know each other from Mama's questions, asking if the shoes were done. Daddy finally announced he would only complete the shoes if she would agree to marry him. By this time, their feelings were mutual, and she agreed. Unlike the redneck advice to new grooms, to "keep their brides barefoot and pregnant", Daddy kept Mom in shoes... and immediately got her pregnant. I became the firstborn child, in Vot-kinsk, 10 months after they married. When my brother was born nearly 3 years later, in a DP camp in Germany, we became an entire family with each member born in a different country.

Not only did my parents pronounce Yiddish differently, but also (when there was food), ate differently. Some dishes we grew up with were Polish, and some Ukrainian, some Yiddish, and some Russian. ALL of them were delicious, and filled with love.

273

Two of Daddy's favorite Polish dishes (that Mama learned to make for him) were:

Sweet Lokshin Soup
dairy

In the middle of the hot summer, when blueberries grew as large as small grapes, and as sweet as sugar, when biting into a plump, tight-skinned blueberry was the sensation of your sharp teeth cracking open the bursting berry and flooding your mouth with incredible sweetness, Mama made this soup. She made her own homemade noodles, rolling the dough thinner and thinner, until you wondered if it would break. Then she took the sharpest knife in the kitchen, and hand sliced narrow lines of noodles, and cooked them.

After cooling the cooked noodles by running them under cold water in the colander, she portioned them out to each soup bowl, added the yagehdehs* (*blueberries) (about 2-3 oz, and preferably hand-picked from Farmer Myer's farm next to Weitzman's Bungalow Colony in the Catskills, where his cows were the reason for the munificence of his blueberries), added a cup of cold milk, and then a lot of sugar, or in Daddy's case, even more sugar.

It was served as a cold soup, but somehow, when the noodles still retained a bit of warmth from the cooking, it was even better. A zoy git!* (*So good!) **Hahk a seder!*** (*Bon Appetit!)

Schipyeh
dairy

These are the basic proportions, adjust to taste, for all ingredients. This is especially nice as a summer lunch or breakfast, served with slices of cucumber and tomato on the side, and perhaps a nice sweet-fleshed juicy slice of cantaloupe. **A Mechayah*** *(*a pleasure).*

> 1/2 cup or more diced radishes
> 1/2 cup or more diced scallions
> 1 c. small curd cottage cheese (drain liquid)
> pinch of salt and pepper

Margarete's parents, Sara & Ted (Towia) Diener, when they lived in Maryland, 1986

Daddy's Bubele
(in his original handwriting)

4 Eggs
1/4 cup matzo meal
1/4 cup sweet wine
1/4 teaspoon salt (if margarine is used, no salt needed)

1) Beat the egg whites stiff
2) Pour in the yolkes and mix
3) Pour in the matzo meal and mix
4) Pour in the wine and mix alltogether
5) Preheat a pan with a little fats, unsalted butter or margarine or oil
6) Pour the mixture into the pan, let it fry by a low heat, when the bottom is brownish, turn it over. With a spoon mix through the mixture each time before pouring it on the pan so the mixture will be even

Dr. Gideon Frieder
Potomac, MD, U.S.A.

My parents were Zionists, but they did not immigrate to Israel before the Holocaust because my father, a rabbi, thought it important to stay with his flock during those harsh days. His story, and that of his family (including myself) and his times, is preserved in Yad Va Shem Archives (under catalog number M.5_191 thru 194). A book based on the diaries, "To Deliver Their Souls" by Emanuel Frieder, (originally in Hebrew "L'Hacil Nafsham") is publicly available. Here I elected to relate only one story that seems appropriate for a recipe book, and appropriate to this particular recipe that was used to both assure the sanctity of the Shabbat, and to provide hot food during the Shabbat.

Food was scarce in Slovakia. All, both Jews and Christians, were affected by the shortage. Therefore it was a cause for celebration when our Christian neighbor secured chicken meat and offered a portion to my mother. My mother refused the gift as the meat was not slaughtered in accordance with the laws of kashrut. Our neighbor protested first arguing that kosher meat was outlawed. When this argument failed, she reminded my mother of her two young children, my sister Gita and me, and our need for protein to grow. But my mother did not relent; she conveyed her appreciation but refused the gift. It turned out that our neighbor, Mrs. Lipka, was a righteous gentile amongst the nations. A short time later she returned at great risk to herself with a live chicken for my mother so that she could have the chicken slaughtered according to religious requirements and so that we children would have food for our survival.

My mother Ruzena Frieder and my sister Gita were killed before my eyes - Hashem Yikom Daman. I was wounded, but saved by a Jewish partisan, Adam Henry Herzog, and by righteous Christians, Jozef and Paulina Strycharszyk. My father, HaRav Dr. Avraham Abba Frieder Zichron Tsadik L Vracha, was credited in saving hundreds of lives. He died shortly after the Holocaust.

This recipe is dedicated to my wife Dalia, to my children Ophir, Tally and Gony - the symbols that Am Israel Chai - and to my friends and many others that gave their lives in the wars of Israel, assuring the continuity of our people.

The recipe has been in my family since I was a child - it is a typical Jewish mid European dish. The ingredients were put in a clay pot that was deposited in the hot central (and typically, only) bakery stove on Friday. As the oven cooled very slowly after it was shut on the entrance of the Shabbat, the food would be slowly cooked, and it was still hot on Saturday, providing a hot meal without the need for cooking or heating on the holy day.

275

Cholent, Sholet

parve

(or Tshulnt, or Chamin as it is called now)

Dry beans -
   one type or variety, including chickpeas and similar legumes
Grain has to be coarse. Barley, Jobs tears, Wheat berries
Carrots, Potatoes, Onions
Salt, pepper, cumin, or caraway
   (seeds or ground - adds some of the characteristic flavor)
Garlic powder or minced garlic and or paprika

See remarks about optional ingredients, spices and amounts in the text

Directions:

1.) Soak beans, chickpeas and other dry, large legumes - lentils (see later) not included for one night in cold water, discard water.
2.) Cut carrots and potatoes into large chunks, peel onions and use them without cutting. Clean grain, using cold water.
3.) Mix all ingredients in a slow cooker - if you do not have one, see later -
4.) Add water to cover solid ingredients.
5.) Add spices, using your judgment, possibly adding your own spicing.

If you have a slow cooker, cook on low setting for 24 hours. If you do not have one, use a clay, Pyrex or Corning covered dish, and use your oven in a below boiling temperature – 200 degrees Fahrenheit will do.
If you are in a village, and have a big, brick built bakery stove, do use it...

Serve piping hot.

Me in my high 20's, when, as a member of the research arm of the Israeli Ministry of Defense, I was accepted to an audience with David Ben Gurion. I was part of a project that warranted his attention, and I am very proud of it.

Me, at age four

The more carrots are used, the sweeter tinge will be in the dish. It will not be as sweet as baked beans, as no sugar or molasses are used. The more grain is used, the more porridge, non chunky like consistency - use your family preferences. The type and amount of onions also affects both taste and aroma - sweet onions support the carrots, sharp onions will support the garlic side of the spicing.

I recommend using both beans and chickpeas, and recommend using small amount of additional variants as additives - such as dried peas (yellow or green), lentils etc. These will add a mushy type of consistency – so beware… Tofu skins (NOT Tofu) add a resemblance of eggs, and an unusual texture.

In any case, the dominant amount should be the beans and all else should be used in moderation. There is a major variant that uses meat. If you do, use relatively low quality meat - it will be tender anyway. One can also use (Kosher…) Kielbasa or other type of sausage, or Kishka – if you know what it is….\ No poultry, please, as it will disintegrate in the cooking process. If you like meaty taste, but would like to keep the dish a vegetarian one, use soy-meat or wheat-meat substitutes. Do not use regular tofu, as it disintegrates in the long cooking process..

An interesting "side effect" is to put eggs into the pot before starting it – do not forget to wash them! As they will be cooked very slowly immersed with the other ingredients, they will acquire a typical brown color and a unique taste. They are quite decorative when peeled, halved and put in the middle of the dish with the yolk showing…

The possibilities are really mind boggling, and the variety of tastes is very rich - it depends on the relative amount of the ingredients, and the spicing.

Bon Appetit…. Enjoy!!!!

This photo is of my family - myself, my children and their spouses and my two grandchildren - Gita who is named after my sister, who perished at the age of four in the Holocaust, and Avi, who is named after my father HaRav Dr. Avraham Abba Frieder who saved many lives during the holocaust and died at the age of 36 immediately after WWII. The picture was taken at the wedding of my youngest child Gony.

Gina Hochberg Lanceter
Upper Montclair, N.J, U.S.A.
Submitted by her daughter Dina Cohen

Gina Hochberg Lanceter grew up in Brody, in eastern Poland, now the Ukraine. As a child in pre-war Poland, she lived a comfortable middle-class existence. Her family was modern Orthodox; her father owned a business. Brody was somewhat protected from the initial Nazi onslaught as it had been annexed by the Soviet Union in September 1939 as part of the Nazi-Soviet anti-aggression pact. However, in June 1941, when Gina was 12 ½ years old, the Germans conquered the area and anti-Jewish regulations were instituted, followed shortly thereafter by the establishment of a ghetto. In May 1943, Gina and her family were put on a train to the death camps. Her life was saved by her parents, who talked her into jumping off the train. Gina is the sole survivor of her immediate family.

Although Gina was only 14 ½ years old when she was separated from her parents, her memories of her life with them are vivid. This recipe for stuffed cabbage is her recollection of her mother's recipe, one that was usually on the menu for Sukkoth. She remembers Sukkoth as a fun holiday, with a Sukkah her father constructed right outside the kitchen window so it was convenient to pass food from the kitchen to the Sukkah. Gina and her brother Zygo, 6 years her senior, decorated the Sukkah. Since the roof of the Sukkah was made from branches since it had to be open, when it rained (which often happened on Sukkoth), eating in the Sukkah was not all fun. However, Gina's father never strayed from the custom, eating all his meals in the Sukkah. Sometimes he even ate while holding an umbrella! Although Gina's mother would eat with him even in the rain, the children only joined them on nice days.

When the German's invaded Russia in June 1941, Zygo and a group of friends decided to flee to the east. He left on June 25, 1941 was last seen in Zloczow, where a pogrom had taken place at that time. Although he and his friends were not listed among the dead or the living, none were ever heard from again.

Lanceter Family Bar Mitzvah
(Gina in center, parents on either side, brother behind)

Pirogen Recipe:

Pirogen were a typical Polish dish, consumed especially during the cold winters and often in Gina's home during Chanukah. Since winter came early in eastern Poland, the streets, roads and parks were covered with snow. Some secluded parts of town looked like a wonderland. There were people who suffered in winter; poor people who could not afford to heat their apartments and who did not have proper clothing. But Gina's home was comfortable and full of warm feeling at Chanukah.
Her mother had the shochet (ritual slaughterer) slaughter the geese she was fattening up. The fat from the geese was rendered to preserve for Passover. It was stored in earthenware used only for this purpose. The goose meat was roasted or stewed with dumplings and of course potato latkes or kugel. The greaves (Griben), pieces left from the rendered fat, were crunchy and delicious; they were often mixed with mashed potatoes or put into potato knishes or pirogen.

While this recipe does not use griben, it is similar to the potato pirogen made by Gina's mother.

Pastry Recipe:

This pastry recipe was a favorite among all the members of my large extended family, most of whom perished in the Holocaust. However, it is still made by the few family members who survived, including one cousin living in Israel who is 96 years old. I remember it as one of the many pastries made for her brother Zygmunt's (Zygo) Bar Mitzvah on a Thursday morning in 1935. After the prayers in the synagogue, my father invited the entire congregation for a feast of herring in all forms, honey and sponge cakes, cookies, fruit and drinks. This was followed on Saturday at our home with an afternoon open house for relatives and friends. My mother had been busy all week preparing for the party, baking delicious tortes, pastry and strudels and making hundreds of canapés. I was very excited. Not quite 7 years old, I still wanted to help, so my mom let me crack walnuts and chop chocolate. Since I had quite a sweet tooth, I sampled quite a bit of the nuts and chocolate. My mother had to remind me to stop eating.

Gina's Pirogen
parve, dairy, or meat

2 cups flour
1 large egg
a few spoons lukewarm water

*Mix ingredients together and work dough until firm. Divide in 2
and roll each piece thin on floured board. Cut out circles with
pastry cutter or glass. Mix fillings.*

Potato Filling

2 lbs potatoes, cooked and mashed
1 lg onion, minced and lightly browned
salt to taste

*For potato-cheese or potato-sauerkraut, substitute 1 lb farmer
cheese or 1 lb sauerkraut for 1 pound of the potatoes.*

Kasha Filling

2 cups cooked kasha
2 onions, minced and browned
salt

Meat Filling

3 cups cooked brisket, ground
1 large onion, minced and browned
2 ribs celery, minced and browned
salt to taste

- *On each dough circle, place 1 tablespoon of filling mixture. Fold over into half
  moon shape and seal edges by pressing dough together tightly.*
- *Cook in large pot of boiling water, partly covered, for about 5 minutes or until
  pirogen rise.*
- *Drain and fry lightly in oil or moisten with butter, if without meat,
  or margarine, as desired.*

Gina's Kindeln (Pastry)

dairy

9 oz (250 grams) unsalted butter or margarine
2 egg yolks
   reserve 1 egg white for brushing at end
4 cups flour
2 tsp baking powder
1 tbsp sour cream
1 tbsp cognac or brandy
3/4 cup sugar

Filling
6-8 oz Apricot jam
6-8 oz Orange marmalade
8 tbsp grated apple
1 cup ground walnuts or hazelnuts

Mix dough by hand until ball forms.
Divide into four parts and wrap in plastic wrap or waxed paper.
Refrigerate dough overnight.

Directions:

Preheat oven to 350 degrees

1.) Mix jam and marmalade together.
2.) Roll out one ball of dough in rectangle.
3.) Spread jam mixture and 2 tbsp apple thinly on dough.
4.) Top with ¼ cup grated nuts (or more to taste).
5.) Roll into jelly roll and place on greased and floured cookie sheet.
6.) Repeat with other 3 pieces of dough.
7.) Beat 1 egg white and brush on each roll.
8.) Bake for 35-45 minutes until nice and golden.

Slice while warm.

Gina's Stuffed Cabbage

meat

5 lbs cabbage

1 1/2 lbs chopped meat

1 cup uncooked rice

1 cup raisins

3 large or 4 medium apples, peeled and grated

1/2 cup cold water

1 egg, optional

2 lbs packaged sauerkraut

1 1/2 lbs cubed beef or chuck steak

2 large onions, chopped coarsely

dried prunes, optional

1 15 oz can diced tomatoes

two 8 oz. cans tomato sauce

two 6 oz. cans tomato paste

1/2 cup maple syrup, or more to taste
 (brown sugar may be substituted)

1/4 cup lemon juice

salt to taste

ketchup

282

Directions:

Preheat oven to 350 degrees.

1.) Rinse cabbage.
2.) Remove top leaves as necessary.
3.) Cut 4 slits around the core.
4.) Immerse head of cabbage in boiling water and boil until leaves start to separate.
5.) Remove separated leaves and continue process until most of the leaves are removed. Drain.
6.) Combine chopped meat, apples, raisins, water, rice, salt and egg if using.
7.) Place about 1 large tablespoon of meat mixture in center of each leaf, fold sides in and roll up leaf. If leaves are large, use more mixture to make a plump roll.
8.) Rinse sauerkraut in colander under cold water.
9.) Cut remaining cabbage into small pieces.
10.) Mix cabbage, sauerkraut, onions, cubed meat together with prunes, if using.
11.) Line large roasting pan with sauerkraut-meat mixture and place cabbage rolls on top.
12.) Mix tomato sauce, paste, lemon juice, maple syrup and diced tomatoes together in bowl.
13.) Add four 8 oz. cans water and mix again. Pour this mixture over rolls.
14.) Cover pan with heavy-duty aluminum foil.

Bake for 2 hours covered.
Uncover, add some ketchup over the cabbage and bake for 15 additional minutes .

Makes 30-32 cabbage rolls – Enjoy!!!

Eva Weigl Shankman
Olney, MD, U.S.A.

Eva and Judy, 1945

My name is Eva Weigl Shankman. I was born in Budapest, Hungary on October 29, 1941. At that time my parents were 31 and 35 years old, they told me even though the war was beginning to spread they did not want to wait any longer to have a child. I grew up knowing that I was really wanted and my father even wrote and published a poem celebrating my birth. By 1942, he was sent to the Ukraine to a labor camp. He survived because he always thought of his wife and child back home, never trading his wedding ring for food or shoes as many others did. He came back to Hungary because several of his toes were frozen and had to be amputated.

As a toddler, I did not recognize him when he returned, a thin, broken man. My mother and I hid with false papers. She was living as the cleaning woman and caretaker of a big apartment house. My grandparents and a great aunt were living in the ghetto in Budapest. This great aunt was taken to Bergen-Belsen and though many didn't, she returned home after the camp was liberated. My mother's brother-in-law, Dr. Imre Freund, was taken to a labor camp in Hungary and was shot to death when, due to illness he could not march West with the rest of the men. The fact that he was shot to death was revealed to us only recently. His child, my cousin, Judith Freund Shanberg, was born after his death, so she never knew her father or the rest of his family, they all perished in Auschwitz.

After the war, my family tried to live as well as we could under Communism. Our chance to escape came in 1956 when, after the Hungarian Revolution we were able to leave the country. My father and I took a train to the border and then walked across wintry farmlands, dodging searchlights from the border-patrol, to Austria. We each carried one suitcase, that's all. My mother joined us shortly, leaving Hungary legally because she was a Polish citizen, not Hungarian, and so she could get a visa. We were not able to come to the USA right away because by January 1957 the quota was full. We hoped to come with the help of American relatives but that did not happen until much later. In September 1957, when I was 15, my mother died, after months of suffering, from ovarian cancer. She was 47 years old and never saw the place she longed for years to be-- America. My father and I arrived in America in March 1959 when I was 17 years old.

In 1964, I became an American citizen, graduated from Kent State University in Ohio and got married to Bert Shankman who is second generation American. Today, I am a retired Librarian with two sons, their wives and 4 grandchildren. My parents taught me, by their example, to be a survivor. I overcame 2 breast cancers and now I am ready to celebrate my 65th birthday.

Eva and Judy, 2005

284

Nut Crescents

dairy

Dios Kifli

2 boxes of ready-made pie crusts
1/2 c. sugar
2 c. walnuts, ground
2 T. milk
2 egg whites, slightly beaten
1 egg, slightly beaten
2 T. confectioners sugar

This recipe is modified to make it simple and still delicious by using pie crust for the dough. The crescent shape is popular for cookies, stemming from the long ago Turkish occupation of Hungary.

Directions:
Preheat oven to 375 degrees

1.) Lightly grease cookie sheets.
2.) Prepare filling by mixing together walnuts, egg whites, sugar and milk.
3.) Roll out pie crusts a little thinner than they are.
4.) Cut circles with a glass or a round cookie cutter 2-3 inches in diameter
5.) Put 1 tablespoon of filling in the middle of the circle, fold it in half and press down the edges with a fork, making a little pattern.
6.) Brush each crescent with the beaten egg.
7.) Bake at 375 F. for 15-20 minutes till lightly golden.
8.) Just before serving, sprinkle with confectioners' sugar.
   (I use a small strainer for that.)

Makes about 4 dozen

Lady's Whim

parve
Noi Szeszely

6 tsp oil (but not olive oil)
1/2 c. sugar
1 Tbsp vanilla
2 eggs- separated
1 1/2 c flour
1/2 tsp baking powder
1/4 tsp baking soda
1 c. chopped walnuts
   (pecans or hazelnuts are ok)
apricot and raspberry preserves
   (mixed or other preserves of your choice)

This is a great recipe because most of the ingredients one has on hand. Also, no butter is used so it's good for people who can't have butter for health reasons.

Directions:
Preheat oven to 350 degrees

1.) Cream oil and sugar.
2.) Add vanilla and egg yolks.
3.) Sift dry ingredients and add.
4.) Knead dough in bowl until well blended.
5.) Pat dough into the bottom of a lightly greased 9x13" baking dish.
6.) Spread a thin layer of preserves on top, sprinkle with 1/2 c. nuts.
7.) Beat egg whites until stiff, adding 2 T. sugar during the beating.
8.) Spread egg whites over the mixture in the dish.
9.) Top with remaining 1/2 c. nuts.
10.) Bake at 350 F. for 25-30 minutes.
11.) When cool, cut into squares.

Halina Herman

Cincinnati, OH, U.S.A.

Halina was born in Warsaw, Poland, just as World War II was beginning. Her father was a physician and was killed during the war. Her mother lost her whole family, including her parents and four siblings, during the war. Halina lived in Krakow after the war until 1949, at which time she moved to Paris, where she spent two years, and then moved to Montreal. She moved to Cincinnati in 1966. Not until she was 10 did she find out that she was Jewish. Here are some recollections from her early childhood.

Glimpses from long ago. They call me Dzidzia. My real name is Halina, but nobody really calls me that. My nickname by which everybody call me is "Dzidzia" which is an endearing, diminutive term, literally meaning "baby"

1942
I am very young, maybe two or three years old. My mother and I ate sitting high up in the attic of a tall building in Zakopane, which is a resort place high up in the mountains in Poland. It is winter and there is snow all around. My mother and I are looking at some books, my very favorite thing to do and I am supposed to be very quiet. Every time I raise my voice to say something, my mother puts her finger to her lips and whispers: "Let's see how long we can be quiet." Way down outside below us, I see a group of small figures, standing out against the brilliant white snow that is all around. I see that they are soldiers and have rifles. They are going from house to house. My mother tells me that they are German soldiers and we need to be very quiet so they will not find us. Sort of like playing hide and seek, I think to myself.

1943
I am about three or four years old living in Chernichow, a tiny village near Krakow, with a woman and her adult daughter. None of the streets are paved. It is mostly farm country. My mother works in Krakow, and from time to time she comes to visit me. She always comes by ferry, a river runs through the village. When she comes, she always brings some things to eat, but most important she brings me books. I just love books.
I am with another family now. They treat me somewhat better than the first family with whom I stayed. I have no shoes and wear an old nightshirt. The other children pick on me because I am small.

1944
I am four and I just recovered from typhoid fever. I was very ill and even delirious at one point. My mother came from Krakow and brought a doctor to Chernichov. I said, "You smell like my Daddy," meaning the antiseptic smell in my physician father's office. This frightened my mother because she is on false papers and is supposed to be an unmarried woman with a child. She is afraid that the doctor will turn us in so she tells the doctor I am delirious.

1945
I am five years old. I am in Krakow, Poland. My mother is putting me to sleep in our cold flat. She dresses me warmly as she anticipates some air raids. I see the chimney and the roof collapse on the building next door because a bomb hit it. I am afraid yet I still have the confidence of a five year old that everything will be all right.

1949

I am ten years old, my mother and I live in Krakow. I go to church every Sunday. This Sunday, my mother tells me we are moving far away. She also tells me that I will not be going to church anymore "Why I ask?" "Because you are not Catholic, you are Jewish!" I cannot believe this. Only much later do I begin to understand that my mother was so frightened by the war, that she delayed telling me that I was Jewish even after the war ended.

The pictures were all taken right after the war around 1945-46. I lived in Krakow with my mother (on one of the pictures I am walking with her). I thought I was Catholic and even went to a kindergarten run by nuns. I did not find out I was Jewish till we left Poland for France (Paris) in 1949.

Easy apple cake

parve

apples
1 1/2 c. flour
1/2 c. oil
2 well beaten eggs
1/2 t. baking powder

Directions:
Preheat oven to 350 degrees

- Slice apples into a round greased Pyrex dish at least 1/2 full.
- Mix ingredients and pour on top of apples.
- Bake 50 mins at 350 degrees.

Mock chopped liver spread

parve

2 cups cooked lentils
1 cup walnut pieces
1 medium onion
Salt (to taste)
Pepper (to taste)

Directions:
Process in food processor to a coarse consistency

Potato onion soup

parve

2 large potatoes
1 onion
1 large carrot

Directions:
- Put in a pot of water and season to taste.
- Cook until tender (about 1/2 hr).
- When done, add ½ cup sour cream or yogurt. (Can also add sliced celery.)

Kuba (Jack) Glotzer

Livingston, N.J, U.S.A.

Submitted by his wife Beatrice Glotzer

Jack and Beatrice at tribute to Holocaust survivors in 2003

Kuba Jack Glotzer was a Holocaust Survivor. He was the only member of a large family who survived. He was born in Poland (now Ukraine) in Rohatyn. He was fourteen years old when his nightmare started. His father had emigrated to the Untied States in 1938 with the intention of relocating his wife and three sons to America.

Unfortunately, however, the war broke out and it was too late for Jack and his mother and siblings to leave. Instead of enjoying freedom of America he had to witness his mother and nine year old brother being shot to death at the liquidation of the Rohatyn Ghetto.

All of the remaining members of his family were also killed there. He was ordered with a few other young men to bury the victims of the March 20, 1945 massacre. He and his one remaining brother escaped to the woods and survived, but his brother was betrayed by the Lithuanians and was murdered just two weeks before the liberation.

After the war Jack was finally able to come to America, but when he arrived he learned that his father, his last living relative, had passed away at the age of 53.

In June, 1998 Jack returned to Rohatyn with 25 people from three continents to erect the monument in memory of the victims of the massacre. When it was suggested that he could look for his family Jack said, with tears in his eyes, "I buried my cousin in a mass grave right where this monument is erected."

Jack found the strength to make it in America and eventually met and married Beatrice. She had hidden during the war with her family and also came to America. They were married for 54 years before Jack passed away on December 31, 2005.

Jack is in the far left. This photo was taken in 1938 after Jack's father had left for the U.S. Jack's mother (second from left in this photo) and his youngest brother (far right) were murdered in June 1943.

This recipe was Jack's favorite. Because he had diabetes Beatrice would substitute sugar free apple sauce for part of the sugar in the recipe.

Apple Coffee Cake
dairy or parve

Jack (Kuba), age 80

2/3 cup butter or margarine (room temp.)
1/3 cup sugar
1/2 cup sour cream
1 tsp. vanilla
1 1/3 cup flour
2/3 tsp. baking soda
1/8 tsp. salt
2 eggs
1 chopped fresh apple (about a cup)
1/3 cup raisins (optional)

Topping
1/4 cup flour
1/4 cup brown sugar (firmly packed)
2 Tbsp. butter or margarine (room temp.)
1/2 tsp. cinnamon

Jack (Kuba) Glotzer, age 19

Directions:
Preheat oven to 350 degrees

- In mixing bowl, cream butter and 1/3 cup sugar until light/fluffy.
- Beat in sour cream, vanilla, and eggs.
- Combine the flour, baking soda and salt. Mix into creamed mixture. Blend well.
- Combine all of the topping ingredients until mixture forms coarse crumbs.
- Spoon half of the batter into a greased 8 inch round cake pan.
- Sprinkle with apples and raisins and half the topping mixture.
- Top with remaining batter and raisins and half the topping mixture.

Bake at 350F for 25-30 minutes.
It's best served warm! Also very nice with vanilla ice cream.

291

Bea (Beatrice Walzer) Glotzer
Livingston, N.J, U.S.A.

Beatrice Glotzer, age 17

Bea was born in 1928 in Jaroslaw, Poland, about two hours ride for Crakow. Jews were about 1/3 of the total population of 30-40 thousand. There were many affluent Jews and also some poor. Her parents Jacob and Regina Walzer were merchants who owned a grocery and candy store. They were among the well to do Jewish families.

When Bea was in grammar school and her brother Alexander was in high school things became extremely uncomfortable for Jewish students because anti-Semitism was rampant. Although Bea was an excellent student, her father had to bribe her teaches in order for her to get better treatment and fair marks.

Jacob had a great desire to go to Palestine but her mother wanted to stay in Poland. When the Germans marched into Poland on September 1, 1939 it forever changed the lives of the Walzer family.

When the persecution and killing of Jews began the Walzers were forced to go into hiding in the village of Moloducze, her father's birthplace. They were helped by some of Jacob's non-Jewish friends. They lived in a cold dark basement of a family who, although they were paid, risked their own lives to hide the Walzers. Food was scarce.

In 1941 when the Soviets took over part of Poland the Walzer family was forced into a Soviet labor camp in Siberia. They suffered from hunger and cold and were on the verge of death. From 1941-1945 they moved to several labor camps where the adults worked in the woods cutting down trees. Bea and her brother went to a Polish school filled with Russian propaganda.

In 1945 the war came to an end and the Walzer family returned to Poland. There they discovered that their entire extended family had been murdered by the German beasts. They stayed in Zagorze on the Polish-German border. There they joined Kibbutz Mizrachi, a Zionist organization in preparation to make Aliyah to the Land of Israel.

They spent six weeks in the former Austrian Death Camp, Ebensee and then lived in a Displaced Person Camp Velmedon, Herzog, in the American Zone. Bea wanted to get the education she had been deprived of, so she went to a Secretarial school in Arolsen. They then decided to come to America where they had relatives, as President Truman had opened the US borders to Displaced Persons. Bea and her family arrived in the United Sates in July of 1949. Bea met Jack Glotzer in 1950 and they were married in 1951. Jack passed away on December 31, 2005. They had two children, Terry and Mitchell. Terry is married to Scott Arons and they have two sons, Jeffrey and Michael. Mitchell is married to Dori Kirk.

Bea and Jack made certain that their children were given the education they were denied. There are three lawyers in the family, their son, son-in-law, and grandson. Bea loves to write poetry and together with her brother she chronicled the life of her husband Jack and his experience during the Holocaust.

In 1998 Bea and Jack went to Poland, a very painful trip for both. They went with a group of 25 to honor those members of Jack's family and the other Jews who were massacred in Jack's hometown of Rohatyn, Ukraine. Monuments were erected to honor the dead. Bea went to Jaroslaw where she and her family lived before the war. She stood in front of her childhood residence but she did not go in because it had a White Power sign on the garden wall. Bea visits schools and speaks to young people to remember the Holocaust.

A Journey Home

From a journey to our home towns
We just returned.
Places where our loved ones
    Were killed and buried.
No relatives came to greet us.
    By "them" we were not expected.
On the mass graves, where they are buried
    Two monuments were erected.
They were not convicted of any treason.
To be born a Jew was their death, the only reason.
Driving through the familiar towns
    Once thriving Jewish population
What happened there is beyond any ones imagination
    Under the blue Ukrainian sky
Surrounded by beautiful country sites
    Of God's creation.
Thousands of men, women, and children
    were murdered.
Providing the Nazis and the natives
With Fun and recreation
We stood there reciting the Kaddesh and crying
    Seeing before our eyes their horrible way of dying
We left feeling sorrow and pain
Making a promise not to forget or forgive
What happened there.
    And not to let it happen
    Never again

Betrice Glotzer
June 13, 1998

293

Passover Brownies

dairy

1 stick unsalted butter
1 cup sugar
5 eggs separated
8 oz. bittersweet chocolate
6 oz. finely chopped almonds
1/8 tsp. salt

Directions:

Preheat oven to 350 degrees

1.) Cream the butter & sugar.
2.) Mix in the egg yolks.
3.) Melt the chocolate over double boiler or in the microwave.
4.) Cool and add butter to the mixture.
5.) Add the almonds.
6.) Beat egg whites until stiff but not dry and fold into the batter.
7.) Pour into a 9 inch square greased baking pan.
8.) Bake at 350 degrees F for 50 minutes.
9.) Check for doneness by inserting a toothpick.

Let cool on baking rack before cutting into squares.

Beatrice Glotzer, age 76

294

Ilse Loeb
Monroe Twp, N.J., U.S.A.

Ilse Loeb was born in Vienna, Austria. In March, 1938 the Nazis annexed her country, and in November, on crystal night, they terrorized the Jewish population. Her parents then sent her to Holland to provide a safe haven for her. When she said goodbye to them at the Vienna railroad station she did not realize that this was their last goodbye. She was just thirteen at the time, and in Amsterdam a Jewish family adopted her as their foster child.

Soon after the Nazis invaded Holland in May, 1940, they began to round up Jews there also. When in June 1942 she received a letter from the German authorities ordering her to report to the Amsterdam train station for shipment to a German labor camp she realized that she had escaped to the wrong country. Her foster parents and friends urged her to defy this order and go into hiding. It is noteworthy that Anne Frank's sister Margo received the identical letter on the same day.

With the assistance of her cousin Edi and his Christian fiancée and the Dutch Underground movement, which supplied her with false papers, Ilse was able to hide with different Christian families in Holland from June, 1942 until the end of the war in May, 1945. They risked their lives to save her.

One of her rescuers, Johanna K. Vos, saved 32 Jews throughout the war. Mrs. Vos has been honored by Yad Vashem, the Queen of Holland, and now lives in upstate New York. Her story is prominently displayed at the United States Holocaust Museum in Washington, DC.

In 1947 Ilse came to the United Sates. In 1966 she moved to New York State. She was a board member of the Holocaust Museum and Study Center in Spring Valley, NY for 19 years. Fifteen years ago she became co-founder of a "Hidden Children" organization which includes Jewish children from German occupied European countries who were hidden from the Nazis during World War II.

Subsequently she was instrumental in the creation of a special award-wining exhibit depicting 17 "hidden children" during World War II which is now touring the United States.

Currently Ilse lives in Monroe Township, NJ with her husband Walter. They have four children and seven grand children and have been married for 57 years.

This photo was taken 3 days before my departure to Holland. My brother is on the left. After that I never saw my parents again.

Ilse has told her story in synagogues, to many public, private school, and college students. She received three Congressional citations for her outstanding public service to the community. Her war time story is chronicled in "We Survived the Holocaust" by Elaine Landau, Franklin Watts Publishing, 1991, "The End of the Tunnel", by Johanna K. Vos, Book Masters Inc., 1999, and "Kristallnacht- Prelude to Disaster" by Sir Martin Gilbert, Harpers, 2006, and "Moment in Time". Drew University, Madison, New Jersey.

Noodle Pudding
dairy

1 lb. wide noodles (cooked but firm)
3/4 cups sugar
1/2 cup margarine
1 Tbsp. lemon juice
6 tsp. vanilla
6 beaten eggs
1 pint sour cream
1 pint cottage cheese
1 can crushed pineapple
1/2 cup orange marmalade
2 cups cornflakes

Directions:
Preheat oven to 350 degrees
1.) Mix all ingredients except cornflakes, enough for a 9x12 greased glass baking dish and a greased 8x8 baking dish.
2.) Mix cornflakes with melted butter or margarine and cinnamon.
3.) Sprinkle over top of noodle pudding so it makes a nice decoration.
4.) Bake in greased dish at 350 degrees for 1 hour, or till it's light brown on top & bottom.

Ilse's Viennese Sachertorte
dairy for Passover

9 eggs, separated
1 1/2 cups sugar
4 1/2 ounces unsweetened melted chocolate
Lemon rind (1 tsp)
1 1/4 cups very finely chopped almonds

Ingredients for Glaze:

2 ounce packages of unsweetened melted chocolate
1 Tblsp margarine
1/2 cup powdered sugar
Fresh lemon juice

Directions:
Preheat oven to 350 degrees
1.) Separate eggs. Blend only yolks with the sugar and chocolate. Add lemon rind.
2.) Put whites in a separate bowl. Whip the egg whites until fluffy. When whites are fluffy, add the almonds to the chocolate and sugar mixture. Then very carefully, fold the whites into the chocolate mixture.
3.) Place mixture in two well greased cake pans. Bake for about 45 minutes to 1 hour. Let cool and remove from pans.
4.) Spread raspberry jam in between the layers. Make glaze by melting the chocolate, margarine and then adding the sugar and lemon juice only until moist.
5.) When cake is cool, pour glaze over the cake. Serve with whip cream and enjoy!

Key Lime Pie

dairy

2 eggs
15 oz. can sweetened
Condensed milk
1/2 cup fresh lime juice
1/4 tsp. salt
1-2 tsp. grated lime rind
Few drops green food coloring

1 pre-baked 9 inch pie shell
OR graham cracker shell
(I prefer the later)
1 cup dairy sour cream
1/3 cup sugar
1-2 tsp. grated lime rind

Directions:

Preheat oven to 350 degrees

1.) Beat eggs until light.
2.) Add condensed milk, lime juice, lime rind and salt.
3.) Beat at medium speed for 2 minutes.
4.) Add enough food coloring to tint mixture a pleasant green.
5.) Pour into pie shell and bake at 350 degrees for 10 minutes.
6.) Blend sour cream, sugar, and salt.
7.) Spread over pie and return to oven for 5 minutes at 425 degrees.
8.) Sprinkle rest of grated rind around edge of pie and cool.
9.) May be wrapped in Saran and frozen.

Regina Freeman

New Jersey and Cape Cod, U.S.A.
Submitted by her daughter Margie Freeman

Regina Freeman was born in 1911 in Staszow, Poland. When she was about 3 years old, her family moved to Proszowice, where her father joined his father's wholesale textile business. Regina grew up as the middle of nine children, with 4 older than her and 4 younger than her. The family moved to Krakow when Regina was about 10 years old, as her father was starting his own wholesale textile business there. From that time, Regina started tutoring children who needed help with mathematics and other subjects. She attended Hebrew High School in Krakow, after which she earned a Master's degree in Languages(English and German) from Jagiello University in Krakow. After her Master's degree, she also got her Certificate for Teaching.

When the war broke out, she lived with her family in Krakow. She had been accepted to teach at the Hebrew High School from which she had graduated, a great honor, as she was offered the position over several people who were her senior. (She had already developed a reputation as an outstanding tutor.) However, the school did not open due to the war and she did not have the opportunity to teach there. She continued working as a private tutor.

The small town of Staszow was the center of the Frydman family, where Mathys Frydman owned a leather tannery and fathered 13 children. The oldest of these children was Necha, Regina's mother. The youngest of the children was Elias, who later became Regina's husband. Alexandra was among the middle children.

Regina's Aunt Alexandra, a dentist in Staszow, had come to Krakow to buy dental supplies. When her aunt saw written announcements that all Jews in Krakow had to leave by a certain date, she invited Regina to be her companion and move to Staszow. (Aunt Alexandra had lost her husband during the war.) The rest of Regina's family planned to return to Proszowice, but after she left Krakow with her aunt, she never saw or heard from the rest of her family again. Except for her older brother, Meir, and her sister, Hannah, who had moved to Israel before the war, Regina and her younger brother, Eli, were the only immediate family members who survived. (Eli was found in a pile of "dead" bodies about to be burned in the ovens in Auschwitz, but one of the liberators noticed that he wasn't dead and rescued him. Eli moved to Israel after the war, married, raised two children, and now has 8 grandchildren!)

Regina and Alexandra lived in Staszow for a couple of years. Regina continued tutoring, mostly Hebrew and other school subjects, especially mathematics. Her aunt continued practicing dentistry. Then in 1943 the Jews of Staszow were ordered to leave. Regina's aunt paid a number of her patients to hide and feed them (which they did at the risk of their own lives) in attics, basements, and even in fields growing wheat and corn.

After two years of hiding with the aid of her aunt's patients, Regina went into the woods and joined small groups of Jews already there ("partisans") who had learned how to hide and survive. Two weeks later her aunt joined them, and they hid together until the war was over.

Regina was married in 1945 in Poland to Elias (the youngest of the 13 Frydman children.) Elias had graduated from medical school in Warsaw in the spring of 1945. Regina and Elias had known each other since childhood, as they were related to each other. They were both in hiding during the war, he with his brother, Stephen, and Regina with Alexandra, although the groups in hiding tried to keep in touch with one another. Stephen had even built a transistor radio, which helped them get news of what was going on in the outside world. After the war, Regina and Elias, as well as Stephen and his family, moved to Sweden, where they lived for several years. Elias worked there as a physician and Stephen as a dentist. They came to the United States in 1953 with their two Swedish-born daughters, Margie (Margareta) and Sarah. When they came to America, they changed their name from Frydman (pronounced Fridman) to Freeman, because people tended to pronounce the name as Fried-man.

They settled in Cadiz, Ohio, a small town which needed a doctor and which they felt was a good environment in which to raise children. Regina worked side by side with Elias as the office manager/bookkeeper of a busy medical practice. They retired in 1994, after which they moved to Florida and spent summers on Cape Cod. When Regina's husband died in March of 2000, she came to New Jersey to live with her daughter, Margie, her son-in law, Lenny, and her grandchildren, David and Rachel. Beginning in 2006, she moved back to Florida as her primary residence. She alternates her remaining time between New Jersey and Cape Cod.

Regina Freeman

Granddaughter Rachel Levin

Grandson David Levin

Daughter Margie Freeman

Zucchini Patties

dairy

1 lb. zucchini (4 small or 2 medium-large)
4 eggs (beaten)
4 tbsp. matzo meal or bread crumbs
4 oz. cheddar or American cheese (cubed or grated)
1 medium onion (minced)
oil for frying
salt and pepper (optional) to taste

Directions:
- Grate the zucchini.
- Combine eggs (beaten), matzo meal (or bread crumbs), cheese (grated or fine-cubed), and onion (minced) with the zucchini in a bowl.
- Heat oil in pan.
- Spoon zucchini into small patties (about 1 rounded tbsp.-size each). Fry on medium heat on one side until firm. Turn and fry on second side until done.
- If batter becomes too liquidy, add matzo meal (or bread crumbs) to thicken.
- Yield: about 20 patties.

Matzah Meal Pancakes

dairy or parve for Passover

Directions:
- Preheat skillet with butter or vegetable oil.
- Carefully separate egg whites from egg yolks, making sure there is no yolk in the whites.
- Beat egg whites until stiff.
- Add the lightly stirred egg yolks to the stiff whites.
- Add matzah meal (one rounded tablespoon per person, i.e. one tablespoon per two eggs).
- Put the pancake batter on a very hot frying pan, covering the pan.
  - Turn the pancake when lightly browned.
  - Proceed until all batter is used.
  - (The first pancake is usually the fluffiest.)

Per serving:
2 eggs (separated)
1 rounded tablespoon matzah meal
vegetable oil or butter to fry

Sweet n' Sour Cabbage
parve

Directions:

- Shred cabbage and set aside in separate pot.
- In very large pot, sauté cut-up onions in vegetable oil. Gradually add shredded cabbage to pot with sautéing onions.
- Add diced tomatoes and ketchup. If using added fruit, add here.
- Simmer until cabbage is cooked.
- Correct sweetness-tartness (with cider vinegar, lemon juice or sugar) at end of cooking.

1 green cabbage, shredded
1 or 2 medium onions, chopped
1 can diced tomatoes (15 oz.)
1 small bottle ketchup (15 oz.)
Optional:
   Apples or plums to sweeten
   Cider vinegar (or lemon juice) to make tart
   Sugar to taste
Oil to sauté

Swedish Almond Cookies
dairy

Directions:

Preheat oven to 375 degrees.

1.) Sift together the flour and salt and set aside.
2.) Cream together the butter, shortening and extract until softened.
3.) Add sugar gradually, creaming until fluffy after each addition.
4.) Add egg yolk and heat thoroughly.
5.) Blending only until smooth after each addition, add flour in thirds to the creamed mixture. Chill dough thoroughly.
6.) Shape dough into ¾-inch balls.
7.) Roll each ball in egg white and then in chopped almonds.
8.) Transfer balls to a greased cookie sheet.
9.) Flatten each ball by pressing an almond slice onto the top of each cookie.
10.) Bake at 375° for 8 minutes or until very lightly browned.

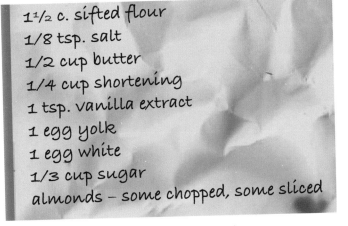

1½ c. sifted flour
1/8 tsp. salt
1/2 cup butter
1/4 cup shortening
1 tsp. vanilla extract
1 egg yolk
1 egg white
1/3 cup sugar
almonds — some chopped, some sliced

301

Wolf Gaister
Columbia, , MD, U.S.A.
Submitted by his grandson Ross Seidman, and mom, Pearl Seidman

My grandfather was called Velvel Geister until he immigrated to the United States in 1950, when his name changed to Wolf Gaister. He died in 1999, but we have his story on audiotape and wanted to share it with you for the Survivor's Cookbook.

Mom and Dad, 1950

My grandfather was born on February 14, 1926 in Belzyce, Poland (near the larger city of Lublin). It was a small city with 400 to 500 other Jewish families. He was one of five children and was the middle child sandwiched between four sisters. In the town there were two Jewish religious buildings. His father was a businessman who sold poultry and eggs. He sold his goods and bought other goods at the market, which was held in different towns depending on the day of the week. Everything that was sold or bought had to be kosher. The family wasn't extremely religious but was observant. They were not wealthy but not poor either, and owned their own house with three rooms: a bedroom, kitchen, and attic. My grandfather went to public school where males and females, Jews and Christians were integrated. He had his Bar Mitzvah in 1939. Not long after, his schooling came to a halt due to the German invasion of Poland. He never finished school.

In Belzyce, a Jewish committee was stood up to respond to Nazi demands, often to supply workers for forced labor camps. When he was 14, my grandfather was sent to a labor camp to dig a canal, where he worked waist-deep in water. Because of his age and because his uncle was on the Jewish committee, he was released after 3 months.

A Jewish work camp and ghetto was established in Belzyce in late 1942. The remaining Jews that had not been taken to concentration camps were moved to the ghetto. In May 1943, the ghetto was liquidated. Everyone was lined up in the yard of the shul. The Nazis sorted people into two groups, one for those who would survive for the time being and another group to be shot. My grandfather, his father, and his oldest sister were among those that were selected to live. His mother and other sisters were selected to die. Twenty men were given shovels and ordered to dig graves. The people that would survive that day were sent inside the shul to wait and watch as family members and others were torn down by machine guns. Those inside the shul were then put on wagons and taken to Budzyn.

Budzyn was a forced labor camp near the town of Krasnik. Two months later, in July 1943, one of the prisoners from Belzyce escaped. The German soldiers lined everyone from Belzyce up. My grandfather was standing next to and holding the hand of his father. The soldiers randomly selected ten men to be killed. My grandfather's father was one of the ten taken into the woods and shot. My grandfather's only remaining sister was taken to a work camp in the town of Krasnik and worked as a seamstress until the end of the war. My grandfather remained in Budzyn where he and other Jews were digging a tunnel to escape. A day before their tunnel was finished, a rabbi threatened to expose the men. He said that if they escaped many innocent men would be killed in retaliation. They decided not to complete the tunnel.

My grandfather was then moved to work at an underground factory in the Wieliczka salt mines, where he removed the working parts from downed planes to be reused for other purposes. After only a short while there, in the spring of 1944, he was taken by train to the concentration camp in Flossenburg, Germany. When those that survived the train journey arrived at night, they were told to strip naked. They showered, were disinfected, and then slept on the cement floor naked until they received their clothes in the morning. Because of his small hands my grandfather's job again was to remove parts from damaged airplanes. The French and Czechoslovakian kapos in his barracks treated my grandfather very well. He traded his ration of chewing tobacco for potatoes. The kapos allowed him to bake his potatoes in the open fire in the barracks.

Two weeks before the war ended in May 1945, prisoners were taken on trains headed toward a destination where they could be liquidated. American planes shot at the train. After three days, the German soldiers abandoned the trains, as they were allied targets, and forced the prisoners to march. Whoever slowed down was shot. The marching continued for three days until they came into the path of American tanks. They were liberated by American troops one week before the war ended. After the war, my grandfather was married in Austria and he and my grandmother immigrated to the United States in 1950, where they had three children. His sister was married in Germany. She and her husband had one son there and then immigrated to Rio de Janeiro, Brazil where they had their second son. My great aunt and uncle still live there, as do their married children and grandchildren.

Mom and Dad, 1990

Mom and Dad, 1960

Pressed and Marinated Cucumbers

parve

2 peeled and thinly sliced cucumbers
kosher salt
1/3 cup white vinegar
1/3 cup water
2 tsp sugar
pepper

Directions:

1.) Place the thinly sliced cucumber in a soup plate.
2.) Sprinkle lightly with salt.
3.) Put another plate on top of the salted cucumber and place a weight on the top plate.
4.) Let it sit for 20 to 30 minutes.
5.) Pour off the excess water.
6.) Mix the vinegar, water, sugar, and pepper.
7.) Stir until the sugar is dissolved.
8.) Pour over the cucumber and let it sit for anywhere from an hour to a few days before it is served.

This can be served equally well with meat or fish but is a particularly good accompaniment with salmon.

Laura Frajnd

Stockholm, Sweden
Submitted by Eva Fried

I was 18 when I came to Sweden with the Red Cross in 1945. I was the only surviving member of my family. I had been through Auschwitz, dachau and Bergen Belsen. In Sweden I married a Jewish man from Poland, I raised two sons and created a new life for myself.

My family name before I married was Codron and I mention this with pride. This name represents a big Sefardic, meaning Spanish-Jewish family. I was born and raised on Rhodes. Jews came to Rhodes already in the end of the fifteens century —due to the expulsion of the Jews from Spain. My first language was Ladino. But I grew up with many languages. I spoke Greek and in school I learned French and Italian. Rhodes was Italian up to 1946. In addition to the Italians there were three big minorities: Turks, Greeks and Jews.

Since there was nobody else with my background among the people that were taken like me to Sweden I became quite alone with my special memories. Nor were there anyone who could speak Ladino in Sweden.

In my home, as a child, we were not especially religious, but for us it was still natural to follow the traditions and to celebrate all holidays. For Pesach the children always got new clothes for the approaching summer and for Rosh Hashana there were new clothes for the winter season. For Sukkot a big Sukkah was built in an inner back yard, the so called kortizo. The Sukkah was beautifully decorated and we had all the meals in it during the holiday week and I loved it. The food in my home had tracks of the Spanish kitchen and of the kitchen of the Mediterranean area. Many dishes were prepared in the big wide pot called the `Paila´. In this pot a lot of dishes with filled and stuffed vegetables were prepared, sometimes with slices of potatoes in the bottom to protect it from getting burned. All the traditional dishes were named in Ladino.

For Saturdays, Shabat, and for all holidays different sorts of pastries with fillings were prepared. Depending on the shape and the filling they were named Pastellikos, Borekitas or Bojos. There were a variety of different shapes and fillings. Very often the meal started with a salad. Casseroles containing vegetables were common, sometimes with meat added. Rice was often the side dish to the meal and it was prepared in many different ways. Different cheeses and yogurts did certainly occur but mostly for breakfast or as snacks. We never mixed meat with milky products in the same meal. Strangely fish was very expensive even though Rhodes is an island. We never used butter for cooking only oil, especially olive oil. We also had a lot of pickled vegetables and olives were on the table for almost every meal. After the meal when the strong Turkish coffee was served there were also small very sweet cakes of different types.

I was almost 18 when the train stopped in Auschwitz. I could not cook and had never shown any interest for the kitchen and its activities. But there, in the camps we were suffering from hunger and we talked a lot about food. These conversations were my introduction to the art of cooking.

Our first stop with the train in Sweden was the little Swedish town Alingsås and there we stayed for a month. Never will I forget the white Swedish bread loafs that we were offered there. I thought that I had never, never eaten anything as delicious as that bread.

During the sixties when I could travel and see relatives still alive, in Israel and other places, I was able to get some of the recipes of the dishes of my home.

Note: Eva Fried produced a book, published in 2002, about Jewish food in Sweden, how it came to Sweden, who the people were that came with the Jewish food traditions, from where they came and when and why. The book also tells about the background to why different food is served at different occasions, holidays etc. It also describes the kashrut roles. But the main issue, running through the whole book, is the stories, memories, that we got by interviewing Jews in Sweden representing the different waves of Jewish immigration to Sweden. The main part of the stories, based on memories connected to food, come from survivors of the Shoah since about 50% of the Jews in Sweden have this background. The publishing house is the only Jewish publishing house in Sweden. By contacting this publishing house one may order the book. The price of the book is USD 50, this is the web address: www.hillelforlaget.nu

It is a beautiful book, 280 pages, with plenty of beautiful color pictures.

This is a photo taken recently with me and my youngest grand daughter, Simone. I have got two wonderful sons, Leo and Arthur, and from them I have two grandchildren in Los Angeles and four grandchildren in Israel.

Laura's Aubegine (Eggplant) Pajs

parve

3 dl flour
1/4 tsp salt
1 dl vegetarian margarine,
   not too cold

3 tbsp of cold water
1 tsp of lemon juice

Directions:

- Mix well all ingredients until the dough is soft.
- Let the dough rest in fridge for an hour before use.

Filling
2 aubergines (eggplants)
1 big onion, chopped
1 tin (5 dl) of chopped tomatoes
150 gram champignons (optional)
2 eggs
Salt
Pepper
Some Parmesan cheese (optional) - dairy

Directions:

1.) Peel and cut the aubergines into cubes.
2.) Put salt on the aubergine cubes and let them drain with the salt for about half an hour. Then, with your hand, press most of the juice out of the cubes.
3.) Fry the chopped onion in oil, when the onion is soft and has a bit of color, add the pressed aubergine cubes and mix in the crushed tomatoes.
4.) Let simmer until most of the liquid is gone, add salt and pepper according to taste.
5.) Let cool a bit.
6.) Add the eggs, mix (if you want to add champignons also add them, sliced and easily fried).
7.) Cover a pie dish with the pastry, add the filling.
8.) Save a third of the pastry to make a grid pattern on top.

307

Esther Lebovits

Stockholm, Sweden
Submitted by her niece Eva Fried

A food memory of my aunt Esti, Esther Lebovits, born in Hungary, Beled, 1928. She was brought to Sweden by the Red Cross in 1945. Since 1998 she lives in Israel.

We were in the ghetto in our little town, Beled in Hungary. I was almost 15 years old. My mother, my two brothers and my grandfather were also there. I found myself to be the oldest daughter in the house. I had always been regarded as the little girl but now I felt a responsibility for my mother. My mother was sad and spent much time praying these days. It was in the middle of the summer and the holiday of Shavuot was approaching. We had hardly any food. There was a curfew, the Jews in the ghetto were not allowed to go out except for a short while in the morning when the men were allowed to go to the prayers.

I got an idea. I wanted to get food for Shavuot. Not far from the area of the ghetto were some farms. I knew who the families were who lived there and I knew which of them I could trust. The morning before Shavuot I slipped out early in the morning and I went straight to one of the farmers. I carried a big basket with me. I bought a big fat goose from the farmer. I put the goose in the basket and I covered it with a towel. So I wandered back towards the gates of the ghetto.

At the entrance of the ghetto I was discovered by a gendarme who pushed me into the office of the gendarmes where he started to yell at me. What did I think, how could I allow myself these kind of benefits! This should lead to consequences he yelled. They wanted to know who had sold this goose since it was forbidden to sell anything to a Jew or to have any connections with the Jews. I did not want to tell the name of the farmer, I said I did not know his name. I understood the seriousness of this situation and therefore I offered the goose to the gendarmes. They shouted that they were not interested in the goose, they were only interested in getting me punished. Anyhow I took the goose out of the basket and put it on the desk in front of the gendarme. The terrified goose immediately produced a big pooh on the desk, right on the papers on which the gendarme was about to write his report of my crime. The gendarme was certainly terribly upset about how this developed and the whole issue ended up with his shouting at me to take the bloody goose and disappear as soon as possible.

This photo of me and my sister Bella was taken about seven months after our arrival to Sweden in 1945 when we had found out that an older sister and our father had also survived. The photo was aimed to be sent to them in Germany. We were brought to Sweden by the Red Cross after the liberation in Bergen Belsen. We had already gained in weight when this photo, the first photo taken in Sweden, was made. I was seventeen and my sister was twenty-one years old. I am to the right with the brace pants.

308

When I came back home with the goose my mother was in total despair. Some men who were on their way back from the prayers had seen me and how I was taken by the gendarmes and had told this to my mother who was by now convinced she will never see me again. But there I was, standing in front of her –and with a goose.

It was not easy to find anybody within the ghetto who could slaughter the goose. When this was done my mother asked me to take it to my grandfather to be checked. My grandfather was a frum and very learned man. He had to check so that the goose was without any wounds or malady so that it was kosher. He checked it carefully and found spots on its lever –it was not kosher. Therefore we could not prepare it. Try to judge my disappointment and my sorrow, indescribable!

We did not have much to eat that Shavuot. We spent about three weeks in the ghetto. After this we were transported to Auschwitz. I and my sisters survived the war. We were taken to Sweden by the Red Cross. Also my father survived. We reassembled in Sweden.

◇◇

Summer gherkins

parve

This pickled gherkin that my mother made has a certain place among the specialities of summer. The pots in which the gherkins are kept should be put in a sunny window. The gherkins get fermented in only a few days. After this they should be kept in a cool place but cannot be saved more than up to 2-3 weeks. My mother called these gherkins in Hungarian `Kovászos uborka,' sour gherkins.

2 kilos of small gherkins
Heads of dill
Approx. 5 spoons of salt
4 cloves of garlic
2 slices of rye bread
Water

Directions:

1.) Clean the gherkins well, brush them until plain.
2.) Make a cut in each ending.
3.) Fill the pots with gherkins mixed in layers with heads of dill and pieces of garlic.
4.) Fill up with lukewarm water and salt. On top put the slices of bread.
5.) Cover the pot with a lid or a plate, put in a sunny window.
6.) The gherkins are ready when they changed color a bit, towards yellowish and they have a freshly sour taste.

Dubi Arie
Toronto, Ontario, Canada
Submitted by Carole Master

Dubi Arie was born in 1940 in Warsaw, Poland. His father had joined the Russian Army. His mother took four week old Dubi and his older brother out of Warsaw just before the Nazi's bombed the city. They wandered Europe and endured three years of confinement in an Austrian refugee camp. Finally, in 1948 Dubi, his brother and mother immigrated to Israel. In 1951, Dubi's mother died and twelve year old Dubi was left orphaned. Dubi found a new home at the Kibbutz Shaar HaGolan in the Jordan Valley. Officials arranged for him to receive artistic training when they discovered his natural talents in drawing. Dubi met his wife, Raya on the kibbutz. In 1957, Dubi volunteered for the elite paratrooper division and served the Israeli army for the next 16 years. Dubi fought in the Six Day War, the War of Attrition and in the Yom Kippur War.

In 1974, Dubi moved to Toronto, Canada with his wife in order to fully concentrate on creating a "The Mission." This massive artistic project is Dubi's contribution to his people. He titled it, "Under the Wings of G-d and the Shadow of Amalek." The research took 13 years, the actual painting took 7 years to complete. Dubi realized the awesome spiritual nature of the undertaking. The painting commemorates 4,000 years of Jewish history. 38 and 1/2 ft. long by 7 ft. high, a brilliant, bold oil painting intended by Dubi, to serve as a dynamic, visual reminder of the Jewish heritage. Dubi's underlying message of his monumental piece of artwork is that out of the darkness comes the light. Dubi hopes his "Mission," will help remind people of their shared bonds of unity amidst a diverse world in order to build bridges of understanding between the Jewish nation and the other peoples of the world.

Dubi's website: www.dubiarie.com

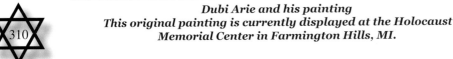

Dubi Arie and his painting
This original painting is currently displayed at the Holocaust
Memorial Center in Farmington Hills, MI.

Genia Aszkenazy Szeflan

Montreal, Canada

Submitted by her daughter, Dana Szeflan Bell

My mother was born in Wegrov Poland, the eldest of three sisters. All were educated and came from a beautiful home where they were loved and sheltered.

My mother married my father Chaim Szeflan. Then her sister Hella, married Michal Werthjzer. I was born 5 years later on May 13, 1938. It was a very joyous time for both families as I was the first grandchild. This wonderful time didn't last long as the war broke out very soon after I was born. At the time we were living in Warsaw, and my parents decided to leave Warsaw, knowing that it would be the first place Hitler would hit. We left 3 weeks before Warsaw was attacked; running and hiding, bombs falling, cities burning, people dying. Life became hell. We eventually got to the Russian border. There my father refused to become a Russian citizen. Therefore we were looked upon as traitors and deported to a labour camp in northern Russia. My father referred to it as Siberia, but in fact it was worse, we were much further north of Siberia. The cattle train that took us to the labour camp was like a death train. We were packed into the cattle cars in inhuman conditions, no food, no privacy. Many people died on the way to the camp. When we finally arrived at the labour camp, most were infested with lice, many were deathly ill, depressed and starving. My parents had to work hard from dusk to dawn on only one meal of black stale bread and a watery soup with potato peels. To my parents, who came from beautiful homes and never had any adversity, this was pure hell. The struggle to survive was immense.

My parents had a reason to survive; their baby daughter. Some gave up the struggle and just died. Very few young children from these camps made it out alive. My mother was multitalented and began to do some extra sewing for the official who ran the camp. In return he allowed us to keep two of their goats in our barrack. She would milk the goats for him, allowing her to keep some of the milk to give to me. My father being a pharmacist brought some medications with him, and that saved me when I came down with whopping cough. The time spent in the labour camp was horrific. When we were freed after 18 months of hard labour, my parents started the journey to Asia. Starving and in ill health, they scavenged for food anywhere they could get it. This was a monstrous voyage...so many obstacles...My father got hoof and mouth disease, and the story of how my mother saved his life is too long to tell, but she managed to get to Moscow to get the penicillin he needed to survive, returning just in time. My mother sewed and made uniforms for the N.K.V.D. (Russian military officials). There was nothing my mother couldn't do, she had such courage and will to live.

At one point both my parents were stricken with typhoid and were taken away. I was 4 years old at the time. Crying alone on a street, a man approached me and asked me where my mother was, I didn't know, then he asked me what she looked like, I responded "my mother is very beautiful and she is tall". My mother was in fact only 5 ft. tall but she was a "tall" woman in every sense of the word. That man placed me in an orphanage. I thought I would never see my parents again. My head was shaved for lice, I looked like a skeleton from malnutrition. After some months in the orphanage I saw an eye looking through a split in the orphanage gate, I yelled "Mama! Mama!" incredibly my mother had found me! She would never have recognized me... I looked so emaciated. Being reunited with my mother was the happiest moment of my life.

311

My first photo in Canada, 1948

When the war ended we made our way back to Poland. On arrival, my parents found out that their whole beautiful family was murdered by the Germans. They never got over that shock.

We ended up in a displaced persons camp in Steyr, Austria. Life began to take on a bit of normality. My mother sewed for people and made a bit of money, my father worked as the camps electrician. I started going half days to a religious Jewish school "Bais Yaakov". We made friends; there was food and clothing given to us by the Jewish agencies. My baby sister Rachella (Ruthy) was born July 15th. 1948. I felt like the luckiest person on earth. Now, I too had family. At the end of that year we got our visas to go to Canada. We landed in Quebec City in November of 1948 and settled in Montreal.

Tragically, my mother passed away at age 45 after we came to Montreal. She was torn from our lives. It didn't seem right. After all she had been through, survived and finally came to a free country...she died. My father, after a long struggle with heart disease passed away at age 75, it was then that I really felt like an orphan again.

Today I have a wonderful life; I am blessed with 2 wonderful children, and 5 delicious grandsons whom I adore, and a loving husband. My sister Ruthy has 3 beautiful daughters and is also blessed with 5 grandchildren. We are a very close knit family. As my father would say, "Our table is getting full once again."

My maternal family and me in Warsaw, 1938

Our Table Is Getting Full Once Again

Nana and the five stars, 2001

Chicken in the pot

meat
a whole meal in one pot

I want to contribute these recipes in honour of my mother, Genia Aszkenazy Szeflan.

Chicken parts, breasts and legs as many as you wish

4 or 5 onions
  peeled and cut into circles

6 carrots
  peeled and sliced into long pieces

4 celery stalks
6 large potatoes
  cut in half or 10 small potatoes whole

1/2 cup of olive oil
Paprika and Onion Powder

Directions:
Preheat the oven to 350 degrees

1.) Cook in a large Dutch oven or large pot with cover.
2.) Pour in the olive oil evenly spread at bottom of pot.
3.) Add the onions spreading them evenly at the bottom of the pot.
4.) Then add the carrots and celery also evenly spread.
5.) Place the chicken parts on top of the veggies.
6.) Sprinkle them evenly with the onion powder first.
7.) Then sprinkle the paprika, make sure the parts are all covered with the paprika.
8.) Place the potatoes around the chicken parts and in between the parts.
9.) You can also sprinkle the potatoes with paprika.
10.) Bake in a pre heated 350' oven for an hour or an hour and a half.

You have a whole meal in one pot, and it's delicious, one of our favorites.

313

Sweet and sour meatballs

meat

1 lb. lean ground beef
1/3 cup matzah meal
1/2 grated onion
1 large egg
Salt and freshly ground pepper to taste
1 28 oz. can of tomato puree
1 ten ounce jar of chili sauce
1/4 cup of brown sugar or to taste
Juice of 1 lemon

Directions:

1.) Mix ground beef in a bowl with the matzah meal, onion, egg, salt and pepper.
2.) Roll approx. a tablespoon of meat mixture into small balls and set aside.
3.) Combine the tomato puree, chili sauce, brown sugar and lemon juice in a heavy saucepan. Adjust seasoning- bring to a boil and simmer, then gently add the meatballs one by one at a time. Simmer covered, about 20 min.

Makes approx. 35 meatballs

Vegetarian chopped liver

parve

3 large onions chopped
2 tablespoons vegetable oil
2 cups green beans
1 3/4 cups green peas
3 hard boiled eggs
20 Tam Tam or other salty crackers
Salt and freshly ground pepper to taste

Directions:

1.) Sauté onions slowly over low heat in vegetable oil for about 20 min. or until golden.
2.) Combine onions with remaining ingredients in a food processor, grinding until well processed.
3.) Add salt and pepper.
4.) Serve on great bread.

Yields: 4 servings

315

Butter Cookies

dairy

1 1/2 sticks (3/4 cup) unsalted butter
1/2 cup plus 3 tablespoons sugar
1 large egg
1/2 teaspoon vanilla
1 teaspoon baking powder
3 cups all purpose flour
Dash of salt
1 egg yolk
1 tablespoon heavy cream
3 tablespoons chopped blanched almonds

Directions:
Preheat oven to 400 degrees

1.) In food processor mix butter and ½ cup of sugar.
2.) Add whole egg and vanilla and process.
3.) Mix together the baking powder, flour and salt and add to the butter mixture, whirl until the dough comes together in a ball. Set aside covered in refrigerator for a few hours.
4.) Roll the batter out ¼ inch. thin on a floured board and cut into round shapes, 2 inches in diameter.
5.) Place on greased baking sheet, brush with egg yolk mixed with cream.
6.) Sprinkle with 3 tablespoons of almonds and remaining sugar.
7.) Bake in a pre heated 400 degree oven for 5 to 7 minutes or until light brown.

Makes about 45 cookies

Chicken Breasts in Dijon mustard

meat

> 6 chicken breasts de-boned
> (you can make as many as you want)
> Jar of Dijon mustard
> 1 cup of all purpose flour (or more)
> onion powder
> olive oil, or vegetable oil (for frying)
> salt and pepper to taste

Directions:

On a board lined with waxed paper place one chicken breast at a time. Cover it with wax paper and pound it to make it thinner, not too thin. Do the same with all the other breasts, sprinkle them generously with onion powder on both sides.

1.) Distribute the Dijon mustard and flour in separate dinner plates.
2.) Dip one breast at a time first in the Dijon mustard, you can use a basting brush for this, or do it with your hand. Spread the mustard evenly over the whole breast back and front. Dip it in the flour, evenly back and front.
3.) In a large skillet pre heated with olive oil, place the breasts one at a time, fitting in as many as you can. Fry each side till golden brown. Take out of skillet and place on paper towels to soak up excess oil. You can use 2 or more frying pans if you need to make a big batch.

I make these for the holidays, they are so delicious. You can make them in the morning and heat them up in the oven just before serving...or you can freeze them. They freeze beautifully. You can serve them with a green vegetable, and wild rice...

Yummy...Enjoy

May we always have good times and enjoy special meals with our families.

317

Annelie Sherwood
Denver, CO, U.S.A.

My name is Annelie Sherwood. In Germany my name was Anneliese Loewenstein. I live with my husband of 62 years in Denver, CO. We have 3 children and 8 grandchildren, and I feel myself very fortunate. I was born in Giessen, Germany in December 1922. I had 2 brothers who were 9 and 12 years older than I, so I was pretty much raised as an only child. My father sold laundry and cleaning equipment and we led a comfortable life when I was young. In 1931 we moved to Cologne. The political atmosphere was already getting uncomfortable, so my parents sent me to a Jewish grade school. By 1933 my older brother left for Palestine and my other brother left for Chicago to American relatives. They were then 22 and 19 years old.

My father, who by then was 59 years old and did not speak English, felt that he could still provide for his wife and young daughter. Besides, my parents and many others didn't think Hitler could last. But slowly through the years my father's business got squeezed out. Customers were afraid to deal with Jews. In early 1939 all Jews had to bring their good jewelry and sterling silver to the Police. When my father went to his bank he was told "Sorry your account is closed". By then my brother had moved from Palestine to the U.S., and my parents were anxious to get to the U.S. as well. But the U.S. made it very difficult to get visas, and we were given quota numbers. Since the U.S. allowed children to bring parents over and vice versa with preferred visas my brothers got affidavits hesitantly from wealthy American relatives, who did not realize just how dangerous life was for German Jews. They received their visas in the summer of 1939, but the U.S. Consulate wouldn't issue a visa for me, and they wouldn't leave without me. My number finally was called in November. We went directly from the U.S. Consulate to Holland and the U.S. 1938 and 1939 were the worst years for me, I was used to signs of "No Jews Allowed" at recreational places etc. One morning my mother sent me to a fish store and suddenly an SS officer came and had all Jewish customers line up against a wall and then marched us outside and along with other Jews we walked single file to an SS Office. We were frisked and held for hours. I raised my skirt to make me look younger, even though I am short anyway. They finally let me go at 2 p.m. I called my parents, they were frantic. That day I loved the Lunghash my mother had cooked to eat for the midday meal, which I used to hate. Another experience took place in our apartment. The doorbell rang and an SS officer came into the apartment, obviously drunk, and threatened my parents while I hid in my room. My father was a mild man but my mother, though scared, was tough and he finally left. We were all trembling afterwards. We were fortunate though.

My mother's sister and brother-in-law did not make it out. They had sent their only child on a Kindertransport to England where she became a nurse and has a family. My father's youngest brother was crippled since birth and a sweet man. During the 30's he was put into a nursing home in Frankfort, and we suppose he was killed. He must have been about 60. During 1938 and 1939 some parents of my classmates made plans to emigrate, but were afraid to tell their children. So slowly some of my classmates disappeared.

We later found out where some of them went. Several went to some South American countries that provided minimum housing etc. I had no contact with former classmates. However a book was written about my High School in Cologne "The Jawne" in early 1990's, and through a coincidence I learned about it and found a group of former class mates in New York. It was an actual healing experience to have found these girls, a bridge between my childhood and today.

Matzo Dumplings for soup

parve

for Passover

6 matzos
2 eggs
small onion
salt and pepper
ginger

Directions:

1.) 6 matzos, soak in warm water, then squeeze out as much water in your hand, and put handfuls into cheesecloth and squeeze more liquid out.
2.) Put it into a bowl, add 2 eggs, 1 small onion, chopped and browned, salt, pepper, a little ginger, and enough matzo meal to form balls.
   * (I use an ice cream scoop and then cut it in half.)
3.) Try one ball out in boiling water for a few minutes to see if it holds together.
4.) Roll the balls out in the palm of my hand.

This makes about 28 dumplings and people eat about 3.

I usually double the recipe. The mixture can be made the day before and then roll the dumplings the day you serve. Any leftovers can be frozen.
I make the soup with chicken, a little beef soup meat or soup bone (it gives the soup more flavor) some carrot, celery, cut onion, and a little tomato. I use lots of chicken and just cover all the ingredients with water. The chicken meat can be used at another time. I make the soup previously and freeze it until needed.

319

Margaret Kohlhagen
Bergenfield, N.J., U.S.A.

Otto and Hilda Friedman from early 1920's

Margaret and Alfred c. 1935

The following story came to us handwritten by Margaret Kohlhagen, and we decided to print it exactly the way we received it . . .

I was born in Salzburg, Austria, a city made famous by the movie "The Sound of Music".

When Austria was taken over by th Nazis in March 1938, I was no longer allowed to attend my school, as Jews were not allowed in "public" places. I was 7½ yrs. old and in 2nd grade and was sent to attend the Catholic School that was part of the "Cloisters" featured in the "Sound of Music" where "Julie Andrew" was studying to become a nun (all the jewish kids from our synagogue also went — we only had to participate in secular studieds & did not have to partic pate in religious instructions)

After "kristall nacht" (Nov. 1938) it was no longer safe to remain in Salzburg. Through my father's connections (he owned an Import-Export Lumber Co,) he made arrangements for my brother Fred (age 12) and me to be smuggled into Switzerland, with a Swiss National, who posed as our "mother," and had "obtained" a false passport registering Fred and me as her children. Since I was too young to understand this "delicate" situation, and the possibility of my saying the "wrong" thing at the "wrong" time, to the "wrong" person, I was told I was going to camp with my brother, and a "lady" we did not know, a friend of my parents. I had no fears, because I was with Fred and everything seemed O.K. We first took a train to an

unidentified destination and then we had to
cross the border over a bridge (on foot)
just like the TRAPP family in "Sound of Music".
    We met my father in BASEL, Switzerland.
He had gone there already several weeks before on
a business trip and at that time was told by his
business associates NOT to return to Salzburg, but to
get us out in this way. He immediately called my
mother to tell her that we arrived safely
without complications after about 12 hours, and
she was greatly relieved. She later told me
those were the worst 12 hrs. in her
life, not knowing exactly where we were
and if everything went according to plan.
It took about 3 months until arrangements
could be completed for my mother's safe
escape, which was arranged by the police
chief of St. Gallen, Switzerland, who was
also known as the ~~Swit~~ "Swiss SCHINDLER"
because he saved about 1,000 Austrian Jews
by falsifying documents to help them
cross into Switzerland. He was later
convicted of TREASON by a Swiss
Court and sent to Jail, he was a
"RIGHTEOUS GENTILE" and a tree
is planted in his memory in YAD VASHEM
    In Feb. 1939, my mother finally arrived
in BASEL after 3 months of harassment by
the Nazis who constantly asked her, where
my father is and she told them that he
abandoned her and took the children. The
Nazis gave her 24 hrs. to evacuate our home

and then they confiscated our beautiful house,
which had 4 tremendous apartments, one
on each floor - the bottom floor was my
father's business offices, we lived on the
second floor (8 rooms) and my parents
rented out the other 2 apartments. My
mother had to move in with friends after
she was "thrown-out" of HER home!

When we were finally together, Feb. 1939,
our "stop and go" travels began. LICHTENSTEIN
was our first stop - a tiny country.. I went to
a "one-room school" on skis (a lot of snow
and NO CAR POOLS!) and my brother sat behind
me - one teacher for about 20 children aged
6 to 14. When our temporary VISA expired, we
moved to MÜLHAUSEN (Alsace-Lorraine) for a
while and then to Besançon (France). Every
time a VISA expired (only temporary) VISAS
were issued in by the French because they did
not want Jews either and only because my
father had business connections and had always
traveled throughout this area, he was able
to obtain these VISAS. Agen (near Bordeaux)
was our next destination where we stayed
until Spring 1941 when we found out that the
processing for our emmigration was beginning —
this would take us first to Marseilles, then to
Madrid, Spain and our final destination in
Europe, Portugal. We spent several weeks at
a beautiful resort in ESTORIL, Portugal
waiting for our departure, from LISBON in
July 1941, when only 2 tickets were available

④

so my father and brother left first and then one week later, my mother and I sailed on the S.S. EXCALIBUR (an American LuxuRy LINE) ~~to~~ Crossing the Altantic was my most unpleasant experience of our entire ~~"~~ "adventure". I was continuously sea-sick and so frustrated because, after having lived on food rations during the war, here the ship offered any kind of food you wanted, especially ice-cream with so many different flavors I never heard of, but I was too sea-sick to eat anything.

On July 22, 1941, we landed in N.Y. and I will never forget the excitement of seeing the Statue of Liberty. My father + brother were waiting for us and we went by train to Ferndale N.Y. where we lived next door to my aunt + uncle who were here 3 yrs already, and we stayed until end of Nov. 1941 when my parents, brother and I moved to Queens, N.Y. where I lived until we married + my husband + I moved to New Jersey where we reside now.

In all our travels, from Nov. 1938 until Nov. 1941, I lived in eleven different homes, in seven different countries (or cities) and ~~st~~ speaking four different languages.

Now, I am happy to say, we have lived in Bergenfield since 1954, having moved only once about a 5 blocks distance. I do not want to ever have to move again!

324

Some of my family's favorites:

Cold Fruit Soup (can be kept in frig 1 week)

apples - peaches - plums - grapes - cherries (any combination whatever is in season
1) Cut up ab. 3 lb. into bite size
2) put in 2-3 qt. pot + cover 1" w. water
3) Cook till soft - stir into hot mixture 1 pkg. any red KOJEL
4) Cool till set - when firm, mix w. fork + add O.J. until desired thickness
5) Refrigerate

Noodle Kugel - Preheat oven 375°
(can be wrapped in foil and frozen)
1) Boil 1 lb. med. noodles until tender + drain well
2) Combine w. **6** eggs well beaten + 1 can drained crushed pineapple + ½ cup veg oil + ¾ cup sugar + 2 cut up apples
3) pour into greased baking dish + sprinkle w. cinamon sugar
4) Bake covered w. foil until set, then uncover - total 45-60 min

Chocolate Mousse

1) melt 1 pkg. (6 oz) choc bits (PARVE) in double boiler or microwave
2) Cool - add 4 oz red kiddush wine (sweet)
3) Stir in 4 egg yolks (beaten)
4) gently fold in 4 well beaten egg yolks
5) line dish w. parve lady fingers or sponge cake
6) Cover w. choc. mixture - refrigerate till firm

325

David Nathan Schechter

Lakewood, CO, U.S.A.

Submitted by his wife Eileen Schechter

David Schechter, my husband, passed away from complications of Alzheimer's Disease on November 6, 2006. A Holocaust Survivor from Poland, Dave, along with his Aunt Sara, also a Holocaust Survivor, made their way to Denver in late 1946. Aunt Sara took on the role of Dave's mother as he had lost all of his immediate family in the War.

Sara was an outstanding cook and baker but NEVER used a measuring cup! As Dave's new bride, I was getting lessons on how to cook and bake from someone who didn't believe in measuring ingredients or writing down recipes. Over the years I did learn quite a bit from Aunt Sara and from Dave. Attached are a few of Dave's favorites: Aunt Sara's Mandel Bread, Challah and Potato Knishes.

In addition to our active role in the Jewish Community, Dave and I were members of the Colorado Child Survivors of the Holocaust Group.

I appreciate the opportunity to submit these favorites in his memory.

David on a horse with his brother
Leibshin in Poland, 1934

My name is David Nathan Schechter and I was born on the first day of Passover in the Spring (March) of 1929. I spent the early part of my life in Mikulince, a small city of approximately 5,000 people located about 18 kilometers south of Tarnopol, Poland.

I was the youngest of three children in my family and one of only three (myself, an aunt and an uncle) Holocaust survivors from a very large and extended family of grandparents, aunts, uncles and cousins.

In 1941, the war progressed in our part of the world and the Germans took over our entire area. The Russian soldiers just couldn't hold them back. I was 12 years old.

As Mikulince was being taken over, my mother took me into the attic of the house and hid me in the chimney. My brother had already been taken to a work camp. The Germans and Ukrainian soldiers stormed into the village and into our homes. They wanted everyone – men, women, children. They took my father, my mother and my sister. That was the last time I saw any of them.

I stayed in that hiding place in the attic all day.
I guess I should have been terrified but, I didn't know how to be terrified.

In the years that followed, I lived in ghettos, forced labor camps and hid deep in the forest surrounding the camps – including a time spent with my brother until we were captured in an underground bunker. We were taken to a nearby camp where we were loaded onto railroad cattle cars – 120 or more people in a car. We walked a gauntlet to get onto the cattle cars. The Polish, Ukrainian and German soldiers just stood there and hit you as you walked through the line. At the end of the line, two German soldiers decided who went where.

To the right, labor camp.
To the left, gas chamber.

My brother was sent to the right.
I was pushed to the left.

As the train moved through the forest, someone broke open a small hole in the side of the cattle car. A man came over to me, grabbed me and took me over to the hole in the wall of the car and threw me out.

The fall from the moving train broke my left arm, but the actions of that man likely saved my life. Myself and others who had jumped or been pushed from the moving train were captured and turned over to the German SS at a nearby camp. The SS soldier took me and a woman with a broken leg over to a wall in the camp.

He shot the woman as I stood next to her.
Then, he pointed the gun at me.

All of a sudden he puts the gun down to his side and walks away. I guess he decided he'd had enough target practice that day.

He looked at the Kapo, the Jewish commander for the camp, and told him to keep me for target practice in the morning.

The next morning came but, instead of sending me to the wall for target practice, the Kapo sent me to work.

After surviving 1943 in the labor camps, I had escaped hidden deep in the forest. I lived there, with other survivors, for nine months before being liberated by the Russians in March 1944.

327

I continued to survive in several post war camps for Jews and ended up in a displaced persons camp in Austria. I eventually made it to the United States, arriving in New York on Dec. 20, 1946 and into Denver on December 25.

I attended The Emily Griffith Opportunity School where I earned my citizenship and learned to be an upholsterer. Over the last six decades of my life, I have lived under the freedom of the United States, with my wife, three children and, most recently, six grandchildren.

David Schechter's Obituary:

Just before the soldiers took his family away to their deaths, David Schechter's mother pushed him into the chimney and left without saying a word. When he climbed down that night, the 13-year-old was alone. That's how he entered the Holocaust.

For two years, he was sent from one labor camp to another. Mr. Schechter saw people get shot and whipped to death. He broke stones with an ax and was beaten so badly he couldn't get up for days. After escaping, he hid for nine months in a forest, walking barefoot through snow and ice to find food until the war ended.

By the time he was 17, he found a new home in Denver. The redhead with long ears and a warm smile learned to make furniture, working for two companies before retiring in the mid-1990's. He married and raised three children with gentle encouragement, quiet devotion and a proud connection to Judaism.

Mr. Schechter died Nov. 6 at age 77.

Aunt Sara

328

Aunt Sara's Challah Dough

parve

(No Eggs in Recipe)

1/2 cup warm water
1 1/2 tsp sugar
3 packages dry yeast
7 1/2 cups unsifted flour
1 3/4 tsp salt
1/3 cup honey
1/4 cup oil
2 1/2 to 2 3/4 cups warm water

Directions:

Preheat the oven to 375 degrees

1.) Sprinkle yeast and sugar over water- let stand approx. 10 minutes.
2.) In a large bowl add honey, oil and water.
3.) Add 1/2 of flour mixture.
4.) Add remaining flour.
5.) Knead approximately 10 minutes until you have a smooth/satin look.
6.) Grease top of dough and place into a greased pan.
7.) Cover with Saran wrap – let rise until double in size/bulk.
8.) Divide dough into 3 equal parts.
9.) On lightly floured board and hands, roll the dough into 3 strips of equal length.
10.) Braid strips together and place in baking pan.
11.) Cover and let rise until double in bulk.
12.) Brush Challah with 2 beaten egg yolks, 1 ½ tablespoons water and 1 teaspoon salt. Sprinkle top with poppy seeds.

Bake in oven at 375 degrees approximately 50 minutes or until brown.

This dough can also be made in any shape for rolls.

329

Eileen's Potato Knishes

a Favorite

parve

2 pounds of peeled and cubed potatoes
2 medium chopped and drained onions
1 tsp paprika
6 tbsp vegetable oil
1 tsp salt
1/2 tsp pepper

Directions:

Preheat the oven to 400 degrees

1.) Place potatoes in a large saucepan and cover with water.
2.) Bring to a boil, cover and reduce heat to low. Simmer until tender.
3.) Saute onions in oil until golden brown.
4.) Drain potatoes and mash.
5.) Add slightly drained onions, salt and pepper.
6.) Mix well and cool.
7.) Using any bread dough recipe – roll out and cut into 4" X 4" squares and place 1 ½ to 2 tablespoons of potato mixture in center of each square.
8.) Pinch edges together, place pinched side down on greased baking sheet.
9.) Brush with egg mixture – 2 egg yolks beaten and mixed with 2 teaspoons water.
10.) Bake in preheated oven at 400 degrees until golden brown (approx. 18-20 minutes).
11.) Can be frozen when baked and cooled. Wrap knishes separately in plastic wrap.

Note: A more convenient version calls for frozen puff pastry dough thawed. Use Pepperidge Farm pastry dough, sheets cut into 18 squares. Makes a very flaky crust. About 3 dozen knishes.

Aunt Sara's Mandel Bread

parve

1 heaping cup of sugar
3/4 cup of oil
3 eggs
1 to 2 tsp of vanilla
3 cups flour
1 1/2 tsp baking powder
1/2 tsp of salt
1 heaping cup of walnuts or pecans

Optional ingredients include:
pecans, walnuts, orange peel, chocolate chips, butterscotch chips, white chocolate chips, toffee chips, dried cherries or cranberries, mint chips, apricot brandy, etc.
(I usually use chocolate chips and butterscotch chips, cranberries or pecans.)

Austria after liberation

Directions:
Preheat the oven to 375 degrees

1.) Blend sugar and oil in mixing bowl.
2.) Add eggs and beat into mixture.
3.) Add vanilla and mix again.
4.) Sift together the flour, salt and baking powder.
5.) Add to mixture.
6.) Then slowly beat in the optional ingredients (nuts, berries, chips, etc.)
    * You will have a very thick, sticky dough.
7.) Shape batter into three separate logs by rolling it on a lightly floured surface.
8.) Place logs on cookie sheet. Place only two logs per sheet, as the dough will spread.
9.) Sprinkle with cinnamon and sugar mixture.
10.) Bake at 375 degrees for 20 minutes or until brown.
11.) After logs have cooled slightly (approx. 10 minutes), slice logs across or diagonally for longer, biscotti shaped cookies.
12.) Spread out the individual pieces on the cookie sheet as you cut them.
13.) Sprinkle them again with the cinnamon and sugar mixture.
14.) Brown again in the oven for approximately 3 minutes.

Sarah Haras, 1990

Sarah, 1946

Rosalyn "Reyzele" Kirkel

Denver, CO, U.S.A.

President, Colorado Jewish Child Survivors of the Holocaust

Reyzele, 1949

Jews and Christians had co-existed relatively peacefully in Lithuania (a Baltic country the size of Ireland) from 1316 until 1941. Then the onslaught. With Hitler's forces' imminent arrival, Lithuanian nationalists and right-wing extremists armed and funded by the Germans and driven by ideological anti-Semitism, began a bloodbath of the Jews. The following is my story.

I was two months old when the Nazis invaded Lithuania on June 22, 1941, defeating the Russian Communists who occupied the country one year before. The Lithuanians welcomed the Germans with garlands and open arms.

The Jews fled for their lives -- from the small villages to the bigger towns. From the cities to the Russian border, to no avail. Fear and premonitions of doom filled their hearts. Restrictions on civil liberties were instituted immediately.

Jews had to wear yellow stars, walk in the streets, close their shops. Children were not permitted to go to their schools or play in parks. Acts to humiliate Jews, random shootings, and looting of homes -- even by neighbors, took place.

Panicked, my parents Avrom and Frida Kirkelis bundled up their three young children - my sister, my brother and me - and in a horse-drawn wagon taking few possessions fled to the Russian border. Too late. They were turned back. Fortunately, they were not shot like some others.

On June 25th a group of Lithuanian partisans in a three-day rampage against the Jews in smaller towns and villages, wiped out the populations of over 150 Jewish communities – Shtetlech.

By August the Jewish community of Siauliai (Shavel - my town), the third largest city in Lithuania, had been herded into two ghettos (Kaukaz and Traku, later reduced to just Traku). Several families were crowded into each little house. A barbed wire fence enclosed the ghettos. Guards stood watch. Twice daily roll call was early morning, and evening after work; workers lined up in rows to be counted sometimes for hours, in the heat, rain, or freezing cold. While parents were at work younger children were left in the care of older children or old people unable to work.

The Jews in the ghettos suffered from hunger, insecurity and fear, teetering between despair and hope. Death from starvation, cold and disease occurred daily. Or the dreaded transports from which nobody returned.

November 5th, 1943 was the infamous day of the "kinderaktion," (children's action). My mother got wind of it and before she went to work, hid us three children in the attic, admonishing us to be very quiet.

Rosalyn

Once the workers left, large empty tarp-covered trucks drove through Traku Ghetto, loudspeakers blaring orders that all the children were to be loaded on the trucks immediately. Orders alternated with loud music to drown out the screams of children. Dogs were brought in to sniff out any hidden children.

At first a thug, (Lithuanian collaborator) assisting the Germans did not find us and left the attic. But then Leibel, my four year-old brother pulled away. "I have to pee."

The thug heard the commotion and ran up the steps, grabbed the terrified child and threw him on the truck. Eight hundred children and 23 adults were transported to Auschwitz that day and murdered.

When my mother returned home and found her son gone, she fainted. The next day she decided that since I was still small, maybe a Lithuanian family would take me for safekeeping.

My mother beseeched Bella, a ghetto acquaintance who had smuggled out her little girl. She talked to her Lithuanian in-laws. Her father in-law's sister Elena Yakubitiene and her husband agreed to take the risk and hide me.

Bravely, Bella smuggled me out early one morning, hidden inside her coat. She positioned herself in a middle row for roll call. I had to be very quiet. The first guard she encountered in Frankel's leather factory, (where she worked) looked her over and waved her on.

Luckily, the German guard outside was away. She crossed the street to hand me to Elena, who welcomed me into her arms, and into her life.

I spent the next two and 1/2 years in a one-room cottage in the near-by town of Radvillskis. I remember the aroma of smoked sausage from the smokehouse. I was called Zulita. Father Justinus Lapis baptized me, and I wore a cross. I lived a Christian life.

A childless middle-aged Christian couple, they showed me love and kindness. Yet fear gripped us all when there was pounding on the door. I would run to the trunk in the closet.

In July 1944, when the Russians returned to liberate, the Germans liquidated the Shavel gheto. My mother, father and ten year-old sister Leja were transported to Stutthoff Concentration Camp. From there my mother and sister were sent to Auschwitz.

Six weeks later my father was sent to Dachau Labor Camp in a transport of men. The Americans liberated him while on a death march in April 1945. Following hospitalization, he went to Feldafing, a German DP Camp.

In 1946 he returned to Siauliai (shavel), Lithuania, to look for me. I was all he had left. I did not recognize him and clung to the woman I'd come to know as my mother.

Upon our arrival to Feldafing, my father began his search for our American cousins. In May 1949 I said good-bye to my best friend Mirale. America had opened her doors. We were off on a long journey to freedom and a new life.

Potato Knaidlach

parve

These dumplings are part of my childhood in my Eastern European American home. Whenever I was sick my step-mother Sarah would make them and pour warm milk over them. They are also good in soups and as a side dish with meat or dairy. Add fruit and it's a dessert.

3 large raw potatoes, peeled
1 cup matzo meal
3 Tbs. canola oil
3 eggs or egg substitute
2 quarts boiling water with 1 tsp. salt or simmering broth

Directions:
1.) Grate potatoes or put them into a blender.
2.) Squeeze out the water with cheese cloth as dry as possible.
3.) Combine potato pulp with matzo meal and oil.
4.) May refrigerate for an hour or drop from soup spoon (about walnut size balls) into boiling water.
5.) Simmer with cover aslant for 25 -35 minutes.
6.) Test a knaidel after 25 minutes.

Serves six to eight for a soup.

Gribines (Grivines, Gribens)

a delicious favorite snack

meat

Ingredients:
- *Skin from one chicken*
- *1 cup chopped onion*

Directions:
- Cut the chicken skin into one inch squares and sauté with the onions.
- Start with one half of the onions and gradually add the chicken skins and the rest of the onions.
- Reduce heat to medium and sauté until skin and onion are brown and crispy.
- No additional fat is needed. May add salt to taste.

Sally Rosenberg
Brooklyn, NY, U.S.A.

Sally

My name is Sally Rosenberg. I presently live in Brooklyn, New York. I was born in Poland, in the town of Sosnoviec. I will briefly tell you what I remember from my childhood years.   My family was quite comfortable. We had a wholesale dry goods store, and had a good life. And then the war broke out and everything was taken away.   We were sent to the Ghetto, and then in 1943, the ghetto was liquidated, and we were sent to concentration camps like Auschwitz and others. After the war we went back to Sosnoviec, where I found my 2 sisters, but the rest of my family did not survive. What I remember from my childhood is too much to mention but I do remember an apple cake my mother used to bake. Here is the recipe and I hope that you enjoy it.

Sally

Apple Cake
parve

2 eggs
1 cup of sugar
1 1/2 sticks of margarine
1 tsp vanilla
2 tsp orange juice
2 cups flour
6 apples
raisins (optional)
2 tsp sugar
sprinkle of cinnamon

Directions:
Preheat oven to 350 degrees

1.) Mix the eggs, sugar and margarine together.
2.) When well blended, add the vanilla , orange juice and flour.
3.) Roll out the batter so that it fits into a 9x13 baking pan.
4.) Grate 6 apples and add raisins (optional).
5.) Spread apples over the batter in pan and cover the apples with the remaining dough.
6.) Sprinkle with sugar and cinnamon.
7.) Place in 350 preheated oven for 45 -50 minutes.

Enjoy!

335

Zelda Sonnenberg Birken

Coconut Creek, FL, U.S.A.

Submitted by her daughter Marilyn Barth

Zelda (Zozia) Sonnenberg Birken with her three sisters, Shaindel, Zipra and Golda and her parents Simcha and Miriam in Poland. This picture was taken during the war in 1941 in her home town of Zdunska Wola.

My mother, Zelda Sonnenberg Birken, daughter of Miriam and Simcha Sonnenberg, was born in Zdunska Wola Poland in 1923. Growing up, her father was a barber and her mother a homemaker; always instilling within her children good values and life skills. My mother was the second to youngest out of four girls. Each sister having their own unique personality, my mother was extremely nurturing and caring. Her take charge personality, always making sure her parents and sisters were safe, made her who she is today.

Although my mother rarely spoke about her experiences in the Holocaust, the few stories she did share are integral to who she is today. She was 16 years old at the time the war broke out. At age 19, my mother was separated from her mother and two sisters who were taken to be shot at a mass grave.

Encouraged by my grandmother to escape, the two sisters safely reunited with my mother, youngest sister, and her father. In an attempt to rejoin the rest of her family, my grandmother was caught by the Nazi's and shot in a mass grave. Not too much later, two of my mother's sisters were gassed to death in a bus which they believed was transporting them to another camp.

Together, my mother stayed with her father and remaining sister, until they were taken to Auschwitz in 1945. It was there, that my mother and her sister were separated from their father, never to see him again. Together, my mother and her sister Cesia remained by each others side for the rest of the war. They were both then transported to Berlin to work in the Krupp's factory, where they lived in ditches with five hundred other girls during the Berlin bombings.

My mother Zelda Sonnenberg Birken at 25 in Sweden after the war.

In 1945 my mother and her sister were liberated by the Swedish Red Cross, sent to Sweden first to be quarantined, and then to a kibbutz where she remained until 1947. There, she met the love of her life, my father, Natan Birken.

From the kibbutz, my mother and father were sent to a town in Helsingborg Sweden to work in a rubber factory. My father and mother married in March of 1948, immigrated to the United States in 1951, and are now the PROUD grandparents of four beautiful grandchildren, Dana, Jennifer, David and Samantha Barth. Despite their experiences of horror during the Holocaust they were still dedicated to bringing their children up as observant Jews. May my parents both continue to be an inspiration to our family and to Klal Yisroel until 120.

This photo is of Zelda Sonnenberg and Natan Birken at their weddings in March, 1948 in Sweden.

Bubby's Stuffed Cabbage

1 head green cabbage
1 lb. chop meat
2 eggs
1/2 tablespoon onion powder (or to taste)
1/2 tablespoon garlic powder (or to taste)
1 teaspoon salt
1/8 teaspoon black pepper
1/8 cup uncooked rice

Directions:

1.) Freeze the whole cabbage.
2.) Place the cabbage in boiling water until soft.
3.) Combine all ingredients into chop meat really kneading well.
4.) Separate leaves from cabbage head.
5.) Place leaf in palm of your hand and place some of the chop meat mixture in the middle.
6.) Fold cabbage and tuck in the ends.

Sauce

1/4 cup sugar
2 small cans tomato paste
Juice from 1/2 lemon
Water to cover
1 can whole berry cranberry sauce
   * (add 1 hour after cooking)

Directions:

- Place all ingredients except for the whole berry cranberry sauce in a pot and bring to a boil.
- Add the stuffed cabbage and simmer for at least 3 hours.

Myra Genn and Sabina Herbst

Tenafly, N.J., U.S.A.

I was born in Trembowla, Poland and was 1 year old when the Germans invaded Poland. I saw my father for the last time when I was 3 years old, at which time he became a victim of the Nazis. My mother and I, with the rest of the Jewish community, were subsequently forced to leave our home and all our belongings and move to the Ghetto of the town. We saw many of our dear relatives and friends taken by the Nazis. Despite many close calls, we miraculously survived the "aktsias, " (the systematic round-ups of murder by the Nazis). The third and final round-up was intended to liquidate the Ghetto and make it "Yuden Rein;" (free of Jews). My mother saw mass graves being dug. She grabbed me and her sister-in-law, and somehow we managed to escape from the Ghetto. We made the dangerous trip (by foot) to the Rajski family. They were a religious, Catholic family who had 2 little girls, Stacia and Irka, who were around my age. Mr. Rajski had been a customer in my parents' leather goods store; he was active in the Polish underground. Despite some understandable initial reluctance they hid the 3 of us in an underground cave for a week and then in an attic (with a straw, thatched roof) over their barn. Mr Rajski had constructed a false wall in the attic where we could hide in moments of particular danger. We remained in the attic for nearly a year, until we were liberated by the Russians. After a 2 year stay at a DP Camp, my mother and I made our way to the USA -- to begin our new life.

We continued our relationship with the Rajskis -- letters, packages. Then all correspondence stopped; despite my mother's efforts, they did not answer her letters. It was the 1950's', a time of Political turmoil in Poland. Years of silence followed, when only my very closest friends knew of my Holocaust experience. In 1991 I was urged by my family (husband and daughters) to attend the first International Gathering of Hidden Children. After becoming active in that group, and with my mother's support, I became determined to locate the Rajski family and have them honored by Yad VaShem.

It was truly a momentous moment in my life when I received a letter from Yad VaShem informing me that the Rajskis were to be honored as Righteous Among Nations. For their courage, humanity and sense of justice, they would receive a medal of honor and their name would be inscribed at Yad VaShem on the Wall of Remembrance.

Yad VaShem, in cooperation with the Jewish Historic Institute in Poland were able to locate Stacia and Irka . Mr. and Mrs. Rajski were no longer alive but their children would be able to accept the honors on behalf of their parents. Joined by their brother (born after the war), Stacia and Irka came to the U.S. in December of 1996 for a reunion with my mother and me! I went to the J.F.K. airport with my family to greet them. We all met with hugs, kisses, tears and bouquets of flowers. It was a milestone in my life. How does one thank the people who saved your life?! Mr. and Mrs. Rajski were also honored in a beautiful ceremony by the ADL/Hidden Child Foundation, receiving the Courage to Care Award.

Myra and Sabina in D.P. camp, 1947

I am very grateful to Yad VaShem and the ADL/Hidden Child Foundation for making this possible and helping me put some closure on a dark chapter of my life. There were more visits to follow that included attending a wedding of one of their children. I continue to be in touch with the Rajski family.

My mother, to whom I was very close, was not only loving and courageous, but also a good cook. I wish I had saved more of her recipes. A staple of our diet when I was growing up after the war was kasha. She ate it as a cereal with milk; put it in chicken soup; ate it with sautéed onions and lima beans. In addition to her wonderful chicken soup with the lightest matzo balls ever, I enjoyed the following recipes.

Through a Hole in the Attic

By Myra Herbst Genn

The sky is so high! A powder-blue sky over infinite space in the vast outdoors. The farm is bathed in sunlight. The birds are chirping and some chickens roam the grassy paths. I see it all through the tiny hole in the straw roof of the attic, over the barn, where we are hiding from death. The quarters are cramped because we are behind the false straw wall of the attic. Here there is more protection from eyes that must not see us. The hiding place is small; I can touch the walls; I can touch the slope of the roof. If I reach through the hole, would I be able to touch space? We talk in whispers because my voice is too big for the space and we might be discovered. I want to soar in the sky, feel the freedom of space, away from small places and whispers. I ask my Mother, who is beside me, why the chickens can roam free and we must hide. Her eyes fill with tears---and I know. I wish I were a chicken, roaming freely on grassy paths.

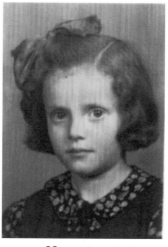

Myra at age 7

My mother's "lightest matzo balls ever"

parve

3 eggs separated
1/2 tsp water
salt and pepper
3/4 cup matzo meal

Directions:

1.) 3 eggs -- separated.
2.) Beat whites with 1/2 tsp water.
3.) Add yolks, salt and pepper.
4.) Add 3/4 cup of matzo meal and stir to combine.
5.) Let stand 5 minutes.
6.) Make into small balls and put into boiling, salted water.
7.) Boil for 20 minutes.

(I could never quite duplicate the lightness of these matzo balls; she had a magic touch!)

Sweet and Sour Chicken Balls

meat

1 ground breasts chicken
1 tbs bread crumbs
1 chopped medium onion
1 egg
sugar
salt and pepper

Myra with parents

Directions:

1.) Mix all ingredients together and form into balls.
2.) Slice 1 large onion.
3.) Boil in water with a little salt and pepper for 15 minutes.
4.) Add meat balls, 1 can of tomato sauce, sugar and honey.
5.) Liquid should cover the meat balls.
6.) Cook for 3/4 of an hour.
7.) Adjust seasoning to taste (optional -- a little fresh lemon juice).

340

Cooked Fish --
carp (or yellow pike)
parve

1 1/2 lbs fish
1 large onion,
        cut in circles- sliced
1 celery stalk
2 carrots
salt and pepper

Directions:

1.) Cook vegetables in water for 20 minutes.
2.) Add fish.
   * There should be enough water to cover the fish.
3.) Cook for 30 minutes more.
4.) Refrigerate.
5.) Fish should be eaten cold.
   * Can be eaten with horseradish and makes a nice alternative to gefilte fish.

Rajski family that saved
Myra and her mother

Edith Jacobs

Sarasota, FL, U.S.A.

A SILVER SOUP SPOON

I believe there was nothing sweeter for my teacher, Dr. Berlinger, and myself than his daily, terse, 4 P.M announcement. "You are dismissed." Since I was both the youngest and shortest student in our one room classroom, he seated me directly in front of his desk. I enjoyed scrutinizing his every move, and observed, our teacher consulted his watch, and sighed multiple times up to one hour before we were discharged for the day.

Dr. Berlinger and I had both been displaced. I, as a first year student from the town of Schweinfurt's public school, and our professor, was terminated from his cushy university position as dean of the history department. New Nazi laws had been passed forbidding Jewish children from attending public schools, and Professor Berlinger was fired and lost his pension; Jews were no longer allowed to hold government positions.

The Jewish community, numbering one thousand or so souls, wasted no time in organizing and establishing a one- room school for the Jewish children of the town, ages seven through fourteen. Our classroom was located close to the center of town, in a small building adjacent to our synagogue. Since the new odious law came on the heels of other odious laws pertaining to Jews, I did not dwell on these events, and accepted them as the meal that fortune had set on the plate in front of me.

The only adverse ripple this change caused in my life was that now I no longer had any friends to accompany me on my way home from school or to play with. Since I was by far the youngest student in the Jewish school the older students benignly ignored my presence. But being alone had its advantages. After 4 P. M., I was free to roam through the town on my own.

It was barely a ten minute walk to the center of Schweinfurt, and I frequently passed through a dark narrow thoroughfare called a gasse. I had seen small cars carefully navigate this tight cobble-stone street. Some of the town's oldest buildings were squeezed together on either side of the gasse. Its apartments were teeming with tenants, and many were occupied by succeeding generations of the same family. The back of my family's department store faced the gasse. This was where my grandfather had elevated his career from Peddler, with a small outdoor stand, to owner of one of the largest department stores in town. Grandpa told me, "I hadn't even been an unpleasant itch for the previous owner's son. He had little interest in his inheritance, and paid no attention to my insignificant business. Eventually, I was able to buy that store and transform it into one of the largest and most popular department stores in Schweinfurt." Raising his forefinger Grandpa said, "in part, your grandmother and I became successful because we never looked down our nose at any customer. We greeted the farmers with the same courtesy as our town's nobility." Grandpa could also boast that he occupied the best location on the Markt Platz, right in the center of Schweinfurt's hustle and bustle. This, of course, all occurred before I was born.

My grandmother's sister, Aunt Lena, lived in a first floor apartment on the gasse directly across the street from our store. Aunt Lena was a tall, slender woman and a picture in black. She always wore a long black dress, heavy black stockings, and sturdy black tightly laced shoes. Her hair was white and covered with a black lace cap. My grandmother told me Lena's hair had turned prematurely white overnight, after she'd been notified that her husband Bruno had fallen on the battle front during World War 1. He had given his life for the Kaiser and the homeland. She remained in permanent mourning with only Justin, their six month old son, as a remembrance of their love. Genteel women didn't work in the 1920's and Aunt Lena was added to my grandpa's long list of family he kept afloat financially. The Kaiser had gambled away his country's resources on the War and lost; earning a livelihood in Germany became a challenge. It seemed to me that whenever I passed the gasse, my Tante Lena was either standing in front of the house or leaning out of her window. She'd smile and say, "I've baked some cookies, just for you Heidi--- come-on inside." I would follow her along the dark and narrow passage that lead to her living quarters. Sometimes I wondered if my Aunt spent her days just waiting for me, and if not me, who else, had she been waiting for.

Tante Lena's dining room side- board was crowded with family pictures. I liked to look at her and Bruno's wedding picture. She'd been young and so pretty in a long white wedding dress and a crown of small flowers adorned her head and her dark brown braids almost came past the waist. On the picture her face was turned towards Bruno, she smiled with adoration at her handsome bridegroom; he stood ramrod straight and looked sternly ahead. There was also a picture of Bruno in uniform, and in the front of that picture, on a piece of black velvet, was the medal, for which he had cashed in his life. There were many pictures of my cousin Justin, at different stages of his life, and even one of me and the rest of our family. We were all smiling then.

In 1940, my father, mother, brother and I, slid through a small sliver of opportunity and escaped to the U. S. Our cousin Justin, a grown man now, had also been able to immigrate. He met us at the boat along with our three American cousins. Although we had never met these cousins, they knew of our existence from their deceased father. Papa had written them that our lives were in danger and asked them for visas. They didn't believe Papa at first, but in 1938 all Jewish men in Germany were arrested. This event made headlines in the New York Times. The cousins finally understood. They began the convoluted journey toward obtaining our visas.

1941 was not a good year for our family. My father became ill and died within two weeks. America entered the war. Cousin Justin enlisted and became one of the first American casualties.

"Like father, like son," my Mama had bitterly lamented.

We no longer heard any news from our family in Germany. A curtain of silence descended over Europe. Towards the end of the war we began to hear terrible rumors about concentration camps and atrocities, but we barely spoke about these things. Mama and I were busy. The wheels of life were turning, food had to be put on the table, and all those related mundane things that make up an existence ate up our days.

As soon as the war ended, Mama began a fruitless, exhausting search for our family. For a long time she didn't give up but, one sweltering July evening she collapsed in our living room club chair and said, "Poof, Poof, Poof, they're all gone; ashes to ashes and dust to dust." Then she began to cry. Mama cried a lot after that, and she didn't want to eat any longer. My mother became thin and gaunt. I was afraid that she wouldn't survive, and my brother and I would become orphans. I had to become my Mama's mother; I gave her no time to think. I kept my Mama busy from morning until night. I got her out of bed each day and gave her orders. I just kept her marching along like an army sergeant. I wasn't always kind. One day Mama rebelled and asserted herself; it was a good omen. She soon became top sergeant again.

I believe it was in 1955 that my mother mentioned that she needed me to accompany her on a business trip to Schweinfurt. She wanted to reclaim our family's property. The German Government had passed laws pertaining to the restitution of confiscated Jewish property.

"I don't ever want to go back to that town," I had said to Mama.

"Do you think it's a pleasure trip for me? " She said. "Who else can I ask, except my daughter? They have taken enough from us. I will reclaim what is ours."

Mama and I flew to Frankfurt and then took a train to Schweinfurt. I remembered every street of that town. The new owner of our family's department store invited us to see our former store and to have a bite to eat with him and his family. They were ensconced above the store in my grandparent's former living quarters. Mama accepted their invitation, but I refused to go. She had been born in that house and to my surprise the visit didn't upset her. It seemed Mama had gone on with her life, and her passionate goal was to reclaim our property, while I only spun my wheels and worked at remaining permanently angry. One afternoon Mama and I were invited to visit a very old lady. Mrs. Herman heard through the town's grapevine that Rose Schloss and her daughter were in town. She'd been my mother's former sewing teacher. Mrs. Herman was known to have been anti-Nazi, but miraculously, she'd been spared the deadly venom of the Gestapo. Perhaps, the secret police left her alone because of her age. Or perhaps, they considered her a harmless, crazy, old lady. Who else, but a lunatic, would have made their feeling about the Third Reich known in those days. As soon as she seated us in her cozy little living room, and brought out tea and kuchen, she said,

"I have been waiting for you. I couldn't die until one of the Schloss's arrived."

My mama politely smiled at her strange comment, but Mrs. Herman's eyes remained sad.

"I have the remainder of your Aunt Lena's estate." She brought it to me in the dead of the night, the day before she was deported with the rest of the forty old Jews that remained in Schweinfurt."

"Give this to any of my family that will come looking for me after the war." Aunt Lena said to the old lady.

"Lena, I will hold these things for you until you return."

"No, I will not be returning; I know it's the end for me, and I don't care. When I heard my son had been killed, it was over for me. They can do with me as they please."

"How do you know any of the Schloss's will ever return to Sodom?" I said to Lena.

"Of course they will come back. They will come back to look for me," she had said. "I know my family."

I began to cry and cry; I couldn't stop. My mother and Mrs. Herman ignored me. I was an embarrassment, but I couldn't stop. Mrs. Herman left the room and came back with my Aunt's estate. There were some towels, an old antique, tarnished brooch, as well as a large silver soup spoon and the gold wedding band that had joined her life to Bruno's, and some trinkets. I momentarily, stopped sobbing and asked,

"Is that all there is?"

"Yes that's all there is," she answered.

"Where are her family pictures?" I said.

"There were no pictures, "Mrs. Herman said. " They'd been allowed to take only one small suitcase with them." And I knew that my Aunt took the pictures with her in that small suitcase.

Now, I use that silver soup spoon all the time, and I remember my Aunt Lena. I also think about Mrs. Herman. She put her life on the line when she opened the door to a Jewish woman. She could have very well have been deportee number forty-one the next day.

344

Edie at 7 years old

Lemon Wine Cream

parve

(Serve with Matzo Pudding on Pesach)

4 eggs separated
1/2 cup sugar
1 envelope gelatin- Kosher
1/4 cup water
3 tablespoons white wine
one lemon --juice and grated rind

Directions:

Preheat oven to 375 degrees

1.) Soften gelatin with water in wine.
2.) Beat egg yolks with sugar until lemon colored, add lemon juice and rind.
3.) Cook egg yolk mixture in top of double boiler over hot water until thick (about 8-10 minutes), stirring constantly.
4.) Add gelatin mixture and stir until dissolved.
5.) Cool.
6.) Beat egg whites until stiff -fold into egg yolk mixture.
7.) Serve either in chilled glasses or with a matzo Pudding.

Selma Lindeman Frankel

Columbia, MD, U.S.A.

Submitted by Dr. Connie Rubler

Just before World War II when Hitler was rounding up Jews, my great grandparents, Selma and Harry, started making out affidavits to get Jews out of Germany. They made out 40 affidavits (applications that were sworn out in front of a judge) not only for relatives and friends but also strangers. They were able to save 29 people's lives; a few of them were even in concentration camps. They spent tens of thousands of dollars doing this, which in those days was a lot of money. They also promised to support these people that they brought to the United States.

Many of these people lived with my great grandparents; some of these people they didn't even know. In those days there was also anti-Semitism even in the United States and the US embassy in Stutgart, Germany rejected 11 of the people that my great grandparents made out applications for. These people eventually died in the Holocaust. Even in the United States, the judge wouldn't let my great grandparents make out any more affidavits, saying that they couldn't support that many people. Selma always cried because she couldn't save all the people.

If not for him I would have been killed by Hitler and I was able to save 29 people from this monster

I came in 1921 Selma's uncle Michael Lorig, her grandmother's brother who lived in Chicago brought my mother to the U.S.

Selma and Harry Frankel 1943

Dr. Connie Rubler's Strawberry Sherbet

parve

> 1 pound bag of frozen strawberries
> 1 12 oz. can of frozen apple juice

Directions:

1.) Place the bag of frozen strawberries into a food processor and pulse until chunky.
2.) Add can of frozen apple juice and process until smooth and a lighter shade of pink.
3.) Pour into a 13 X 9 pan and freeze.
4.) Scoop it out and serve with cake, cookies or just by itself.

Grandma's Mürbe Teich (pie crust)

parve or dairy

> 1/4 lb butter (dairy)
>   or margarine (parve)
> 1/2 c sugar
> 1/2 c orange juice
> 1 egg yolk
> 2 c flour
> 1 tsp baking powder

Directions:

Preheat oven to 375 degrees

1.) Mix all ingredients together.
2.) Place in a pie dish.
3.) Add fruit filling.
   * Typically my grandmother used small plums. She cut them in half and sprinkled them with sugar.
   * You can also make a lattice on top of the pie with extra dough.
4.) Bake at 375 degrees for approx. 40 min.

Andy Bate's Mock Crab Cake

parve

Directions:

1.) Thaw and coarsely chop/ flake imitation crab and mix with thawed g-fish and other ingredients.

2.) Make into patties and fry in oil 4-5 minutes on each side until brown.

3.) Serve with tarter sauce and/or cocktail sauce.

1 - 24 oz log frozen gefilte fish
(I like unsweetened Raskins best)
1 - 16 oz package imitation crab/seafood
(you can find in a Kosher grocery store)
1 Tbs Old Bay or other seafood seasoning
1 egg beaten
4 Tbs mayonnaise
2 or 3 stalks celery finely minced
1/2 sweet red pepper finely minced (optional)

Zeidy's Favorite Kugel

dairy

1/2 lb medium noodles
(cooked and drained)
6 eggs, well beaten
1 cup sugar
1 lb creamed cottage cheese
1/4 lbs softened cream cheese
1/2 lb farmer's cheese
1 cup sour cream
2 cups milk
6 tbsp melted butter
1 tsp vanilla
1 tsp cinnamon

Topping
1 cup Corn Flakes (crushed)
1/2 cup dark brown sugar
2 tbsp melted butter

Directions:

Preheat oven to 350 degrees

1.) Cream eggs and sugar in large bowl.
2.) Add rest of ingredients (except noodles) and mix well.
3.) Pour in noodles.
4.) Bake at 350 degrees in a 9x13 inch pan for 45 minutes.
5.) Sprinkle top with topping.
6.) Bake an additional 15 minutes.
7.) Let stand until firm.

Easy and Delicious
Fish Ball Noodle Soup

by Joanne Caras

parve

One bottle Mothers Fish Doeuvres (fish balls)
1/2 bag of Radistore Noodles or other of your choice
Carrots, celery stalks, onion and parsnip any
combination your family likes
32 OZ parve NO-Chicken broth (found at organic
markets) or vegetable broth
Fresh parsley
Salt and pepper and other favorite spices to taste
Oil and vegan butter (Earth Balance) to fry in

Directions:

1.) Cook noodles as suggested on package.
2.) Chop vegetables and sauté over high heat with olive oil and vegan butter.
3.) Drain noodles, pour fish balls over noodles, add vegetables and broth and fresh cleaned parsley.
4.) Simmer over low heat.
5.) Season to taste.

349

Conversion Table for Cooking

U.S. to Metric
Capacity

1/5 teaspoon = 1 ml
1 teaspoon = 5 ml
1 tablespoon = 15 ml
1 fluid oz. = 30 ml
1/5 cup = 50 ml
1 cup = 240 ml
2 cups (1 pint) = 470 ml
4 cups (1 quart) = .95 liter
4 quarts (1 gal.) = 3.8 liters

Metric to U.S.
Capacity

1 milliliter = 1/5 teaspoon
5 ml = 1 teaspoon
15 ml = 1 tablespoon
30 ml = 1 fluid oz.
100 ml = 3.4 fluid oz.
240 ml = 1 cup
1 liter = 34 fluid oz.
1 liter = 4.2 cups
1 liter = 2.1 pints
1 liter = 1.06 quarts
1 liter = .26 gallon

Cooking Measurement Equivalents

16 tablespoons = 1 cup
12 tablespoons = 3/4 cup
10 tablespoons + 2 teaspoons = 2/3 cup
8 tablespoons = 1/2 cup
6 tablespoons = 3/8 cup
5 tablespoons + 1 teaspoon = 1/3 cup
4 tablespoons = 1/4 cup
2 tablespoons = 1/8 cup
2 tablespoons + 2 teaspoons = 1/6 cup
1 tablespoon = 1/16 cup
2 cups = 1 pint
2 pints = 1 quart
3 teaspoons = 1 tablespoon
48 teaspoons = 1 cup

Our Goals...

Raise money to feed hungry Israelis

Raise money for Jewish Organizations
all over the World

Preserve great Jewish Recipes

Keep the stories of Holocaust Survivors
alive for generations to come

כרמי העיר

CARMEI HA'IR

**Proceeds from the sale of this
cookbook will benefit**
The Carmei Ha'ir Soup Kitchen,
**which serves over 500 meals each day to
poor and hungry Israelis.**

www.survivorcookbook.org

"I survived because God wanted living witnesses."

– Ann Eisenberg, Michigan

"On November 4, 1943 all of the workers in our factory were taken to Poniatowa, where they were made to dig their own graves. They were all shot. One of the victims was my step father Stanislaw."

– Edyta Klein-Smith, England

"I had no idea even how to make a good soup. I do not remember exactly what my mother looked like, but I remembered the smell of her chicken soup. I worked on it till I felt I had my Mom in my kitchen."

– Ruth Steinfeld, Texas

"We were starved in Auschwitz and to alleviate our numerous hunger pangs, we invented frequent "dream meals" ranging between coffee klatches, luncheons, informal and formal dinner parties. This may sound delusional I know, but during these meal planning sessions, we were briefly transported to a normal world, a world that was so far from our miserable reality."

– Lillian Berliner, New York

"I was almost 18 when the train stopped in Auschwitz. I could not cook and had never shown any interest for the kitchen and its activities. But there, in the camps we were suffering from hunger and we talked a lot about food. These conversations were my introduction to the art of cooking."

– Laura Frajnd , Sweden

"Without one penny we married, and we built a life together in America that produced three children, twelve grandchildren, and twelve great grandchildren."

– Leah Friedman, Maryland

"Sadly, Sol passed away in 1999, but in his memory, and to honour him, I am submitting the following recipe for your cookery book."

– Ruth Filler, New Zealand

"My parents had a reason to survive; their baby daughter. Some gave up the struggle and just died. Very few young children from these camps made it out alive."

– Dana Szeflan Bell, Canada

"The only food they had every day was a loaf of bread and a brown liquid similar to a soup. There were no spoons so they had to lick it, just as dogs do."

– The daughters of Agnes Mandel, Argentina

US $36.00